THE TERMS OF ORDER

Political Science and
the Myth of Leadership

THE TERMS OF ORDER

Political Science and

the Myth of Leadership

CEDRIC J. ROBINSON

State University of New York Press

ALBANY

For Winston (Cap) Whiteside, grandson of slaves
a man of extraordinary courage and profound understanding
. . . my grandfather and my first teacher.

Published by State University of New York Press, Albany

© 1980 State University of New York

Printed in the United States of America

For information, address State University of New York Press,
State University Plaza, Albany, N.Y., 12246

Library of Congress Cataloging in Publication Data

Robinson, Cedric J
   The terms of order.

   Bibliography: p.
   Includes index.
   1. Political science.   I. Title.
JA71.R59   320   79-15023
ISBN 0-87395-411-4

Men who do not know what is true of things take care to hold fast to what is certain, so that, if they cannot satisfy their intellects by knowledge (*sciencza*), their wills at least may rest on consciousness (*conscienza*).

Punishments were called *paradeigmata* by the Greeks in the same sense in which the Latins called them *exempla*; that is, exemplary chastisements.

Giambattista Vico

Contents

THE TERMS OF ORDER

Political Science and

the Myth of Leadership

Preface

The histories of the societies rooted in Western civilization are a 1500-year record of unrelieved perturbation. Indeed, the past four hundred years, the period marking the emergence of the modern world system, are witness to profound upheavels of wars, revolutions and social disintegration. Currently, at the centers of this civilization, what are now frequently referred to as the core-states: America, Britain, France, Germany and Italy, social crises are extensive and structurally quite deep. Paradoxically, that intelligentsia which has marked as its special province the explication of social organization, has in large measure ignored both the disruptive character of our times and the fundamental nature of social disorder. Its members persist in the delusion that, beneath the chaos, ordered systems reign administered by stable political institutions and fundamentally resilient cultural and economic integrations. As such, the existential experience of the individual is denied by resorting to an heritage as citizen of a politically maintained social order rationalized by the authority of leadership. Greater social cohesion, we are instructed, is dependent upon better leadership.

This book critically examines those intellectual traditions in Western thought which have contributed to the illusions of social order. Its purpose is to expose the historical and philosophical foundations of the myth of social order which compel dependence on tradition-bound forms of authority. In an era dramatically characterized by capricious, incompetent and mischievous social leaders, it challenges the total paradigmatic construction of leadership as a basis of social order.

Not content to rest upon the contained confrontations between Liberal and Marxian theories, I have probed the ideational structure which both bourgeois and radical thought share: the pre-eminence of political order. I have sought to expose from the vantage point inherited from a people only marginally integrated into Western institutions and intellectual streams, those contradictions within Western civilization which have been conserved at the cost of analytical coherence.

This book like most has an indefinite point of origin . . . the issue to which it is addressed is an ancient one. Of the book's writing I can be more precise. It was begun in 1970 in England with the support of the Leverhulme Foundation. A very different sort of support was provided by Charles Drekmeier and Margo Drekmeier, two uncommonly gifted individuals. Without Elizabeth, my wife, however, the work would have never been finished or assumed any proper form of presentation. She shared her sense of the exact with me in work and in principle. To Dominic Sankey and his family, to Terrence and Gloria Hopkins, to Immanuel and "Bea" Wallerstein, I extend love and appreciation: such friendship is invaluable.

xii

Introduction

In the history of ideas of the West, concomitant to the development of Mediterranean and European political thought, there was the development of an *anti-political* tradition. Just as North Africa, Asia Minor, Greece and Rome contributed traditions to the foundation of the political as a concept in medieval and modern Europe, those same traditions contained within them its antithesis.[1] While the political came to fruition in modern thought with the theory of the State as the primary vehicle for the organization and ordering of the mass society produced by capitalism, its opposing element evolved into the anti-state theory of anarchism.

Yet it was in the natures inherent in these two developments—one an organizing principle, the other, its contradiction—that they would not compete on historically equivalent levels. The peculiarities of history did not allow each to be compared to the other on its own terms or in the context most favorable to it. Political societies and nonpolitical societies, that is those societies in which there was an attempt to contain power by routinizing or institutionalizing it and those societies in which this question did not arise, could not be expected to have been encouraged in their development by the same forces.

Instead, the political, as an idea dominated by the positivity of the State, found convenience with the exigencies of certain sectors of the population of the new, class-conscious society. The functional interests of these classes fell within the capabilities of the State as an administrative apparatus, thus confirming its significance in utilitarian terms. On the other hand, and again in historical, economic and ideological processes, the antipolitical was translated and transformed into ethical theory, theology and philosophy, that is into forms of idealism.

These were not, however, simple processes. As the structural transformations of European society became more explicit, that is as traditional formations became less effective in maintaining institutional and structural coherences, these processes responded through crisis-specific, situation-specific permutations. The political and nonpolitical in dialectic consistently assumed historical forms. The persistence of their dialectic resulted in an opposition complicated by the transitions in European societies from theocratic institutions to constitutional and parliamentary ones; from feudal economic organization to capitalist modes of production; from agrarian societies to manufacturing and then industrial concentrations of production; from rural life to urban life; from peasant-dominated populations to proletarian ones; from regional integrations to national centralizations. It was, in fact, out from the very center of these transformations that the modern notion of the political emerged.

The young Karl Marx addressed himself to this development perhaps no where more brilliantly than in his short essay, "On the Jewish Question." In it, Marx indicated that he believed that the civil society, which had emerged from the ruins of feudal society, had been fixed by political transformation and revolution. The State had emerged, and in its most progressive form, that is as a secular projection of the bourgeois class and its interests, had founded its existence on the ideology of political liberty. *The State in its highest form had achieved political emancipation.*

In this short essay, Marx was anticipating by more than thirty years what T.H. Green would write in 1879:

To ask why I am to submit to the power of the state, is to ask why I am to allow my life to be regulated by that complex of institutions without which I literally should not have a life to call my own, nor should be able to ask for a justification and what I am called on to do. . . . I must be able to reckon on a certain freedom of action and acquisition. . .and this can only be secured through common recognition of this freedom on the part of each other by members of a society, as being for a common good.[2]

2

But Marx saw the relationship between the State and *true* emancipation quite differently. He argued that the relationship between political emancipation and human emancipation was not a true one. For him, the political was at best a "devious" instrument to be *used* for human emancipation, ". . .by emancipating himself *politically*, man emancipates himself in a *devious way,* through an intermediary, however necessary this intermediary may be."[3] Ultimately, the political was such an instrument because the State could not attack or change its base: the civil society. This civil society (which Marx would later identify as bourgeois, capitalist society) was exploitative and oppressive for the mass of its "citizens." Yet the State could not dissolve it without destroying itself. The State, despite its capacities for guaranteeing political liberties, could not transform its social basis.

In realizing this contradiction, Marx achieved the insight which was the precondition for his later concern with the social revolution (*The Economic and Philosophic Manuscripts of 1844*), "the withering away of the state" (*The Communist Manifesto*) and the transitory democracy described as the "dictatorship of the proletariat" (*The Civil War in France*). In his "On the Jewish Question," Marx insisted on the limitations of that which had come to be designated the political. He understood that *by itself*, it was incapable of transforming bourgeois society. He also understood that in the historical process of this transformation, the political would have to be transcended. Writing in 1844, in his essay, "Critical Glosses," Marx would put the relationship of the political to social transformation in the following terms:

> Revolution as such—the overthrow of the existing power and the dissolution of the old conditions—is a political act. But without revolution Socialism cannot carry on. Socialism needs this political act in so far as it needs destruction and dissolution. But when its organizing activity begins, when its ultimate purpose, its soul emerges, Socialism will throw the political husk away.[4]

With these realizations, Marx, for the time being, achieved a reconciliation of the political and the antipolitical: though a useful instrument, the political itself would be transformed by a deeper, more profound process—social revolution.

Yet the problem of the political was and is not merely a programmatic one. It is also analytical-conceptual, metaphysical and epistemological. If, in terms of one liberationist tradition, mechanistic or vulgar Marxists have understood the political in terms much more shallow and much less ambiguous than Marx himself, it is also true that, in the meantime, the political has come to dominate Western social thought. It has become a basic grammar, a mediation, through which the outlines of social reality have been generated. In other words, the political has become a paradigm.

> The inquiry into the nature of politics probably demarcates most accurately the boundaries of our intellectual landscape. The evolution of the state toward what Max Weber called maximally politicized society, the unprecedented concentration of bureaucratic and technological power which economically and culturally dominates the rest of the world, creates a climate in which all problems cast a political shadow. We may flee from the political dimension of our experience or we may embrace it in order to do away with it, but we are obsessed by politics.[5]

In current Western social sciences, there are many ways of approaching or using the political as a paradigm. For example, there is formal and organizational theory, political history, systems analyses, normative theory, institutional analyses, political sociology, behavioral analyses, etc. Each presupposes aspects of the political as reality. However, they are *contained* explications, that is they are paradigmatic. They are exercises through which the political persists rather than instruments by which that persistence might be explained. As such, there is a restriction of insight into the nature of social organization. It is with this persistence and its concomitant restriction that this essay is concerned. The concept chosen through which to make the deep incision is political leadership. This concept is at the root of the paradigm, and, as such, demonstrates the contradictions resident in political order.

The declared and/or implicit goal of most historical societies has been persistence; persistence in terms of social integration, biological continuity and cultural integrations. By "historical," I mean here those societies which have existed in reality over time. Vico called them nations. I mean to exclude those illusory entities often mistaken for nations which have maintained a sense of continuity by constructing "histories" (e.g. the English Commonwealth, the United States of America, etc.).

With regard to persistence, however, the concept of political leadership is dysfunctional to the social sciences as a social and analytical instrument. The presumption that political leadership is a concept through which the *event* of social organization can be made recognizable is a specious one. Yet it is this same presumption which underlies both liberal and radical attempts at social reorganization and "perfection."

An historical evaluation of political leadership would render at best an ambiguous judgment of its functionality. Yet the model persists in the absence of a precondition for its abandonment: a critical historical evaluation requires an alternative model of organization. The absence of this alternative would appear to be consistent regardless of the political culture or political tradition and institutions involved.

As well, detrimental impacts of political leadership on a society are qualitatively intensified the more concerned its ideologists are with those liberal, bourgeois freedoms that Marx and others have addressed themselves to—that is, those "freedoms" posited on principles of individualism. More specifically, in psychological and analytical terms, the forms of political leadership tend increasingly to subvert the capacity of the individual to respond to his or her environment creatively, intelligently and ingeniously. In short, one impact of political leadership is sociopathological—sociopathological in existential terms and ultimately for the attempt to recognize the nature of reality. This is so since political leadership is an affirming element basic to the ideological nature of Western social science.

The task, then, is to capture in its most fundamental terms, in its most authentic dimensions, and in its various institutional forms, an explanation for the retention of political leadership as a social instrument. The task requires that one look at the means by which our species recognizes and characterizes the significant phenomena of its reality: the identification of *objects* which anticipates the identification of *problem-objects* which, in turn, anticipates the identification of *solvent-objects*. This seemingly extraordinary dimension appears appropriate since political leadership is posited as cross-cultural (not merely across *apparent* cultural boundaries such as between England and France, but presumably across *real* boundaries as between Lapp and Amhari) and *almost* anthropological.

Paradigmatically, political leadership seems related to political authority which is, itself, related to the larger and inclusive concept: Authority. Authority, in turn, relates to Order. But, I would argue, Order, as a logical element, has two prior epistemologies—one rooted in perception, and the other rooted in the psychological. The task requires that the phenomenological process of each be traced systematically and deliberately, not merely for their relatedness but for the character of that relatedness. One must estimate continuously the coherent and its context, the incoherent, considering constantly the seminal influences of the irrational on the rational. In short, the nature of knowledge as it relates to choice must be explicated—in this instance the choice for political society, political organization, political structure, political culture and institutions.

As a consequence of the nature of this investigation into the interstices of Western political thought, I have chosen, as instruments, approaches which have a marginal relationship to the "world hypothesis"[6] of political order—approaches which convene critically if not exactly with what Michel Foucault called the "Counter-sciences".[7] Specifically, these are the sciences and arts of the mind: psychoanalysis, analytical mythology, neurophysiology, gestalt psychology and structural linguistics, ethnography, and philosophies of history (Marx, Hegel, Freud, etc.). Through these I intend to abuse the political consciousness.

CHAPTER I

The Order of Politicality

In perceptual terms, the concept of the political has no precise, corporate image. Certainly, there are objective phenomena which we identify with the political because of association, but they are aspects or elements of it rather than its actual nature. Figures and institutions —presidents, congresses, bureaucracies, parties, armies—can be recognized as being of the nexus of the political, but they are by no means identical with it. These are not the substance of the political but its phenomenology: the objects which express the presence and influence of the political.

Yet the political seems to have as a characteristic the quality of arranging the relationship of things and of people within some form of society. It is an ordering principle, distinguishing the lawful or authorized order of things while itself being the origin of the regulation. We associate, then, the political with power, authority, order, law, the state, force and violence—all of these are phenomena which restrict the outcome, deflect the extraneous, limit the relevant forces. We speak of the political both as an instrument for ordering society and that order itself. It is both a general way of acting on things and the consequences which follows having acted upon things.

But further, as consequence, the political presupposes the possibility of continued action:

> . . .in the political context the end is altered from a purpose to an effect, and the vision of power as a process scaled down from the realization of the good to the production of a faithful mechanism of response. As a corollary, the finite tendency of potentiality, in its original sense, to

surpass every stage of itself toward its end becomes, in the political context, the tendency of power, bereft of its purpose, toward infinite expansion of itself.[1]

The political is always there, it would seem, absorbing and being itself absorbed, penetrating and being penetrated. It is a strategem of behavior directed toward a certain consequence, an act founded on specific sociological presumptions, a pattern of role-interactions selectively scattering the existence of human beings by some estranged, arbitrary definition of the positivity. It is an active definition of the situation.

Yet there is no doubt that the political is a phenomenon of force and thus of significance. But what exactly is the nature of that force? What forms, what substances do its regularities assume? Where are they to be sought, how are they to be found?

If one were to reach toward the materials of contemporary political science in hopes of identifying that very force, one might withdraw with the secure insight that the force is in essence the phenomenon of governing and that political science was the record of the art, science and/or failure of governing. Governing justly, unjustly, singly or by elite, "democratically" or dictatorially, momentarily or for imperial durations, consensually or by force,[2] wisely or wrongly, but nevertheless, governing.

But there could be seen, too, a more particular preoccupation evidenced by the science. One could come to the understanding that governing is realized through elements consisting of boundaries, rulers, administrations, decision-making apparatus, formal and informal parties, patterned negotiations, interest conflicts, executing, legitimating institutions, all mitigated by crises, creeds, ideologies, public opinion, conditioned and modeled responses, primary and idiosyncratic as well as quite literally the enigmatic and the extraordinary. Yet governing still. And governing, in turn, could be defined as the rule of some specified community by some form of authority. At a not much higher level of abstraction and distillation, our ambitious nominalist might subsequently decide that what he was discovering in the political was the habits, forms, histories, and characters of authority.

Such would surely be the mean result of a behavioral analysis of the field of contemporary American political science. With respectful consideration given to the antiquity and sociology of Aristotelian thought, our researcher would find that this science would present to him a "paradigm" quite clearly the consummation of Aristotle's declarations on political philosophy and artifact. Man is thus intended by nature to be a part of a political whole, and there is, therefore, an immanent impulse in all men towards an association of this order. "But the man who first *constructed* such an association was none the less the greatest of benefactors."[3]

But be certain, the question here of the meaning of the political is not one of antiquity or parentage, but one of relevance. It is not so much a question as to whether the foundations of modern political science can be discovered in the work of Aristotle as it is a question of whether modern political science consciously addresses the political. Sheldon Wolin's assessment appears appropriate:

> . . .a wide variety of theories exists for the political scientist to choose among. To call them political theories is, in the language of philosophy, to commit something like a category mistake. Systems theories, communication theories, and structural-functional theories are unpolitical theories shaped by the desire to explain certain forms of non-political phenomena. They offer no significant choice or critical analysis of the quality, direction, or fate of public life.[4]

And so one would be led, finally, to the conclusion that one cannot resolve the question of the nature of the political by the process of distilling it from a science of politics. For, at some point, one would have to confront the science of politics in its epistemological, metaphysical and methodological terms. That is, those terms themselves which would suggest that the first order of inquiry would be some close explication of the philosophy of science, since it is there that the relationship between epistemology, metaphysics and methodology is assigned.

Two major contemporary voices in the fields of the history and philosophy of science are those of Karl Popper and Thomas Kuhn.[5] Regardless of their attempts to argue otherwise,[6] it appears certain that what each describes as the true nature and essential processes of knowledge growth in the sciences are at odds, representing fundamentally different and opposing schema.

9

Popper's thesis is closer to the folklore of science, postulating a systematic, deliberate and conscious process for the development of larger inventories of knowledge proceeding through the construction of falsifiable hypotheses and their confrontation with empirical reality: "We invent our myths and our theories and we try them out."[7] Popperian science is then most clearly identifiable with speculative philosophy—conjecture and refutation:

> I do admit that at any moment we are prisoners caught in the framework of our theories; our expectations; our past experiences; our language. But we are prisoners in a Pickwickian sense: if we try, we can break out of our framework at any time. Admittedly, we shall find ourselves again in a framework, but it will be a better and roomier one; and we can at any moment break out of it again.[8]

Popper thus argues for the rational man who imposes procedurally his ethic of rationality onto the very character of discovery in the larger adventure of making human experience rational. And "rational" presupposes, imposes in fact, a self-consistency, an internal coherence.[9]

Kuhn, on the other hand, has read the history of science quite differently and proposes that in the sequence of creative thought, Popper's perception is that of only a single episode in the sequence. He argues that science proceeds in its development of fundamental insight through the replacement of one paradigm by another, e.g. Ptolemaic astronomy being replaced by Copernican astronomy. Paradigms are discarded for several reasons: *awkwardness* (the computational correction of Ptolemaic theory had proliferated by necessity into unmanageability); *impatience* (Copernicus presented to his colleagues a system which could explain little, if any, more than its predecessor, yet it was simpler, and the other had been given a fair amount of time to prove itself); *anomalies* (in a different episode, an experimenter unexpectedly released a gas which would later be known as oxygen— to a follower of the phlogiston theory, the gas was an unacceptable result); and *multiplicity of competitive theories.*

It is during periods of crises, in the transitional periods—and more specifically when competitors have been severely reduced in number, most importantly to one—that "extraordinary science" (Kuhn's phrase) occurs. "Extraordinary science" is a testing, challenging procedure which is identical in its significant aspects to Popper's version and generalization. Once the crisis is resolved by the selection of the new paradigm, Popperian, extraordinary science ends and "normal science" (again Kuhn) or "puzzle-solving" begins. The creative moment is over and scientists now get down to the proliferation of games, techniques and instrument-designs which will be used to confirm their paradigm-induced presumptions.

"Normal science" is thus in large measure the actualization of tautology. Full sequences of inquiry and responses have been proscribed while other sequences have become prescribed. One knows what to ask of one's data and how to produce that data because one knows "instinctively" the boundaries and the range of correct and acceptable answers.

Kuhn's paradigms thus represent several levels of actualization. They are *metaphysical*: sets of beliefs; *sociological*: universally recognized scientific achievement; and *artifacts*: tools, instruments and analogies.[10] They thus relate closely to Polanyi's "justification of personal knowledge" (which are the commitments and responsibility for making certain choices and assertions the foundation of meaning and understanding), and Louch's "warrant" and "entitlement" in his refutation of the predilection for generalization as explanation and his assertion of the truer authority of *ad hoc* explanation.[11]

Kuhn thus rests to some extent in the tradition of Wittgensteinian and Cartesian linquistics while Popper is more identifiable with some "objectivists" who posit a Kantian philosophical development. It is of less significance for the purposes of this essay that Kuhn would now prefer to refer to his sociological paradigms as "disciplinary matrices" and his metaphysical and artifactual paradigms as "exemplars" than that his insistent declaration is that he is attempting to describe the critical force of values in the choice of theory, explanation, meaning and logic in science:

> What I am denying is neither the existence of good reasons nor that these reasons are of the sort usually described. I am, however, insisting that such reasons constitute values to be used in making choices rather than rules of choice. Scientists who share them may nevertheless make different choices in the same concrete situation. Two factors are deeply involved. First, in many concrete situations, different values, though all

11

constitutive of good reasons, dictate different conclusions, different choices. . .More important, though scientists share these values and must continue to do so if science is to survive, they do not all apply them in the same way.[12]

Additionally, Kuhn's use of revolution as a metaphor of the change of paradigms signals the assumption of the panoply of constructs with which most political analysts are quite familiar: conservative-radical factions, alienation, resistance, violence, waste and a certain sequence of the dynamic of change (e.g. from disequilibrium to equilibrium). It represents, too, a "proof" of his thesis that scientific explanation is often profoundly affected by historical phenomena presumed external to it, for certainly the imagery of revolution has displaced evolution as the dominant impression of change in Western experience. To the contrary, the Popperian interpretation is fundamentally that of an evolutionist.[13] Again, according to Kuhn, we would anticipate evolution being the character of the mode of analysis to which Kuhn's work is negation. The analyses of Kuhn and Popper are thus related dialectically and historically.

That both Popper and Kuhn continue to assert that the criteria of change in the scientist's construction of rationality are accuracy, simplicity, scope and fruitfulness seems more to demonstrate the irony of the formal convergence of paradox than to be a display of the former "truism" that "all roads lead to Rome." However, if Kuhn's reconstruction is to be chosen over Popper's, there first needs to be the declaration of a formal qualification that perhaps the choice signifies that Kuhn is an apostle of this time, with its biases, bold impressions and hysterias in its attempt to make change recognizable.

Yet within the confines of a consideration of political science, other reasons for the choice also seem powerfully convincing. These reasons can be articulated through a simple demonstration. This demonstration has to do with the role played by the concept "power" in political science. If we assume for the moment Popper's prescriptive history of science, for the science of politics, do we find—as we would be led to anticipate by Popper—theories of power which take the form of falsifiability (e.g. the presumption of an organizing principle within human groups alternative to power which would obviate the puzzle-solving business of political scientists)? We, of course, do not discover the latter, but find instead that power as a conceptual tool corresponds most closely to the "background knowledge" of the "methodological falsificationists" (see note 6), and remains an "unquestionable" basic statement among political scientists.

Even given power as a natural phenomenon of human society, is the "conjecture" that it is a causative of order posed so that it might be refuted or is the presumed concomitance between order and power so thorough in the investigations of political analysts that it functions as an identity and consequently might be suspended from critical consideration? Once more, there is no refutation possible since we are told again and again that order in human society cannot be obtained without the presence and subsequent use of power.[14] But perhaps we should draw Popper's attention to a more concrete problem in American political science. How is it that in the celebration of democracy as the institutionalization of Just power that Western political science seems to have become, is there never the slightest suggestion of the absurdity of identifying this construct with the reality of mass societies as they exist in North America, Western Europe and elsewhere? Let us pursue this example in some detail.

Democracy and the Political Paradigm

Robert Dahl's work is an interesting instance of the metaphysical paradigm of power's inevitable relation to order. In an historical essay, he argues that the American civil war is of interest to "students of politics" because it is a dramatization of the nature, failure and success of the American political system:

> *Failure*, because there can be no more convincing evidence of the breakdown of a political system than reversion to the barbarism of internal war, particularly among people of the same origins and language, already become a nation after living under the same government for nearly three quarters of a century, or if we count the Colonial period, for two centuries.[15]

13

One paragraph later, he appears to identify political systems with the nature of civilization, ". . .because some problems have recurred ever since civilized men have tried to live together, every political system. . .has had to deal with some of the same problems."[16]

But as might be objected: this is politics, the political, not power which Dahl is associating with order. Again, Dahl writes with a certainty which frustrates apologists; he knows he is talking about power and is unafraid to write his mind:

> . . .countries with democratic regimes use force, just as other regimes do, to repel threats to the integrity of the national territory. . .large minorities are virtually "compelled" to remain within the territorial limits of the nation.[17]

But what of Dahl's much-written about "pluralist democracy" (shared to some real degree with Nelson Polsby, Aaron Wildavsky, William Mitchell, Austin Ranney, etc.)? Of what does it consist? Dahl understands it as power:

> Because one center of power is set against another, power itself will be tamed, civilized, controlled, and limited to decent human purposes, while coercion, the most evil form of power, will be reduced to a minimum.[18]

Thus Dahl has displayed for us the basic metaphysics and mythology of his system. He has argued that the integration of a people (nation) is achieved by the *praxis* of the state ("living under the same government"). If we forget the specious nature of Dahl's history; that is if we forget his presumption that Americans had "the same origins and language" (a notion which Dahl confirms by mentioning Germans under Germany, Indians only under India; the Irish, Scots, Dutch, etc.—all of whom make up substantial proportions of this early population—are not mentioned at all); if we forget that Dahl is confused by socioeconomic stratifications (he finds incomprehensible the delegates to the Constitutional Convention in their discussion of factions and their preoccupation with attacks on their property: "Curiously enough, none of the men at the Convention ever seems to have stated exactly what he had in his mind."[19]); and if we join with him in forgetting the presence of slaves (an "exception"), it is still obvious that Dahl has founded civilization on Just force by a contradiction. The contradiction consists of the suggestion that the state acting for the nation has the habit, right and duty to protect itself from dissolution by, paradoxically, proceeding at its limit into "the barbarism of internal war." It never occurs to him that the state and its political system is that same "barbarism" under the conditions of applied and potentially applicable force.[20] For Dahl, barbarism is violence in the *absence* of the state to be qualitatively distinguished from that violence which is the prerogative of the state.

Western historical experience seems to have sufficiently falsified for any deliberate, reasonable intelligence, any presumption of order (if it is to mean anything more than severely momentary regularity); the power-order dyad; participant democracy (a term itself which is an unashamedly needful redundancy since the "understanding" of democracy has become so expedient); representativeness and constitutionality; yet studies continue to proliferate in deathly replica in attempts to probe the infrastructure of these hypotheses *cum* presumptions.

It does then seem that in as far as political science is a science and Popper is taken as one of that science's philosophers, there is something lacking and profoundly awkward in the anticipated articulation between political science, science and the philosophy of science. Unquestionably, the Popperian "myths" are there, yet instead of becoming the very stuff under investigation, they are transformed into the presumptive generalities and universalities which lie unchallenged beneath any subsequent analysis. Certainly Kuhn as the alternative to Popper, in eschewing the notion of a formal "logic of discovery" and drawing attention to the social aspects of knowing, the para-technical determinisms and the process of epistemology narrowing into darkness, has constructed the more salient statement for the particular discipline. But this, too, would seem to require some slight demonstration.

If one were to concentrate, for the moment, on the notion of democracy in Western thought from Aristotle to modern times as a test of the paradigmatic vision, the results would seem to confirm many of Kuhn's insights into the development of scientific knowledge.

Literally, of course, the term democracy is to be understood as "the people rule."[21] Yet that was an ambiguous statement at best since "the people" as a concept was subject for its meaning to a variety of historical circumstances (see below). Additionally, for the concept of democracy in the intervening twenty-five hundred years since its formal construction as a category of governmental form in Western thought, much of the meaning of the world upon which it depended has drastically changed and in so doing has corrupted or augmented what has been called democratic theory.

As a consequence, among the formal guardians of the creed—that is, political analysts and theorists—there has been much controversy and dissembling concerning the significant meaning of the term democracy. Who, for example, are "the people?" If one took the term to imply the majority of a community, society or state, there would still remain undercurrents of meaning to be taken into account. One such undercurrent is the wandering characterization of the people from the *pöbel* (the poor or mob of classical literature) to the *bourgeoisie* who dominate societies of contemporary industrialized nations.

But even here, while signifying a dramatic social and historical change in the character, capacities and resources of the majority, one would, too, have to acknowledge the impact of Christian philosophy as it penetrated political philosophy. For Christianity did have some systematic effect on the meaning of words and philosophical debate.

Primitive Christianity, for example, seized the very same characteristics of the people which classical Greek literature had sadly deplored; that is the people as simple, traditional and ponderous, were honored for those styles, which formerly were seen to be ridiculous, vulgar[22] and obscene. Primitive Christianity stressed the conservative aspects of a people true to their fathers' dogma, unpanicked by eventuality or seduced by novelty. Aristotle had understood those qualities as manifestations of intellectually dull, inferior and naturally subservient classes. As such, Aristotle was antagonistic to the idea of democracy, perceiving it as a perversion among the several alternative forms of political society:

> These [Kingship, Aristocracy, Polity] are the three subdivisions of the class of right constitutions. Three perversions correspond to them.

16

Tyranny is the perversion of Kingship; Oligarchy of Aristocracy; and Democracy of Polity. . .Democracy is directed to the interest of the poorer classes.[23]

Yet the medieval Christian doctrine of the Elect, itself an admixture of Judaic tradition and secular hierarchical presumptions, played its own havoc with "the people," distinguishing once again, as Aristotle had seen necessary, the masses from the elite. As such, following the implosion of the Christian world of the past four hundred years precipitated by the Reformers, the way was prepared for the more contemporary *apologia* of the "majoritarians," and their presumption that the bourgeoisie are the embodiment of the people as an elect and materially favored group.

One would also, then, have to record that at the base of any modern democratic theory and the perception of just what constitutes the people, rests the utilitarian ethic. The people are those for whom the state services the necessary preconditions for the good life (that is satisfaction of happiness, its more primitive and crude equivalent). The architectonics of the state refers then to a spiritual and material well-being which precludes concern for the poor or slaves unless one is addicted to Platonic rationalizations. And since the state may command only a limited quantity of resources, it must choose between and allocate discriminately if distribution is to remain rationally coherent to first principles: the preservation of the state itself and of the bourgeoisie.

Thus it can be seen that merely in terms of what is meant by the term "the people," one moves from democracy as the rule of the mob and of the rabble to its contrary, the rule of the functionally invisible and the invested. And yet there is a third meaning of the "people" which seems to have had little practical value except to the unsophisticated, and that is, of course, the most obvious meaning: "all the people." This sense of the term does, infrequently, invade serious discussion of democracy but its natural habitat is those institutions, literature, and instrumentalities of socialization. It is a manipulative myth. To the degree that any discussant dwells on such an interpretation, to that same extent is he or she perceived as simpled-minded, naive or radical (and thus dangerous because such "neo-realists" tend toward inventive ontologies of masses and populism). In this sense, "the people" suggests a sameness, boundedness, citizenry, continuity, territorial and proximal identifications which are never fully empirical. In short, it is an ideograph.

The notion of democratic rule, however, has had a much more consistent history and singular meaning. It seems not to have digressed significantly from the *sense* that it is a contraction of "ruling through a governmental apparatus a society for its own interests." Instead, the differences found among political analysts and philosophers have concerned the instrumentation or actualization of the creed. On this score, there has been no lack of *schema* in the grand tradition early represented by Rousseau and Thomas Harrington. In the midst of the dissolution of absolute monarchies (or the construction of attenuated monarchical but still elite systems), Rousseau, Harrington and their several ideological companions, sympathetic to the democratic ethic, felt the need, understandably to present systematic explications of democracy. But with the onset of "the democratic creed' as the acknowledgement that democracy was a realistic alternative, liberal thought largely subverted the primitive visions of "participant democracy" into "representative democracy."[24]

Recognizing the effect that political participation would have on the consciousness and morality of the individual—i.e. the realization of a humanity indivisible from the collective relation—liberal democratic philosophers corrupted their ideal of democracy with considerations of wealth and superiority evidenced or recognized by analogy to the dynamics of the market. As the ideologues of a class and a civilization in formation, they subverted the fundamental ideas of the society which theirs was historically succeeding while laying the theoretical foundations for the political of a market society. Instead of tradition, they deposited beliefs in the sanctity of the individual *qua* individual and the ethic of utility. That in so doing they contradicted their primary political and social morality, i.e. equality, was apparently less obvious to them than the requirement that their thought, to be programmatic, would have to reflect the social reality of class society. Liberal political theory presupposed a civil society, that is a stratified, unequal society.[25]

In Locke, the historical renaissance and feudal societies were the "state of nature" within which the bourgeois ("man") had proven himself exceptional. In his organizational, explorative and practical extraordinaries, the bourgeois had earned the right to be certain of the security for which he contracted into civil society. The democratic state of such a society would then have to be a state controlled by those who had discovered in it an instrument for their own preservation (that is the preservation of their lives, liberty to increase and maintain their wealth through the dynamics of the market economy, and protection of their property): a bourgeois state.[26]

Similarly, J.S. Mill, after recognizing the impact of participation toward the constructive development of the individual, turned to the mechanisms of that participation, gravitating *logically* to elitism:

> But it is an absolute condition not to overpass the limits prescribed by the fundamental principle laid down in a former chapter as the condition of excellence in the constitution of a representative system. The plurality of votes must on no account be carried so far that those who are privileged by it, or the class (if any) to which they mainly belong, shall outweigh by means of it all the rest of the community.[27]

In so doing, Richard Lichtman reminds us, Mill was attempting to balance within civil society the interests of the privileged and few with those of the unprivileged and many. But because he did not question the basis of such a society, class stratification, his proposed mechanics served to *maintain* that society. The result for Mill was the compromise whose substance was procedure—a procedure the social utility of which was founded on the presumption that decisions and laws made by individuals of superior quality would have superior effect on the society as a whole:

> The position which gives the strongest stimulus to the growth of intelligence is that of rising into power, not that of having achieved it; and of all resting points, temporary or permanent, in the way to ascendancy, the one which develops the best and highest qualities is the position of those who are strong enough to make reason prevail, but not strong enough to prevail against reason.[28]

Here, again, economic and social presumptions and biases penetrated political philosophy resulting in the discharge of the people ("the masses" of the 18th and 19th centuries) from the processes of consideration and choice. As such, the construction of democratic institutions which translated the people's choices into policy for the people had come to resemble a more modern equivalent to Plato's timocracy. As theory went, "the people" made choices for men who were thought somehow to incorporate specific and constant ideals and who, in turn, when confronted with issues, constructed laws. That is, the proper bourgeoisie and the upper classes could construct laws for all because their political institutions and their procedures of decision-making were the constitution of the people. Not withstanding Rousseau's reservations, the theory argued, an instrument could be found to replace (or economically distill) the people in the processes of their own rule: representation.

By the mid-twentieth century, however, representative democracy had largely been itself subverted by the behavioralists (having, of course, effectively withstood from its inception declarations of theorists and philosophers who called it logically absurd and morally contradictory) whose electoral studies suggested an electorate largely distant by any meaningful criterion from the political process.[29] Procedural democrats, needing another theory, affected a new similitude between fact and value with the theory of pluralistic democracy. Here it was acknowledged that, indeed, mass society did consist of a plurality of social groupings with varying proximities to power. In addition these social groups had not only competing interests but also differing interests. These social facts seriously brought into question the descriptive value of the Burkean or Jeffersonian models of democracy, for one now had to come to grips with a multiplicity of "people" *within* one state. This difficulty was overcome by the discovery that these peoples (groups, now) were represented by pressure groups which demanded satisfaction from the *political system* through the elite or "notables." The people(s) thus ruled by articulating their demands in such a way that those demands became "mini" crises or "inputs" into the system; thus the character and preference of the people were thought to be system-regular in nature, corresponding (or capable of being made to correspond) to receptors or equilibria gyrators within the system. The democratic ethos was then itself salvaged by replacing concepts of process with system; the people with groups; representatives with pressure group notables (or elites), and all collated somehow (again) under the concensual umbrella of the democratic creed. There seemed (and seems even now) to be little embarrassment over the fact that the people had been removed one step farther from rule by having become essentially claimants.[30]

In using terms like "participant," "representative," and "pluralistic" democracies, one is acknowledging not a special case of democracy but a machinery designed presumably to take its place in the face of what might be considered insurmountable difficulties. These machineries are rationalized as one accepts a tyranny of demographic "facts" (e.g. mass society) or becomes convinced of a critical intellectual or spiritual weakness among the members of any society (e.g. they are moronic). These terms, which would otherwise be redundancies, thus become mature, rational applications of a principle through the repetitious character of its contradictions. Through the transfer of authority from the people to an instrument, a machinery of governing is accomplished which succeeds in reconciling the ancient distrusts and disgusts at the mere suggestion (or model) of democracy while borrowing the symbols of legitimacy from that very same "repulsive" form. Contemporary democratic theory is sheltered, then, beneath the illusion and structure of mass authority while it masks from the view of the ordinary man a political process engineered by infinitely smaller minorities.

Regardless of one's persuasion, the point is clear that there has been a significant sequence of change in the meaning of democracy as a paradigm in political thought which does not, again, demonstrate Popper's understanding of scientific development. But neither has a paradigmatic revolution appeared to occur in Kuhn's terms. The above devolution would seem to close with both Popper's and Kuhn's judgment of the social sciences as immature disciplines but confirms Kuhn's thesis of paradigmatic puzzle-sovling.

Democracy, as a construct, is quite clearly a disciplinary matrix of Western political science and like Ptolemaic astronomy, it has become increasingly overworked by anomalies (it does not explain the political systems which bear its name) and encumbered with addended calculi (a recent one being the fully matured "democratic elitism" in Bachrach's critique[31]) in the hopes that the theoretical and observed orbits will correspond.[32]

Thus it would appear that if American political science is in a "normal science" phase of its development, it is somewhat at the end of that phase, preparing for an overturning of basic presumptions and assumptions. This would fit with the logic of Kuhn's recognition of normal science and its function. As Feyerabend has argued, Kuhn's defense of an exclusivist paradigm (a mature science) is ultimately that "its adoption will in the end lead to the overthrow of the very same paradigm to which scientists have restricted themselves in the first place."[33] Kuhn's thesis that normal science inevitably results in its own refutation is consequently to be understood as a weakened version of Hegel's dialectic: the negation (praxis) of negation (theory and its observational language). Unfortunately, even with his deeper knowledge, comprehensiveness and wit (Feyerabend's characterizations), Hegel's construction of dialectical knowledge, by being cast as historically transcendent, was ultimately as ahistorical as Kuhn's account of theory sequences. Notwithstanding Kuhn's attention to the normalizing tendencies of metaphysical (ideological) systems, sociological (behavioral) structures and artifactual (technical and methodological) inventories, to understand the theoretical conservativeness of political science requires a consciousness of the historical interaction between ideas and the social institutions and structures of Western civilization. The history of American political science has not conformed to Kuhn's succession of normal periods and revolutions because it is implicated in the historical process of the emergence of the modern State from its Late Feudal and Medieval antecedents. The State in the history of Western society, to use Feyerabend's phrase, is "the powerful and non-scientific institution [which] pushes thought in a definite direction."[34]

Kuhn's characterization of puzzle-solving as the dominant (orthodox) activity of normal science does indeed apply to the discipline of political science. It does not achieve, however, the necessary comprehension of the ideological function of political science by the presupposition that paradigmatic revolution follows paradigmatic dominance. For historical reasons and as a consequence of social phenomenology, the metaphysical and sociological aspects of political thought have persisted. As an arrested discipline, political science has been characterized by artifactual innovations rather than paradigmatic transformations. As for example, Samuel Huntington's work demonstrates,[35] the discipline has traveled some notable distance beyond a first-order effort at explication and application of presumptions, model construction and typologizing. Huntington, in the pursuit of a prescription for *ordered rather than democratic* states, leaps over the empiric of his native experience; proclaiming it ordered, he proceeds with a distinguishing typology for those systems in flux in which practically every element fits those nations he considers "ordered."[36]

Conceptually, Huntington has merely contemporized the older distinctions between Western and non-Western, democratic and non-democratic, developed and underdeveloped political societies and supplemented this with his own interests in historical, structural development to explain his specious dichotomization. Yet in comparative politics, his work is considered quite respectable as it has broken new ground in conceptualization and analytical frameworks.[37] As such his study exemplifies the sophistication towards which the discipline has moved and the enormous complexity achieved in the problem-solving aspect of its work. The work now largely describes the background material for political analysis; it has proceeded inappropriately to the point of being axiomatic rather than tendentious. And as this process has continued it has itself left cruel marks on the development of analytic insight and conceptual license.

We may now move from a concern with describing what is meant by a paradigm and a resemblance between that concept and certain representative sequences of political science to a treatment of the epistemological and metaphysical elements which underlie and confirm the political paradigm.

Consciousness of Politicality as Ideology

The political precept as a descriptive capsule for enclosing segments of human experience and organisation has at once become more diffuse in its application while becoming more specific and particular in its definition. The latter phenomenon has itself progressed into lucid absurdity with its concomitant insistence that most significant events of human interaction possess an authentic "political" component referent to an eminently "political" universe. This process has meant the penetration by the "political" of the concerns, interests and phenomena of arenas formerly dominated or characterized by alternative or truly alien instruments of reconciliation or resolution. The anthropologist, Stanley Diamond, in an assessment of the differences between social orders of law and social orders of custom, identifies one such instance:

> . . .law has cannibalized the institutions which it presumably reinforces or with which it interacts.[38]

> Whether the law arises latently, in confirmation of previous usage, or through the transformation of some aspect of custom. . .neither circumstance brings us to the heart of the matter. For we learn by studying intermediate societies that the laws so typical of them are *unprecedented.* . . . They arise in opposition to the customary order of the antecedent kin or kin-equivalent groups; they represent a new set of social goals pursued by a new and unanticipated power in society.[39]

In consequence of this "cannibalization," the discipline's practitioners have not hesitated long enough in their rush to uncover other hidden locations of "the political" to acknowledge or consider the existence or substance of conceptual spaces in their paradigm(s). These spaces, which may indeed be better described as vacuums created by the interruption of one conceptual universe (for example that of kinship, or that of custom) by another (for example that of the political), have remained unremarked upon.[40]

In graphic terms, this vacuum may be thought of as consisting of those loci where these systems, ideologies, dogmas or explanations converge with the result that the "shared" phenomena are not truly possessed by either for each suspends the authenticity and authority of the other. Additionally, of course, there is no reason to restrict the convergence to two systems or even to presuppose that unlike constructs of plane geometry, these systems cannot collide but once. Unfortunately, rationality does often incorrectly imply that coherence or logical consistency is linear, but such a "description" cannot be safely applied to events (of the mind) whose structure consists of language and whose machinery is human thought. In human thought, there are legends, residues and ghosts of logical systems long ago publicly exorcised, which persist, forming a strand here and there of the tapestry of meaning.

Now this is contrary to one level of meaning ascribable to Kuhn's analysis. Kuhn's argument is that paradigms are incommensurable with their competitors because no interparadigm language exists which suspends the beliefs of one and the other so that they might be objectively valued. In opposition, I am suggesting that incommensurability is the consequence of the impossibility of any language being or possibly being paradigmatic in terms of unitary dimensions. Language services human traffic and because of the essentially irrational character of that interaction, language incorporates distinct and different senses of time, history and meaning.

In the contradiction and critique of his own work, Wittgenstein,[41] choosing as a basis for the structure of language first factual propositions and then later tautologies or logical propositions, inadvertently demonstrated this paradox. To be specific, language consists, in part, of "objects" which have long ago ceased to be so, or "objects" which never were so, and "objects" which have still to become so; in other words, beliefs, values, facts and their syncretics. The languages of metaphysics, philosophy and science are and have been obviously no different, pretend as their practitioners have otherwise, but have at their best achieved an order of mathematical precision among some subunits of their interstices.

Thus logical systems interdict on occasion rather than at some point or at some contained series of points, and the resultant antagonism to the presumed nature and character of explanation and meaning resembles that contradiction of physical law known as space or vacuum. We have already seen one example of this experience in the problem of democracy in Western political thought and particularly American political science. This essay, however, requires a more specific explication, or more precisely, a group of such explications, each serving as example, to make its point.

The political, we are told, is a proposition of fundamentally factual properties consisting of the phenomena of force, a force-arena (or community of individuals which may be human or conceptual), choice-in-process and choice-actualized. Imposed on this empirical matrix, we are again instructed, is some declaration concerning order, stability or regularity. In a more integrated presentation, the assertion is that within a collection of human beings, given the "logical" need for order (read as stability), alternatives relating to survival are continuously presented by circumstance (history). These alternatives precipitate a crisis of choice which is resolved by a social instrument, authority, which both tempers the crisis by institutionalizing it, and makes the choice by using some predetermined procedure. The maintenance of this authority itself is achieved through agencies of power. Thus it can be readily seen that power is the *sine qua non* of order. It is not argued, we are assured, that order and power are synchronous or synonymous, but rather that order is a special instance of power. Power, effectively used, provides order.

It follows, then, that as elements of a factual proposition containing power, when one speaks of community, order, history, authority and agencies of authority, one is speaking of political phenomena or speaking of phenomena in a political way—setting off and underlining by those elements which articulate with power, the existence of power, its uses, its effects and its maintenance. While speaking "in the political way" other characteristics of these elements become subordinated or suspended for the moment to ensure a coherence to descriptive and explanatory stratagems. This, then, is a somewhat simplified presentation of how identification and consideration of the political proceeds according to most of its guardians. To them, the political simplifies in terms of revealing an infrastructure behind secondary and tertiary constructions of propositions, hypotheses and frameworks rather than in the sense of providing acceptable distortion for the sake of classification and deductive application. The political is proudly represented as systematic, coherent and logical, in short, scientific, explicated through a language-currency which is itself mathematically precise and bereft of metaphysics. To the contrary, however, I am suggesting that the presence of metaphysics, systemic philosophical errors and epistemological contradictions, can be demonstrated, thus ratifying Kuhn's somewhat rudimentary insights (suggestions, really) concerning the vitality and authority of socio-logical, artifactual, and metaphysical paradigms.

Fundamentally, the difficulties begin with the unsubstantial presumption that, in its origins, the political is a factual proposition, and these misconceptions carry through most of the innumerable vagaries of political thought. This seminal error is demonstrated, but not truly described or explained, by employing once again the nature of a problem encountered by Wittgenstein in his initial investigations of the relationship between language and reality. If reality were determinate, as he first proposed, one would expect that instruments developing from it, to report and reflect it (i.e., language), would bear a basic shared understructure. Instead, with languages, Wittgenstein discovered "resemblances" suggesting the subtle integrations of familial relatedness ("the faces of members of the same family") which, in turn, required that the momentum of his logic reverse the determinism.

Such is the nature of many of the analogues of political history and comparative politics when the literature declares for example the existence of a German feudalism comparable with English feudalism; or medieval European feudalisms with Tokugawa feudalism or with eighteenth-century Bakongo feudalism. There are, of course, superficial similarities (styles of exchange and codes of reciprocity, for instance), but differences strike the analyst's eye as well—for example the existence or absence of alienable land perceptions; the presence of tribal, religious and cultural totalisms preceding the later stage of the state as an organizing principle of the twentieth century in Europe; the presence in one tradition and the absence in another of millenarian outbursts, peasant uprisings, wars of succession, etc.

But even more importantly, one finds also different degrees and totally alien kinds of perceptions, traditions, and beliefs, concerning the *presence* of anything recognizable to participants as the political. One impetus toward the growth of functionalism in modern political science is the confrontation of Western social scientists with people who have realized no distinctly political institutions or traditions and possess no distinct consciousness of the political. This suggests a very different theory of origins for politics. We shall see this contradiction exemplified once again when we talk of leadership. But here it can be demonstrated by the example of apolitical societies (to which we will return in a later chapter).

How does one authentically account for nonpolitical communities, if one accepts for the moment the possibility of their existence? Alternative explanations occur most of which are traditional and as such essentially subvert the significance of the paradigmatic enigma.

It occurs to some analysts[42] that such communities are possible (e.g. in twentieth-century German and American communal movements) if such "experiments" are deposited within the vortex of supremely political states during some crisis which preoccupies the latter. They exist because they do not obtain the attention of the enveloping system though dependent upon its larger economic and social integrations. They are thus quite transitory, quite vulnerable, and fundamentaly dead-end experiences. Their lack of internal political machinery is made possible by the influence and determination of their political hosts and thus they are not truly without politics but suspended proto-colonies somewhere in the interstices of a state.

Another explanation is that such communities may survive among "primitive" peoples who exist outside or are peripheral to political communities; that is people who lack sophisticated stratifications, contain finite populations and possess simple economic relations. Again their persistence is understood as an expression of disinterest (or mometary expansionist exhaustion), or distance (as for example the south-central African people, the Bushmen). Their economic technology is arrested at the hunting-gathering state of subsistence, their living units tend to be extended families. Tradition, habit or religious proscriptions perform the functions of political authority. They are not, then, without politics, but possess a rudimentary or primitive political apparatus. Once again the existence of the phenomenon is finally subverted or negated.

A third possibility is that they do in truth exist independent of any experience of the political either as sufference or embryo through the agency of an entirely different vision of authority from that of the political. But more of this momentarily. The point is that the members of such communities have not confronted themselves with the presumed inevitability of the political facts of existence. Existence is a construct seen as experience consisting of other than politically authoritative choice, value and instrumentalities. The critical substantiation for such a possibility is consciousness.[43] If a people found a consciousness of authority, survival and order without respect to the political, that is without human agencies which embody power and its cognates, then they can be understood to be authentically without politics.[44] Having considered this premise, it will follow despite more amorphous and ambiguous ambitions of functionalist analysis, that it will be possible for them to elaborate and embroider social integrations around quite different prominences in their existential reality than power and coercion, political authority and political history.

Yet such phenomena may be effectively inaccessible to the political scientist whose paradigmatic orthodoxy will, at its furthest stretch, dictate the uncritical application of politics even as metaphor. Both Stanley Diamond and Hannah Arendt have suggested this. Recall the Diamond statement which appeared in the introduction of this essay:

> The inquiry into the nature of politics probably demarcates most accurately the boundaries of our intellectual landscape. The evolution of the state toward what Max Weber called maximally politicized society, the unprecedented concentration of bureaucratic and technological power which economically and culturally dominates the rest of the world, creates a climate in which all problems cast a political shadow. We may flee from the political dimension of our experience or we may embrace it in order to do away with it, but we are obsessed by politics.[45]

Now Arendt:

> . . .to proceed under the implicit assumption that distinctions are not important or, better, that in the social-political-historical realm, that is, in the sphere of human affairs, things do not possess that distinctiveness which traditional metaphysics used to call their "otherness" (their *alterites*), has become the hallmark of a great many theories in the social, political and historical sciences.[46]

The compulsion to subordinate apolitical phenomena to political coherence—just as Marxists conjoin political phenomena to economic and historicist phenomenology—is evidenced repeatedly in studies by political scientists. One instance is the literature of researchers in the "fields" of Southeast Asia and Africa in which the existence of states and requisite phenomena is insisted upon, e.g. nationalism, where they do not occur in any sense authentic to their ontological authority. Yet metatheoretic and epistemological materials do substantiate the logic and possibility of such alternative constructions of reality and in so doing yield not only novel interpretative frameworks but also intimate conceptualizations which could be useful for rationalizing the erroneous system founded upon political authority and political order. But to accept this possibility and to understand the consequence of its logic, one must come to grips with those primal concepts which are no longer for most of us a part of our immediate consciousness. It is time, then, to arrive at some agreement about what one means when speaking of authority and order.

I intend to treat order and authority separately not because they are distinct from each other, but because that is how they are conventionally recognized. There is an analogy here to the use Marx made of the concepts of political economy. He used them not because he accepted them, but because he did not accept them and wished to destroy them before an audience for which they were paradigmatic. Order is not distinct from authority but it is the precept which is authority's precondition. In corollary, authority is the rationalization of order, authorities the rationalizations of orders.

Authority

It is no ordinary handiwork to accomplish some true or trustworthy understanding of the meaning and nature of authority for it is itself the architecture of all understanding. Authority is root and radical, sense and prescience. It is all the events, instruments and organs which contribute the existential boundaries to any and all individuals. There are boundaries beyond which no preceptions, no questions, no presence is suggested. Authority is an absurd, irrational and arbitrarily placed insight which contains the first and last marks in the universe sustained by faith and a fatigued intellectual bruteness in the presumption that there is nothing beyond.

Hannah Arendt, one social theorist who has been concerned with authority for some time, makes for a useful beginning in our pursuit. In an essay which laments the passing of authority from the contemporary stage of mass societies, she translates Theodor Mommsen's dictum of authority which, though specifically concerned with Roman thought, does encompass a sense of the "larger" authority:

> Mommsen called it "more than advice and less than a command, an advice which one may not safely ignore," whereby it is assumed that "the will and the actions of the people like those of children are exposed to error and mistakes and therefore need 'augmentation' and confirmation through the council of elders."[47]

But there are most often more particular experiences of authority all of which are actually Platonic-like projections (in the sense of what Plato did rather than his interpretation of it) of quite tangible, human eventualities and observations. Political authority is one such instance of a particular form of authority which draws upon not only what has previously been distinguished here as the political but also on the metaphysics of authoritativeness previously indicated.

Arendt traces the origins of the two most enduring senses of authority—that is, authority as something which compels human affairs, and as something which is a foundation—to Greek and Roman political thought and philosophy. She argues that Plato, (and in his way, Aristotle) as a major representative of an era of Greek thought, identified authority variously as truth, beauty and lastly as ". . .the highest idea, in which all other ideas must partake in order to be ideas at all. . .that of fitness. . . ."[48] The meaning of authority for Plato was demonstrated in the "rightness" and validity of sequence, in the compelling imagery of fit and in the absence of fundamental contradiction. Just as numbers represented "real" progressions of magnitudes, just as institutions consisted of social and natural phenomena being coalesced through some permanent aesthetic, and just as an all-consuming, self-absorbing wholeness reflected completion, just so authority was to be sensed in its ultimate.

Arendt continues by declaring that Aristotle saw authority as the "natural order of things": an order "which 'established the difference. . .between the younger and the older ones, destined the ones to be ruled and the others to rule.' ''[49] Authority thus assumed the nature of *factual universals* beyond human affairs or intervention but inevitably reflected in the human (for Plato, the philosopher's) eye and often mirrored in social relations. Yet basically, authority took firm hold on the character of *phenomena beyond human meddling* from Plato's Forms—the forms which Plato intended to legitimate lastingly the presumption of rule by the philosopher class by declaring its rule as in the nature of things or in their true order. Plato thus sought to avoid political authority, that is, an authority based on coercion or violence (anathema to the traditional view of the polis) or persuasion (judged inefficient by Plato according to Arendt). Leonard Krieger supports this view of Plato and his intellectual culture:

> . . .the Greeks spawned the generic notion of power and the Romans the political—a circumstance that helps to explain why in subsequent ages utopians have tended to evoke the Greeks and realists the Romans. The Greeks, indeed, had no authentic notion of political power at all, for the simple reason that the notion of political authority is essential to the notion of political power and, as Hannah Arendt has pointed out, the egalitarian polis left the Greeks with no idea of political authority, forcing them to borrow surrogates from the non-political authority of fathers over families, reason over existence, soul over body. . . . In its political context, "power" for Plato simply connoted force. . ."political power" was correspondingly entirely distinct from and subordinate to the intellectual and moral power that was seated exclusively in the rational element and was the only authentic power.[50]

Roman political thought in its form absorbed the Greek precedent and merged it with the Roman tradition and experience of authority in political context. The Romans with their concept of *auctoritas* fittingly established the sense of authority most similar to its contemporary meanings:

> Authority, in contradistinction to power (potestas), had its roots in the past. . .the authoritative character of the 'augmentation' of the elders lies in its being a mere advice, needing neither the form of command, nor external coercion to make itself heard. . . . Thus precedents, the deeds of the ancestors and the usage that grew out of them, were always binding.[51]

32

In pursuing such convictions and statements one becomes aware of a capacity for recognizing distinctions and as well identifications subsequently lost somewhere during the Christian era. Authority, political authority and authority in a political context were not for the Greeks and Romans interchangeable conceptualizations but really rested to some degree on the margins of each other. Plato was concerned initially (as in the Roman understanding) with authority and only subsequently with authority in politics; but he never acknowledged the need for existence of political authority in Greek experience.

The Romans, too, required no such notion as political authority. Until the beginnings of the Christian era, Roman philosophers argued that power related not to Romans themselves but to alien peoples, for the Roman people were subject to an authority integrated by tradition and religion (Arendt is instructive here, as well, as she indicates the origins of "religion" in the Latin *re-ligare*, "to be tied back, obligated, to the enormous, almost superhuman and hence always legendary effort to lay foundations, to build the cornerstone, to found for eternity"[52]). Yet power, in this instance, as that deliberate violence which was to be unleashed upon those outside one's community, was subsequently alienated from authority and this separation issued forth its own kind of crises concerned specifically with political legitimation or its absence.

In turn, these crises nurtured the formulation of political authority so remarkably serviced by Machiavelli. And clearly, political authority was of a species quite different from Greek and Roman authorities or that authority extant in the political context. For Machiavelli, distinguishing his thought from the earlier traditions, political authority rested from its inception in the cradle of power, force and violence. It was, then, a transformation of classical authority into temporal and historical forms, clawing respect not from the bequest of a "true order of things" but from fear, not from a foundation and obligation drawn up in antiquity for eternity but from demonstrated diffuseness. ". . .all political society is based on repressive organized force."[53]

If one were concerned, as Arendt is, with the "death" of authority, it would seem so much more appropriate to begin with the understanding that that phenomenon was not sudden but instead long in

33

vanishing. . .and consequent to the temporalization of authority into its pallid variant political authority. Such would be, however, a specious conclusion for authority as the ontological boundary, the cosmic end-point, has never been abandoned, nor is it ever likely to be, for such limitations correspond and are to be identified with the edges of human consciousness whatever other burdens it may commit upon itself. No, that death has never occurred nor will it ever be recorded. Instead, one must say of those declarations of authority's demise that they lament at an absurdly mistaken graveside. Political authority in Western experience, that monstrous issue of the Christian church and the Christian state, appears, indeed, to have been laid to an abortive rest in place of a much more durable, vigorous and true force. Nor is political authority dead but merely writhing from wounds inevitably self-inflicted—crises of disobedience, disappointment and despair among those who would believe in it.

Arendt insists that the simultaneity and interdependence of the "Roman trinity of authority, religion and tradition" made it impossible for the one to survive without the others; and, she continues, with the default of tradition and religion, authority, too, has ceased to exist. Not too obviously, she is speaking of political tradition, the religion of the state and its authority, not their less particular or historical fraternities.[54]

We recognize, again, the myopia in our analysts and analyses which was suggested and anticipated by Kuhn's paradigmatic vision. Arendt, in the company of so many other social analysts, reasons out from an intellectual and conceptual commitment so precisely articulated in the following lines taken from Herbert Rosinski's writings:

> . . .power. . .is the reverse of a limited or partial concept. Power is nothing less than an objective quality inherent in all that exists by virtue of the mere fact that it does exist. Power is an inescapable aspect of reality itself.[55]

Power and authority are thus confused with one another. Their paradigm relates power to authority by way of political authority. Rosinski has described authority not power because he is conscious of authority in only one way, by way of a politically "ordered" society. This again is an historical consciousness, a consciousness which has emerged through the historical condition of the predominance of the state as an ordering instrument.

Order

We come now to a consideration of order, and, as with authority, we must distinguish social and political perceptions of order from psychological conceptions. Here, too, we discover a deceptive mix between the analytical instruments we bring to bear on the event and the character of the event itself.

The logical analyst will agree with the experimentalist that order consists and is represented to us through patterns, that is, related phenomena integrated by some persistent appearance in time and space. Without some regularity, what we are confronted with remains or, more precisely, becomes senseless—which can mean, contrary to our usual presumptions, that too many of our senses are being activated rather than too few or none of them. Yet even this process of being confused or disoriented by a particle of reality presupposes more primary integrations if we persist in an understanding of it as "our" being confused by something. This primary integration we might consider sanely intelligent yet nothing has been done to avoid an almost inevitable suspension of the critical analysis which follows at some point. Rationality is a stratagem which purports to contain the means of discovering, revealing and articulating certain ordered insights about order, yet it too represents some arbitrary "choice" of which or which not ordered phenomena will be understood and acknowledged.

In such a maze, then, psychological order or the significance of an experience of order for the mind becomes the root instance, that is, the etiological explanation, of any method which would discover political order through an epistemological device. With a not very different purpose in mind, Polanyi has stated:

> Every kind of human knowing, ranging from perception to scientific observation, includes an appreciation both of order contrasted to randomness and of the degree of this order.[56]

and elsewhere:

> . . .it is enough to recognize here that, in affirming these fundamental laws of nature i.e. the laws of statistical thermodynamics, kinetics, thermal motion and natural selection, we accredit our capacity for knowing randomness from order in nature and that this distinction cannot be based on considerations or numerical probabilities, since the calculus of probabilities presupposes, on the contrary, our capacity to understand and recognize randomness in nature.[57]

Experimental psychology has, to a large extent, confirmed this thesis particularly in its *gestalt* studies. Studies which have repeatedly demonstrated the relationship between the eye, the brain and the mind, culminating in, for the individual, the insight or experience of objectness, the figure or order against a background of randomness.[58] Thus, it appears, we are taught or instructed by "simple" biological mechanisms the truth of order, an order upon which our capacity to survive is dependent. This sequence known as perception then lends itself in the development and maturation of the individual in psychosocial terms to a character of knowing and delineates as well the nature of things knowable.

This fundamental intuition for knowing and understanding in orders and degrees of order becomes as well the basis for the experiential projection which we mean by social or political order. Again, according to Wolin, it seems Plato has been definitive:

> . . .he taught later writers to think of political society as a coherent, interconnected whole; he was the first to view political society in the round, to view it as a "system" of interrelated functions, an ordered structure. . . . In short, Plato was the first to picture political society as a system of distinctive or differentiated roles. . . . The harmonization and integration of these roles made of political society a functioning, interdependent whole. . .there must be no confusion of roles, no blurred identities.[59]

This integration, this structuring of society, dependent as it has seemingly always been in Western political thought on an instrument of power is then really a most extraordinary resonation. It is a quite primitive response, a convergence and reiteration of a sense experience from such to an intuited theory of social beings. The lens of the eye given its quite particular capacities and styles for discrimination thus dictates to the mind (as, indeed, Levi-Strauss seems to be saying) its ways of knowing (object and categorization) which in turn proceeds to declare and actuate that same image into a nature of society—a society made intelligible only through the agencies of object, order and regularity in contradistinction to the diffuse and the random. Edmund Leach puts it this way:

> I postulate that the physical and social environment of a young child is perceived as a continuum. It does not contain any intrinsically separate 'things'. The child, in due course, is taught to impose upon this environment a kind of discriminating grid which serves to distinguish the world as being composed of a large number of separate things, each labeled with a name. . . . But how can such certainty of discrimination be achieved if our normal perception displays only a continuum?. . .We achieve this second kind of trained perception by means of a simultaneous use of language and taboo. Language gives us the names to distinguish the things; taboo inhibits the recognition of those parts of the continuum which separate the things.[60]

So social order must consist of integrations, institutions and patterns in order to satisfy the images of the mind and the skills of the brain and the eye. And that coherence, the certainty of that coherence in Western political thought, is obtained by one object, political authority, acting on the others and corresponding as such to another dictate of the perceptual experience, movement and thus causation.

There is, then, to some large degree, a correspondence in their sophistications between a political philosophy (or paradigm) which acknowledges political order through political authority and a geometric astronomical paradigm. Both, quite understandably, are a reflection of the sense of the being, and the discrepancy in the duration of their dominance over human preoccupation can be, in part, explained by the relative inaccessibility of the latter to human intervention and machination. It is, indeed, difficult to escape the mischievous tyranny of a mind which can not only declare but also sculpture the physique of its error into reality.

> The categorical and the abstract replace learning rooted in the perception of structures, thinking takes on a schizophrenic quality as the concept precedes the knowledge that comes from direct experience, and language becomes more and more metaphorical.[61]

But we should also pay attention to another aspect we have discovered in our preceding comments, an aspect in the inventory of perceptual experiences which gives rise to other models of social order. Images projected on screens of time and space are subject, too, to a sense of their stillness, movement, permanence and change. Patterns before the eye maintain stability or permutate, they remain fixed or they flit about the perceptual arena, they persist or they are extinguished. We make from this a sense of their movement or absence of it, awareness of their presence and define the character of their natures as the brain summons its past. Concomitance, the synchronous, causality and existential separateness and unrelatedness are translated into models of change and exchange.

To the Western social analyst social order becomes understandable, in terms of evolution, revolution, incremental integration and disintegration. Ernest Gellner has taken these theories of progress and social order appearing in Western political and social thought in the past several centuries and argued that they have exhibited at least one of three characters: episodic, evolutionary, or neoepisodic.[62] More specifically, he has meant that they consisted of progress as seen as event or process; a total event beginning with an act (e.g. Rosseau's social contract) which propelled mankind from bad to good conditions; or a process of global dimensions (as with Hegelian realization or Marxian historicism) fundamentally entelechic.

The interesting thing here is that whether one can accept Gellner's particular way of characterizing the order of change as they have been encompassed into the concept of progress or not, other analysts have as well remarked on similar epistemological matrices, all of which suspiciously mirror the perceptual experience of patterns in some motion and sequence. As such, theoretical and analytical thought are merely quite elaborate expressions of this "projection":

> Scientists do tolerate uncertainty and frustration, because they must. One thing they do not and must not tolerate is disorder. The whole aim

of theoretical science is to carry to the highest possible and conscious degree the perceptual reduction of chaos that began in so lowly and (in all probability) unconscious a way with the origin of life. In specific instances it can well be questioned whether the order so achieved is an objective characteristic of the phenomena or is an artifact constructed by the scientist. That question comes up time after time. . . . Nevertheless, the most basic postulate of science is that nature itself is orderly. . . . All theoretical science is ordering and, if systematics is equated with ordering, then systematics is synonymous with theoretical science.[63]

And, of course, this immersion in order is an anthropological "truth":

This thirst for objective knowledge is one of the most neglected aspects of the thought of people we call "primitive". Even if it is rarely directed towards facts of the same level as those with which modern science is concerned, it implies comparable intellectual application and methods of observation. . . . The thought we call primitive is founded on this demand for order. This is equally true of all thought but it is through the properties common to all thought that we can most easily begin to understand forms of thought which seem very strange to us.[64]

And so order is not only represented by the visual experience of patterns seen suspended in one space and one time, but perceived as well as suspended through successive dimensions of space and periods of time. That is to say that order can be seen *in design*—in place, or order can be seen *in lawfulness*—over time. And social order, a conception which emerges from order, can presume, too, fundamentally different images of objectness and continuity, Conceptualizations of social order can range from the design of Aristotelian and Burkean "constitutionalities" and anarchistic rationalisms to the law-fulfilling dialectic of Hegel and the historicism of Marx—from station to process. In the end, of course, they amount to the same thing: "the perceptual reduction of chaos," the ensuring of the existence of an identifiable, objective reality.

Thus it can be said that order as a presumption concerning human existence proceeds from looking at things.

CHAPTER II

The Parameters of Leadership

One means by which members of a political community perceive the nature of their political order is through political leadership. It is through the leader that a relationship with what is conceptualized as being the established political order is maintained. Political leadership thus *represents* and *relates* the objective reality of order and authority presumably found in political order and political authority. Consequently, an analysis of the meaning(s) of leadership should allow us to identify the perceived character of political authority and political order extant in a particular community. I believe that the empirical function of the leader is to define the situation of the community and to choose and organize activity in the situation which will benefit the community. The leader is an instrument of rational action where rational action is understood as collective action which extends the survival of the community. The leader is thus an element in the logical-positivist model of reality. The situation of the community is an objective situation accessible to the decoding, rearrangement, and definition of its objects by the leader. But political leadership is also an idea. As such, I will argue, it possesses the properties that Walter Benjamin associated with ideas. According to Susan Buck-Morss, Benjamin

> . . .argued that the particular was not identical to the general. Its essence or truth could not be reached through abstraction. Instead, the general was contained *within* the particular. The smallest unity, the extreme, the detail—these were the source of truth: "The idea is a monad—that is, in short: every idea contains the image of the world."[1]

Political leadership is one such "detail," or "particular." It is a critical idea. Political leadership then becomes an occasion for the testing of the epistemology of political order in terms of the revelation of its substructural components and its functions as well as their structural rationality and integration. Thus in this chapter, political leadership will be dealt with on two quite different levels: its function and its theory.

The Leader as Manifest Idea

In his analysis of political leadership in contemporary American society, Murray Edelman made a number of observations which will be useful in our present discussion of leadership.[2] Equally instructive will be the number of things he failed to say about political leadership; failures which were inherent in the analytical procedure he chose to adopt.

Being concerned primarily with the "meanings for large publics of the acts and gestures of leaders, of the settings in which political acts occur, of the language styles and the phrases that permeate political discussion and action, of law enforcement activities,"[3] the myths and rituals of politics, Edelman relied heavily on psychological and linguistic analyses. This approach might have proven quite powerful except for the fact that it was used in an ahistorical way. Edelman failed to recognize the imprint that the development of institutions and structures made on the symbolic phenomena with which he was concerned. He failed to pursue the significance that socioeconomic and epistemological dynamics possessed for the roles and ideology which are the matrix of American political leadership. Nevertheless, he did produce an outline of leadership which can be used as a starting point in our inquiry.

Edelman identified a number of characteristics associated with the leader. Each of these characteristics relates either to the elite or extraordinary quality of the leader: intelligence, knowledge, skills, certainty, responsibility, capacity to give direction, success, conspicuousness, potentiality. The leader is thus someone who is recognizably set off from the collective mass. The leader is someone who possesses these qualities in larger measure than other members of the relevant population.

In addition to these prescriptive characteristics, Edelman argued that the actions of the leader are also definitive. The leader is perceived as someone free to choose actions—someone who by force of personality or the manipulation of the symbolic culture is capable of "evoking strong emotional response in large populations."[4] The leader is someone who gives to the situation a definition and is capable of identifying a problem and presenting a solution.

The perceived impact of the leader is thus largely implied by the preceding associations. The political leader as symbol for the State brings rationality to the situation. The situation becomes manageable after having been identified by the leader as one of lawfulness and regularity:

> The creation of law and regularity and personal planning where accident, chaos, and impersonality are feared is his key symbolic function. We speak a great deal about our "government of laws and not of men," but we must write histories about culture heroes who established the laws and sustained them.[5]

Implicit, then, in this "key symbolic function" is the presumption of *objectness in* and *objectivity of* the situation. In order to be recognized or understood, the situation must be made to conform to determinate, bound attributes. Its dynamics must be explicit and overt rather than subtle. The situation must be definite, that is capable of being perceived in preceise terms: it is a proposition. The political leader as Edelman describes the role, is an element in a model posited by the epistemology of logical positivism. Theodor Adorno revealed the critical presumption of that model in his criticisms of Karl Popper's thought:

> Popper's celebrated "third realm" of "problems and scientific suppositions about problems" is no more than a normative simplification. Inherent in it, argues Adorno, is the aprioristic and severely reductionist assumption that authentic reflection bears only on soluble problems or, more precisely, on decidable propositions. The Popperian scheme is very likely inadequate to the praxis of the natural sciences with its inevitable admixture of historical, social and epistemological variables.[6]

42

In the context of contemporary American political analysis, the notion of the political leader is a way of talking about a specific process of resolution. And the roots of this procedure of resolution rest in the representation of reality defined by the paradigm of logical positivism. Edelman had recognized this in a particular way:

> Leadership. . .is not to be understood as something an individual does or does not have, at all times and places. It is always defined by a specific situation and is recognized in the response of followers to individual acts and speeches. If they respond favorably and follow, there is leadership; if they do not, there is not.[7]

Certainly, as is pointed out below, Edelman was critical of the leader-follower roles which accrue to the American poltical process: arrogant, dissembling leadership and submissive, uncritical followership. But Edelman's criticism was of the actual political leaders who pretend to perform the role of political leadership rather than of the model itself. He argued that the organizational and structural complexities were such as to void political leadership by obfuscating responsibility and achievement. In Edelman's own terms, unlike the conditions present in "simpler politics," in an "age of large organizations" the analyses of decision-making and the significance of decisions made are of little use in the political arena. The public assessment of leaders is no longer objective:

> Leaders rely increasingly on style differences to create and emphasize an impression of maneuverability, and the impression remains an important political fact even if the maneuverability is not.
>
> The achievement of particular results is therefore not ordinarily a major influence upon the continued incumbency of a leader or upon public restiveness or satisfaction, though it may become so in rare cases of inflexibility or obtuseness. What counts normally is the affective response of political groupings in particular situations.[8]

In Edelman's estimation, malleable, subjective calculi had displaced rational, objective criteria. Concerns for identifying the efficiency of the model in operation had been set aside by its "dramaturgical" impact.

But despite his criticisms, Edelman failed to recognize in his ahistorical analysis several crucial relationships contained in the paradigm of political leadership. He failed to identify in political leadership its relationship with political authority, substituting instead a functional, utilitarian model for this relationship. His discussion of political authority[9] was less a critical discussion of ideology and conceptual systems than a treatment of bureaucratic dynamics.

In contradistinction to Edelman, I will suggest in this chapter that political authority is integrated in the dialectic of the social, economic, conceptual and ideological forces of a society. It is a dynamic, developing aspect of the culture of that society, an historical expression. And political leadership is inseparable from political authority.

In discussing American political leadership, Edelman had also ignored the development of the State and its relationship to the development of capitalism. The conflicts, crises and contradictions are never discussed. The insights which might have generated from a concern with the development of an urban, industrial working-class out of a feudal past are, in Edelman, apparently substituted for by dyadic and group dynamics. A sensitive treatment of the evolution of liberal theory and ideology which form the basis of individualism in contemporary American society and culture finds in its stead the use by Edelman of ego psychology.

In short, what is missing in Edelman's work is the sociohistorical foundation of the psychological and ideographic phenomena he is studying. Political leadership, political leaders, styles of leadership, are all expressions of political authority. They are legitimated, to use a term associated with Weber, by political authority. In its turn, political authority is the consequence and expression of objective, conceptual and ideological processes. The weakness of any analysis which mistakes these relationships is narrow, paradigmatic conformity. In other words, such an analysis is weakened by a form of reductionism. In such instances, recognition of isolated elements of processes precludes comprehension and consciousness of those processes. The *totality* of social change and transformation is missed. As one becomes accustomed to conceptualizing reality in terms of its particular items, the suggestions of fundamental changes become traumatic jolts to be avoided at any cost.

The Relationship of Political Leadership
to Political Authority

I have argued in the last two sections of the previous chapter that order and authority articulate with social or political order and political authority in precisely the same way as Kuhn's metaphysical paradigms articulate with his artifactual ones.[10] The concepts are inherently present in how we have learned to see and what we have learned to see. This would suggest that in the logical order of things these perceptual skills are predispositions or "pre-visions." As predispositions, these perceptual skills are the structures of the experential and analytical resources developed by members of any and all human societies and communities. They are the lattice-work of experience and thinking about experience.

The outcome of this process is that these predispositions, integrated and codified in conceptual and analytical systems, express through language as their text some ideology or some "social construction of reality." The purpose of this last phrase is to bring to mind the acute description of some aspects of this process contained in the work of Berger and Luckmann.[11]

By analogy, just as political authority is a particular construction of authority, political leadership is a particular characterization of political authority. It is leadership that one describes when one is speaking about the influence of one individual over others which results in particular value-, perception-, behavior- and concept-choices. It too is of leadership that one speaks when the question is that of the influence of a finite number of individuals on a mass of individuals.

Political leadership is that which characteristically effects these relationships through the instruments of coercion, violence, domination and the effective usurpation and control of information and communication. Political leadership is that which achieves the pre-eminent manipulation of symbols by political instruments, that is instruments designed to deal with opposition and advocacy. Other dynamics may be recognized in the matrix of a political relationship, viz. persuasion and ideology formation, but the root of the relationship is force.

In contrast to political leadership, political authority is the historical continuity, the social and traditional matrix which relates one leader to his or her predecessors and successors. It relates one elite with its past and future counterparts and, in the minds of all the members of society, appears as a continuity in the experience of domination from what Was to what Will be. Political leadership is the instrument made accessible to a community by the development of and dependence on political authority. Political authority is an adaptation to and an expression of the community's historical experience. All this must be understood, then, in terms of process: from crises to adaptation (or skill) to adaptation seen as the new matrix or milieu.

But if political authority can be understood as a *skill* achieved by a group, then it can be said that political leadership is the actualization of a myth, a legend or, as it were, a social ideology. Political leadership is a way of comprehending which substantially consists in the collective idealization, or said differently, exaggeration of modalities (or characteristics) contained in certain crisis-experiences. These crisis-experiences were those which accompanied the construction of the community historically, its reconstruction, or more descriptively accurate, its reproduction in terms of socialization.[12] In the context of our present discussion, the developments of industrial capitalism, the State and the liberal theory of democracy were such crisis-experiences. Whether they developed from forces within the society (e.g. in the case of England) or were introduced through largely external forces, or something in between (the case of Japan), their significance was to transform the matrix of political authority so that it might accomodate them.[13]

Political leadership is then the reified expression of a tradition of meaning which authorizes and determines the loci, forms and styles of social and economic resolution, and presents the means of their ultimate legitimation or illegitimation.[14] And it is to that particular matrix of political authority in a society's psychohistorical experience that all political leadership is fundamentally referred. This must occur for the matrices assume different consistencies in different societies corresponding to their peculiar origins. Political authority always incorporates particular historical content.

Yet it is not merely the "parochials," "subjects," or

"participants"[15] who subordinate their visions and imaginations to the *dicta* of the particular political authority of their society. The conventional definitions of established political roles within a political society must be extended. The same subordination is true, as well, for the overwhelming majority of those who have presumed to be concerned with, or pretended toward social analysis, i.e. social theorists, critics and analysts.

"Democratic" theorists, too, have emerged as ideologues (believers) and ideologists (makers of beliefs). It is they who have—appropriate to their roles—tempered, obscured and confused the meaning of a "democratic system" in Western thought. When they speak of the processes of decision-making, electoral or legislative behaviors, communication media, public opinion, etc., in a "democratic society," they have had in mind that peculiar notion of democracy discussed in Chapter I. And when they turn their attention to "democratic" leaders, it is this same attenuated construct of a democratic system which becomes the reference point. It is the degree of conformity or degree of conflict with this construct which becomes the basic concern. So we are not surprised when Alvin Gouldner quite uncritically asserts:

> The problem confronting democrats is how to use leadership for realizing their goals, rather than how to get along without leadership. Put differently, the problem is the old one of combining democratic with effective social organization. This would seem to be advanced by enlarging the understanding which rank-and-file members of any group have of their leadership. Such an understanding would entail analytic thinking about leadership and encourage an emotional objectivity that would sap the mystique of leadership. . . . An ineffectual leadership is of no use to adherents of any set of values, let alone to hard-pressed democrats.[16]

The number of implicit and explicit presumptions in such an assessment is quite large. Each proceeds on the back of the other, supported by the first. Each is supported by what Gouldner, the editor of this series of leadership studies, would call twenty years later "background assumptions."[17] In what for most of us is an extraordinarily familiar thought-chain concerning an egalitarian model, several anomalies are just barely concealed:

1. The presence of at least three strata in an implicitly, permanently stratified society: ideologues-ideologists (addressed as "democrats"); leaders; and the rank-and-file.

2. The identification of the first group as the guardians of the social procedures through their manipulation of social organization for the maintenance of the goals and values they perceive as in their best interests, and only by suggestion, in the best interests of the whole ("enlarging understanding" contains no real commitment to transforming passiveness into active responsibility).

3. The reminder that whatever the goals, their realization must conform to certain organizational boundaries.

4. The critical function of the ideology they produce is to fix the arrangement of the political elements of the society to each other.

5. The epistemological commitments which will determine the rules or social or organizational laws with which the structure of the society must conform are situated in logical positivism. How can the effectiveness of democratic organization be "problematic" in American society? No such problematicism exists for a thing in the absence of the preconditions of its occurrence.

These same assumptions and presumptions operate in comparative analyses. The striking independent variable is usually the analyst's degree of sophistication, that is the analyst's capacity to suspend his or her ethnocentrism. This sophistication is more likely to be absent when the analyst is making comparisons between "democratic" and "nondemocratic" systems. But the problems persist even in the instance when work is concerned with "competing" democratic traditions. This is true because each "democratic" tradition evidences its own remarkable and "alien" specializations. To the North American, one example of these specializationis might be Britain's constitutional monarchy; privileged parliamentarians; the relationship between prime minister and other ministries; etc. Yet the allowances which are made on such occasions turn to dread and awe in the instances when confronting "nondemocratic" systems. We discover, for example, analogies being made with disease:

> Should this work wish to articulate with the social tendencies giving impetus to interest in leadership, it must take cognizance of the anti-

democratic direction latent and overt in these tendencies. The forms, techniques, the social and psychological conditions evoking authoritarian leadership, and possible ways of containing it, should come under consideration. This seems as justifiable and vital an undertaking as medical science's study and efforts to control the pathogenic agents impairing the human organism.[18]

Yet the focus of explication consistently remains fixed on a discussion and exposition of the degrees of fit and/or contradiction to the conception one maintains of political authority in one's own social history. That is, whatever tradition of political authority the analyst emerges from is persistent in his or her observations elsewhere. And, again, whatever the particular form of that political authority, it seldom conflicts with the anticipation or existence of political leadership. The political leadership of one's own society seems reasonable according to the accepted tradition of political authority. This is something which is true, too, perhaps more frequently than is generally presumed, for the anarchists and "utopians." The paradigm holds true even when "we" in the liberal democratic tradition seek corrective instruments:

. . .it is plain that no one can be a leader in isolation. It is never enough to ask: Who is this leader? A more meaningful question is fourfold: Who is leading whom from where to where? The leader's character, the expectations of his contemporaries, the play of historic circumstance, and the success or failure of a movement in reaching its goals are equally important parts of the over-all process.[19]

And even when the most extensive of mandates (i.e. charisma[20]) has been proffered and has been seen to have failed by the analyst, no fundamental reevaluation is attempted or suggested:

Names of highly charismatic leaders who failed because they were short of skill come to mind only too readily. What has been said applies to both revolutionary leaders and "reform-mongers." Both need a minimum of skill. . . . Only in this way can they do better for the communities which they pretend to lead than those communities would be expected to do if one were to predict their future on the basis of their average attitudes, perceptions, and misperceptions. This is the ultimate function and justification of the leader: to improve on the *average* prospects for advance of those whom he leads, to raise the expected value of their future.[21]

And so, on and on. The literatures of sociology, political science, history and social psychology stridently substantiate through the plethora of analytical instruments, the metaphysics of leadership. In the historical sociology of leadership, the presumption of the inevitability of leadership as a characteristic of all human association assumes, of course, finally the weight or authority of "normalness". Leadership is thus orthodoxy, reasonable and sane depending upon the analytical frame of reference the observer consciously favors or is possessed by unconsciously. Leadership is not a specific state or condition of social organizations but a characteristic, *sui generis*. Leadership is presumed to augur effective social action just as authority is inexorably related to the social order. In this instance, effectiveness presumably relates to the processes of action or the actualization of the instrument, the group, rather than to the consequences incurred once a group has been mobilized. Eufunction and dysfunction, success of failure, are too often attributed to factors outside the "well led" group, relating ultimately to the historical moment of the group's evolution and appearance. Yet groups are acknowledged as failing because of their particular leadership and/or in spite of their particular leadership but never because they possessed leadership:

> This book presented a theory of leadership effectiveness which takes account of the leader's personality as well as the situational factors in the leadership situation. We have known for some time that the same type of leadership style or leadership behavior will not be suitable for all situations. This theory attempts to specify in more precise terms the conditions under which one leadership style or another will be more conducive to group effectiveness. The theory thus reconciles the sometimes conflicting claims and results which would favor one style of leadership over another.[22]

The Leader as Deviant

Yet despite the ineluctability of the appearance or development of the leader, most of the literature of the social sciences does indicate, suggest or declare that the leader is him- or herself a deviant, an extra-ordinary. One description and analysis of leadership which exemplifies this is cited by Gouldner. The formulation belongs to Mapheus Smith who sees:

1. The leaders as those whose *attainments*, in terms of a set of goals are considered "high".
2. The leaders as those whose *status* is recognized as superior to others engaged in the same activities.
3. The leaders as those who emit stimuli that are "responded to integratively by other people."[23]

To paraphrase Smith, the leader achieves more, possesses a higher status and influences his "contemporaries" to an extraordinary degree. But the wrapping of this quality of the extraordinary into the envelope of a normal event does produce some tension and as a consequence some near absurdities:

If a dichotomized difference is sought between leaders and followers, then there is none. The difference is most probably a matter of degree, regardless of which definition of leadership is employed. This by no means impairs our ability to use such a definition. For in many cases the difference of degree seems sufficiently sharp to make possible a workable distinction among a group of individuals. In other words, given a group of one-hundred people, we could probably be sure that those who were at one extreme in their ability to structure behavior were leaders, while those at the other extreme were followers. . .This inability to dichotomize leaders and followers should also serve to emphasize that no unbridgeable gulf exists between leaders and follow-ers, such as is sometimes implied in certain stereotypes.[24]

Though the "unbridgeable gulf" of some analysts becomes the statisticized "matters of degree" for others, the function of the leader as a role-player remains by definition singular, unique and distinct. There remains to be seen no suggestion that the normativist (here read "democratic" normativist) or behavioralist can subsequently dismiss the category of leader as some sort of distortion in the prescriptive or observational exercise. Because one senses here some confusion aris-ing out of what is essentially contradiction, it is precisely here that one can begin to address the various fallacies or exaggerations which undergird the orthodoxy of leadership analysts.

If we review more closely Smith's formulations concerning the identification and definition of leadership, several problems emerge. Assuming that achievement, status and stimuli must articulate together in order to produce the impression for Smith of an individual *leading* within a community of others, the first of the three criteria, attainment or to a much smaller degree success, does *suggest* the obtainment of an "objective" criterion—of the occurrence of an event beyond question, a fact. Unfortunately, the objectivity of this criterion is merely a suggestion actually and not a fact since it does imply a judgement which concerns the significance of an act or action and thus presupposes someone to judge attainment through the use of an accepted codified "law" of achievement. In other words, Smith does not share with us the means by which he arrives at recognizing something as achievement.

Nevertheless, attainment is the closest that Smith comes to laying down an observable *a priori* to leadership—that is something the person does which precedes acceptance by anyone (including him- or herself) of that individual's preeminence. What follows this quality of extraordinariness, then, or more accurately what may follow since there are other responses available, is a quantum leap in the estimation of that individual by others and their subordination to him or her in specific or nonspecific ways.

Leadership, as such, can then be seen as a strategy for dealing with the appearance and subsequent impacts of extraordinary individuals in a "closed group" (suggesting again that the closure is always arbitrarily bounded in spatiotemporal terms). Status and subordination as ascriptive phenomena serve as the definitional elements in the recognition of leadership, while achievement signifies the identity and identifications of the leader. The difference here is between what one makes of the appearance of an object and what the object as phenomenon actually is. Historical biographies in the field of leadersihp have frequently reconstructed from the figure of the leader individuals hardly recognizable to the particular era's "masses."[25]

Yet what we mean by leader at this point seems to grow in complexity and uncertainty since we acknowledge no inevitability between the event of greater effectiveness and the appointment to leadership. We realize that others may or may not relate to such displays sympathetically or by emulation or through the projections of analogues or even by celebrating its convenience to their own lives and achievements. We know that they may fail to recognize, *acknowledge*, sense or project the representativeness of the extraordinary person. If they indeed do so, rather than attract, it may repulse. And further, if the inevitability of the leader-reaction can be questioned, so too the normality of the reaction. It can be questioned first in its implication of statistical frequency and secondly in its suggestion of psychic eufunctionality.

First of all is it not "normal" that much high achievement go unrecognized? And if recognized, is it not "normal" that high achievement be frequently signified as petty mastery or as specific expertise unrelated to the question of submission? That is, is it not normal that achievement be effectively ignored by resisting the interpretation—or failing to arrive at the interpretation—that it is salient to one's own concerns?

In terms of accessibility to the order of things leading to subordination, high achievement can be quite justifiably said to be "normally" defused. And so it follows that the according of a specific and certain status to high achievement is hardly normal or inevitable. High achievement may be the instrument for transporting such "leaders" outside of one's own life sphere to the status, perhaps, of the alien as the insane, or the alien as criminal, or the alien as a member of some other parallel universe. Or as one alternative, high achievement may be a means of allowing the depositing of such individuals on the top of that sphere. But it is unquestionably an array of circumstance which makes one of these resolutions more accessible than the others. As Sidney Hook put it:

> The rise of capitalism, the industrial revolution, the march of the barbarians from the east, the Renaissance—none, of course, would have been possible without the acts or examples of individuals. But no matter what particular individuals are named in connection with these movements, there is no evidence that the individuals were indispensable in the sense that without them these movements would not have got under way.[26]

However, Gouldner takes exception to our primary premise and emerges with a very different understanding of the leader as that role is prescribed within "democratic" processes. Though Gouldner introduces Smith's formulation as one having "sifted out the essential distinctions that have been made,"[27] he chooses not to recognize their integration or its relevance for the social scientist. He eschews the criterion of attainment as a begging of the question and not "central" to the problem identified in the essays he has edited and concentrates instead on status and the emission of stimuli. This is difficult to reconcile with the fact that he does finally paraphrase as the legitimation of leaders (including charismatic ones) Max Weber's *ideal types* of authority legitimation:

> The leader might be viewed as being a person with unusual endowments; perhaps his stimuli are legitimated by virtue of the legal or traditional system of norms governing his appointment or election, perhaps because of his knowledge of expertise, or because he exemplifies other qualities valued by the group.[28]

And he also "finally" argues that neither attainment nor social status are definitive in the leader-follower situation:

> Individuals, therefore, emitting legitimate, group-patterning stimuli, whether "orders," "commands," "instructions," or "suggestions," will be considered leaders regardless of their degree of attainments or their social status.[29]

Gouldner in such manner reveals the foundations of his working paradigm. He has chosen to recognize in leadership an analogue to industrial organization.[30] Since effective social action depends upon the integrative aspect of the stimuli emitted by the leader, one must presume that the group before the advent of the leader consists of poorly integrated units—collective momentum is lacking. And so the leader congeals these disparate parts, he or she manages the collectivization, ensuring that its resources are coordinated and concentrated in the appropriate arenas and/or on the appropriate issues or problems. However, to see leadership in terms of this particular form or organization is to exaggerate, to over-emphasize and misinterpret the nature of the "individual" member of the society.

Is the individual a discrete phenomenon, a social device, as Gouldner's analysis suggests, subject in the interaction with others of his type to the application of a variant of collision theory and vector analysis? Are his psychosocial boundaries so precise, or so well preserved, or if not precise, so irrelevant to the phenomena of submission, obligation and obedience as to justify an analytical approach which recognizes and manipulates only atomistic and molecular phenomena (and even here an anachronism emerges for the physical model is Newtonian rather than contemporary, i.e. of quantum theory and mechanics)? When he presumes that a stimulus autonomously predetermines an "integrative response," has not this early Gouldner inflated the aspect of the individual as an object into that of a first-order axiom? And has he not simplified the mass of "networks" to a strange parallel of mystical and scientific causalities reaffirming as he does the communication model of political systems with his reliance on stimuli emission?

Suspended between the presumption that democratic society requires a style of leadership for its preservation and the belief that leadership usurps certain critical prerogatives from other members of the group, Gouldner searches for the manager. The manager is the industrial-morphic organizational engineer around whom only rational and economic action and loyalties will thrive. But it is precisely in this form that the resolution causes concern, for, as Anthony Piepe remarks, although ". . .it is absurd to suppose that rational behavior predominates in social action. . .it is easy to underestimate the degree of rationality in social affairs."[31] Piepe goes on to declare that other phenomena get in the way of "rationality," phenomena such as prejudices, traditions, or creeds. In other words, as I read him, it is possible that what Piepe is describing can be understood as alternative rationalities, mutually exclusive but coherent systems, competing for the energies, resources and interest for their exclusive fulfillment.

In such way, we encounter a definitive expression of this difficulty with the "economic society" which replaces the psychohistorical experience of society.

The Conceptual Imprint of the Market Society

Historically, if we trace the formation of the most articulated (if not dominant) notions of leadership and submission as they occurred in Western Europe, we discover three distinct social forces which have contributed differently to our conception of democratic leadership: the Church, the State, and industrial organization. The first two, however, are closer to each other than they are to the third both in the form of leadership (and thus obedience) that they sanctioned and the extent to which they intruded into the lives of their subjects. They were also complimentary while capitalist production proved to be subversive of both.[32]

Neither the medieval Church nor the Absolute State of the late medieval period required regimentation of a total or incessant sort. Their authorities, both because they were absolute and essentially extractive in their appropriations, were only episodically intrusive for the most part. Moreover, to a certain extent, the princes of the Church and the State expected their subjects to be hostile, recalcitrant and given to fits of rebelliousness (i.e. sinfulness or crimes against the crown). The development of industrial organization, however, presupposed a different order of discipline and civility. Industrial production demanded a kind of submission which invaded every recess of the worker's existence. The insularity of the peasant, the serf, the artisan, the domestic handicraft worker was dissolved by the concentration of industrial labor, its standardization and mechanization.[33] This loss of personal autonomy was thus existentially and ideologically authorized by the envelopment of the individual by a rationalized social order and organization. Marx had captured these events and processes in two phases: "The ideas of the ruling class are in every epoch the ruling ideas" (*The German Ideology*); and "The bourgeoisie keeps more and more doing away with the scattered state of the population, of the means of production, and of property" (*The Communist Manifesto*). The bourgeoisie mystified their expropriation of wealth by accruing to themselves the function of rational, scientific management. In this way, the mystification of the ruling class of industrial society became the historical and political basis for the mystification of leadership in contemporary Western thought.[34] Concomitant to this mystification was the conduction of the discipline of the industrial work place to the regions of social and political behavior.

The market society informs the political authority of Western society. It is at its roots. The constructs of the market or economic society are one set of the material factors which service the political authority *episteme*. These factors have transformed political authority as well as supplying political authority with appropriate means of expression. And it is not too difficult to uncover the material basis for this argument.

It would appear that the styles in which individuals are organized to work are often extended beyond the situational boundaries of whatever is the discrete operation. When confronted with a task to be performed against their environment, individuals have also ordered and conformed their interactions, and these systems have influenced their lives sometimes in unexpected ways. Specifically, the techniques, calculations, skills, etc. of a market economy have not been limited to the operations of what bourgeois society recognizes as economics. Thus ideologues and social theorists have sought to expand this experience beyond its empirical and situational prerequisites to encompass social and political phenomena and their institutions in conceptual constructs.

In a treatment of Marx's discussion of labor in *Das Kapital*, Jurgen Habermas has written:

> The nature that surrounds us constitutes itself as objective nature for us only in being mediated by the subjective nature of man through processes of social labor. That is why labor, or work, is not only a fundamental category of human experience but also an epistemological category.[35]

Habermas has been echoed by others: Trent Schroyer interprets Habermas' attempt to characterize the existential significance of modes of production in the following way:

> Habermas argues that the Marxist notion of work is not only an economic category, but also deals with ways in which the material base of society conditions objectively possible knowledge.[36]

These constructs have filtered into the perceptual and conceptual arenas from observations of the empirical make-up of economic and technological relations between individuals. And this process has produced two anomalies.

The first anomaly proceeds from the fact that system and organizational forms borrowed from technical and economic organizations are designed to deal with phenomena of a specific type. The most relevant characteristic of these phenomena is that they have been identified in terms of the interest and intent to control and manipulate. They are thus described in rational and linear terms. For example, when one is building bridges or preparing a fission implosion, explanation is usefully replaced by vector analysis or causative descriptions. And, of course, this structural engineering displays extraordinary ranges of sophistication. But here the subject has a limited range of relevant characteristics and quite often successfully resists any but the most superficial acquaintance with its substance. One is merely concerned with the negation of certain physical laws but not the meaning of those "laws."

The consequence has understandably been to restrict the concern, the instruments, theories and conceptualizations used to accessible qualities and attributes. These are labeled as significant and whatever remains is suspended to the realm of speculative and problematic. One could easily substitute for this example from engineering any mathematical analogue to society (e.g. sociomathematics, historicomathematics, or cliometrics, etc.) and discover that similar approximations and compromises had been made. The consequence is to restrict the imagination to "relevant," "significant," and accessible data. It is usual for the perceived nature of the subject phenomena to determine the "useful" characteristics of those instruments focused upon them. But the outcome is that such instruments are then peculiarly unsuited for the observation or manipulation of phenomena which possess only at their most superficial extremes or at the most manageable complexities rational or mathematical attributes. Human social organization in either historical or structural terms is one such phenomenon.

The full complement of human personality in its individual or collective expressions encompasses irrational and arational elements.[37]

Any operational or analytical framework which presumes as relevant only those aspects of human behavior which correspond with fundamentally nonhuman phenomena (that is formal, analytic, systems-specific relations) inevitably distorts the subject without securing redemptive advantage, that is, explanation. Task-group authority and organizational patterns have demonstrated their own inadequacy by this distortion. Historical violence, dependency and despair have often been the correlatives of organizing human beings for their most productive use.[38]

Yet it does seem clear that one of the social functions of the leader, as seen by these socioeconomic analysts, is to break down the boundaries between those social units known as individuals so that they might cohere in the achievement of certain ends. For these same social scientists, the term and the function of the leader are coterminous. The leader is seen, in Fritz Redl's terms, as the "central" or "focal" person around which a group adheres.[39]

What is suggested is that the particularistic identity is suspended for a moment in a deference to a wider identity, a more plural and immediate identification. This deference, according to Redl, may be the consequence of fear, identification, celebration, projection or awe of his or her skills. The subtle, almost primordial, logical tension between the leader as a deviant phenomenon in this analytical construct, and leadership as a norm persists. At one and the same time, we are given the leader as an extraordinary but a less than qualitatively differentiated personality; the leader is a resolution to the real and/or potential inertia and ineffectiveness residing in any historical community but somehow of the community while somewhat outside its historicity. The leader is a discontinuity which ensures the survival of the community's constituency.

Crises in human affairs differ in magnitude and intensity. But, judging by the history of peoples of whom we have more than fragmentary records, there has never been a period which has not been regarded by some of its contemporaries as critical. History itself may not inappropriately be described as one crisis after another. Whatever the social forces and conditions at work, and they always are at work—*insofar as alternatives of action are open, or even conceived to be open*—a need will be felt for a hero to initiate, organize, and lead.[40]

This interpretation transports us to the second anomaly of the "economic society."

In bourgeois or civil society, economic and technical organizations have as one of their basic presumptions the belief that there are inevitable differences among members of a group. These differences give rise to the development of role differentiation along the continuum of superordination and subordination. Descriptive categories become generally understood as qualitative differences. The larger the group, the more marked becomes the process of the leader-elites and followers-mass differentiation. Inequalities, that is, differences at their least "innocent" manifestation, are expressed in terms of differing capacities to conceptualize, actualize and integrate the full complement of roles required to perform a given task.

Continuing with these arguments, it is presumed that these can be ranked according to the degree to which these capacities are possessed by each individual. The group population being normal in the distribution of characteristics, the elite will prove to be a relatively finite number of its members. In statistical terms, that would mean that the largest number of members formed a mean or average with relatively few members at either of the two poles representing *no* competence and *total* competence.

Within the superior element of the population some individual will possess that happy complex of skills which will distinguish him or her as leader though it is expected that many members of this subgroup (the elite) could perform this role almost as well. In the process of the group's development, the leader, having been designated, chosen or acknowledged, will set out almost instantaneously in accruing a cadre of elites to assist him or her in the organizational tasks. And it is this presumed sequence of development which is one of the fundamental *raisons d'etre* of economic and technical organizations. Hierarchical stratification is therefore assumed to be a natural and inevitable condition of human organization.

This whole analysis rests, however, on the willingness to construct a specific standard—or more precisely, the meaningfulness of ranking differences in such a way as to arrive at a prejudicial scale. Such a scale, I am arguing, is unwarranted. But let us not misunderstand, differences are true phenomena, meaning not simply that they are

60

demonstrable, but rather that they are in the order of the thing (human groups). Yet transposing phenomena *naturalis* into phenomena *de jure* is irrefutably a *transformation*. Giving differences a specific meaning involves moving from fact to value. It critically changes the condition and context of the event projecting it into organizational forms for which it is inappropriate.

Such is the process of creating a kind of empirical metaphysics which stands in the stead of an authentic normative system—a system consciously constructed upon explicit value premises. To put it bluntly, the fact that human nature is variable has yet to be proven, in historical terms, to be an adequate, functional or effective base for human organization. That there are differences in capacities between individuals does not in itself suggest the "correct" form of organization.

For one instance, individuals whose skills integrate rather rudely with their social and cultural milieu have not been known to accept inferiority or subordination as their inevitable condition for long. On the contrary, such "subordinates" have repeatedly become the raw force which, having adopted alternative and competing conceptions of themselves, have overwhelmed their "superiors."[41] The presumption that differences legitimate or make inevitable hierarchical forms of human organization has been demonstrated to be alien to human nature, that is, unnatural and inhuman. Historically, people have failed to accede to such rankings; by their intransigence they have forced elites to resort to violence, deception, and force to maintain their advantages. Such methods, it seems, have ultimately failed. They have failed, in part, because they serve ironically to focus discontent, mobilize opposition and assist in the expression of demands among the "inferiors" against those who employ them. Yet the choice of these methods is quite natural, perhaps even inevitable, since they follow the arrogance implied in the organizational presumption.

Still, there is another aspect which is disturbing when the leader is seen as deviant. It is an aspect that transcends the mechanical or technical concern with the logicoanalytic device. And it is an aspect which ultimately allows for the transcending of that very paradigm which is the central concern of this essay. That aspect is the perception of the leader as a rare, implicitly alien, phenomenon to the group. At the same time, the leader is seen as the product of the social, historical and psychological forces contained in or acting upon the group.

In order to deal with this particular contradiction concerning the nature of the leader, let me return to the interplay of forces, events and phenomena which occur repeatedly in the inquiries of leadership and followership, irrespective of the context or style of those occurrences.

Despite the identification of the leader as a deviant, we are also given to understand that leadership is not a rare event. The leader who provides the implication of true extraordinariness by summoning and summing up the genius and skills of a group or a "people" is not rare. To the contrary, we are told by sociologists and social psychologists that leadership is present as a common occurrence, as an oft-chosen or developed style of organization regardless of the size, culture or historical strain of the group.[42]

We are presented with, then, a kind of "deviance" which is endemic in the societies and associations of mankind—a deviance which is *sui generis*, that is it evolves out of the fact of social integration, and is as such produced by the act of integration. The materials of its declaration in any particular association may be expected to be largely peculiar due to the specific historical continuities. Yet it is somehow and in some way made possible and almost inevitable through the processes of ideology, socialization and rationalization. Within each group, there exists acting over time, a "technology" of leader-production. Depending upon whether the analyst is prone toward sociologism or psychologism, this technology manages the development or the exaggerations of personality through a systematic but "accidental" deposit of experiences which are significant for the dynamics and interaction of the leader role. Though the arrangement of life-encounters is socially random, in the biographies of potential leaders it is orthogenic. The analyst has little difficulty in reconstructing the developmental sequence of the social and/or psycho-historical events producing the leader.[43]

The presence of this technology is substantiated by the occurrence of elite and subelite groups which appear as concomitants to any development of leadership. Such groups, we are told, are often the population from which the individual leader will emerge. And they are certainly, in any case, critical to the future of any movement or organization.[44] Whether the leader is recruited from among them or not, there is a self-recruiting impulse among the elite which provides the substructure to the development, ultimately successful or not, of any leadership. This substructure of elites in the society captures that leadership, institutionalizing it, rationalizing it, translating it and lending to it the critical character of omniscience and expertise. One means by which this illusion of omniscience is established is described by Alex Comfort:

> The individual who possesses concrete leadership-attributes expresses them in fields where only the reality is adequate: he is the sub-leader, the executive front which protects the mythical leader from personal contacts by which his leadership may be tested. Political leadership in large unitary organizations is essentially leadership untested by the dynamic contacts which determine dominance within the group.[45]

But clearly, this sociology of leadership and the historiography of this sociology does not comfortably cohere with the assumption that the leader represents a scarce resource, a finite point upon which all other activities converge. Rather, leaders would appear to be in some abundance. So much so that it takes an effort to obscure the ordinariness of leadership. The leader is actually a social construction; an expedient use by the community of the social, psychological and phenomenological materials contained in an individual. That is as we have heard many social analysts testify, an exterior is created for the leader, and the image of this figure is constructed from the organizational traditions of the community, playing on personality so as to conform to the immediate disposition of that community in a particular historical period. Though it is possible to agree with parts of this theory of leadership (see the discussion of charismatic leadership in Chapter IV), it is inconsistent with an approach to leadership which conceptualizes the leader as deviant.

Recognizing a "sense," a logic and rationality in these construc-tions and selections of the extraordinary ones which proceeds through the various arrangements of this particular "market" myth of authority, it is possible to challenge it in another way by paying close attention to the homogeneity of its material consistency. If leadership

63

is presumed as a social mechanism which provides efficiency within the context of the uncertainties of decision-making, is it not too much to expect that decisions arrived at will prove enduring in their "objective" eufunctionality?[46] Each decision-making event assumes at least the dimensions of a mini-crisis to the system. Decisions are made in order to resolve emergent issues which pertain to the immediate or distant future of the group. As such it can be argued that crises are in the very nature of any social system. Given such an assertion, it would be worthwhile to look analytically at what are called decisions in order to confirm or disconfirm the alleged relationship between leadership and decision-making.

The Decision as a Logical Positivist Event

Within the logical positivist tradition, at least one of its proponents has articulated a relationship between choice and reality which may guide our analysis as we look at the nature of decisions as that nature is treated in the literature:

> . . .so long as we take suitable steps to keep our system of hypotheses free from self-contradiction, we may adopt any explanation of our observations that we choose. . .logically our freedom is unlimited. Any procedure which is self-consistent will satisfy the requirements of logic.
>
> It appears, then, that the "facts of experience" can never compel us to abandon a hypothesis.[47]

If this statement is representative, then the recommended decision is self-consistent procedurally, with a rather ambiguous relation to reality or rather that reality beyond the decision-making procedure. Having established this premise, the types of decisions would appear to be limited only by the imagination. However, the literature of decision-making abounds with classificatory systems for decisions. Some analysts have argued that decisions fall into categories of description, explanation, prediction, evaluation and prescription;[48] others focus on the multiple stages or processes allegedly part of decision-making.[49] Still others have concentrated on identifying the systemic and/or idiosyncratic elements presumably organic to decision-making processes.[50] The richness of models and constituent analyses in the study of decisions is matched by the paucity of theory development. Consequently the literature is in some disarray, providing few consistent guidelines. Yet certain insights can be drawn from this literature for our purpose.

It appears no discussion of decision-making can entirely avoid systems of decision-classification. In the following discussion, I have kept this tendency to a minimum in order not to deflect from the main argument concerning the implications of decision-making processes for the theory of leadership. I have reduced decisions to choices between pure options; semi-choices (incremental decisions); and negative choices (irresolute decisions).

"Pure" decisions are simple ones, that is the choices between clearly understood and precisely-valued alternatives. An example of this kind of decision might be that of choosing between two alternatives, neither of which is perceived as influencing subsequent decisions, nor as being ambiguous in outcome. Such pure decisions require no more resources or skills than most of us develop. In a circumstance of clear choices we are all equally capable. Each of us receives practice in such decision-making daily. The issues resolved range between quite trivial choices to quite momentous ones. Such decisions are made against the background of a lawful universe:

> Laws explain our experience because they order it by referring particular instances to general principles; the explanation will be the more satisfactory the more general the principle, and the greater the number of particular instances that can be referred to it.[51]

So for whatever the reasons one of us comes to be preferred over the others, these reasons can be understood to be arbitrarily related to the rational, manifest task of "pure" decision-making. If the arrangements of our interactions, experiences, and understandings of each other are such as that which assume the nature of a community, the choices will appear to each similarly, with similar consequences. James Rosenau comes very close to this position in his review of decision-making analysis in foreign policy:

> Ordinarily, for example, one does not need to know the details of a chief executive's upbringing or the profession in which he was trained

after completing his formal education in order to explain his decision to arm allies and otherwise contest the aggressive behavior of a potential enemy. The decision is entirely comprehensible in terms of the perceptions and values which any occupant of the role is likely to have.[52]

In contradistinction to "pure" decisions, there exists another genre of decisions for which decision-analysts have prescribed some form of "incrementalism" as the most appropriate response.[53] Though often borrowing the form of its representation from pure decisions, the "adulterated" decision contains elements which range through several degrees of understanding and misunderstanding, and consists of important order heterogeneities. Again, Rosenau is helpful in providing concrete examples. In the process of defending Richard Snyder's decision-making approach to foreign policy, Rosenau states:

> As I read it, however, Snyder's formulation does not suggest that foreign-policy decision-making necessarily unfolds in a rational and conscious fashion. It merely asserts that officials have some notion, conscious or unconscious, of a priority of values; that they possess some conceptions, elegant or crude, of the means available and their potential effectiveness; that they engage in some effort, extensive or brief, to relate means to ends; and that, therefore, at some point they select some alternative, clear-cut or confused, as the course of action that seems most likely to cope with the immediate situation.[54]

Thus the suggestion that all decisions are like all other decisions, requiring no real differences in strategies or formulation is unacceptable here. But the incrementalist approach would presume to reduce the complexity of this type of intricate decision to a series of pure decisions, suggesting that the decision-maker hold in abeyance the understanding of the actual nature of the "series". Charles Lindblom, a frequent contributor to the literature on decision-making, puts it this way:

> Abandoning synopsis, a hypothetical central decision maker would not try for comprehensiveness in his view of the relations among policies but would instead take up in series each of an unending stream of particular problems, dealing with each with a narrow view of the implications of any policy solution, dealing with neglected implications as quite

separate problems, therefore patching up without cease and often anticipating adverse consequences of neglected implications, but in any case dealing with them as separate problems rather than "coordinating." In turning from one problem to another he would presumably turn from one set of relevant values to another slightly different set.[55]

The illusion of pure decision is thus maintained which is used additionally to subsidize the belief in the select nature of the decision-maker. The critical evaluation of the quality of the decision made is postponed or altogether avoided since what has actually occurred is the choice of a stratagem which tampers with the ingredients of the confrontation. Again, Lindblom is quite clear:

> The synoptic idea of problem solving is fairly straight-forward. To solve a problem one must first understand it—one masters it. In contrast, behind the incremental and disjointed tactics we have just summarized is a concept of problem solving as a strategy. In this view public policy problems are too complex to be well understood, too complex to be mastered. One develops a strategy to cope with problems, not to solve them. . . .
> The decision maker makes an incremental move in the desired direction and does not take upon himself the difficulties of finding a solution. . . He assumes that to the extent that his move was a failure or was marked by unanticipated adverse consequences, someone's (perhaps even his) next move will attend to the resulting problem. If policy making is remedial and serial, his assumptions will be correct.[56]

On the other hand, this stratagem reduces complex decision-making to that range of things admittedly accessible to all of us and thus corrodes the argument which would select "superiors" for the role of their manipulation.

But more importantly, the choices made are without durability—their fit with the swelter of issues contained in the decision crisis is most likely fortuitous, convening with artificially "pure" decisions; resolving choice complexes without objective reference to the problem event. One contemporary English anarchist has written of such solutions:

The solution of concrete domestic problems usually calls at some point for expert knowledge and intelligent foresight, and success or failure in performance are concretely evident. But the issues of foreign policy are increasingly imaginary—issues created so that they may be dramatised, crisis requiring sensational acts of personal statesmanship, threats of an emotionally-satisfying kind of liberty of existence, the matter, in other words, of the film and the comic-book. The function of most modern foreign policy is to dramatise the participants. It is conducted under a curious tacit understanding between even the most embittered ideological opponents, for each depends on the other. It has no relation to the solving of real problems—for the recurrent prolonged conferences are not conducted with the intention of settling anything: but they dramatise the participants and satisfy their sense of summit-hood without demanding from them knowledge, judgement, foresight, or even the need to face a reckoning.[57]

Comfort's criticisms of this mode of decision-making are of course deeply influenced by his total rejection of the social organization which he recognizes that it serves to mystify. As such he assumes that as a strategy for the transaction of social and political issues, the purpose is not to resolve but to sustain conflict. Comfort's dissatisfaction with the results of the methodological elegance of incremental decision-making, however, is sometimes shared by others—even its practitioners—whose social and political ideologies are in the convenience of political society.[58]

Still, again, there is as third genre of decisions which transgresses, fundamentally, against that nature common to the two prior forms. This decision is the companion of those crises which are without resolution. None of the objective phenomena in the event can be altered and instead what is required is a readjustment of the actors to the crisis. The choice is in determining how to live with the crisis, which, in a way, is a form of resolution which is thoroughly subjective in its activism. Here, again, the primary function of the leader is symbolic.[59]

Thus operating within the context of these crises which are supposed to legitimate his or her appearance as a solvent, the leader's efficacy is made obviously problematic. So a fundamental premise of leadership is called into question. Decisions are indeed often obtained, but ones which frequently lack definitiveness and in no way confirm the paradigm of leadership as it is presumed to be: a rational instrument of social organization.

And thus we arrive at a point of departure at which basically two alternatives occur. The point is to begin to dismiss political leadership as the manifestation of authority, that is as the instrument through which an authority which manages the integration of a community is maintained. Once beyond this point, we can begin to pursue the alternatives to leadership which bond societies and communities without rendering their members anomic, disoriented, frightened and anxious.

The first alternative suggests that near-leaderlessness in a group can be achieved functionally by the *succession* of leader-guides, a succession which "exaggerates" the capacities of nearly all the members of the community by ensuring to each actual mobility (in contrast to potential mobility) with several delimited periods of eminence. Within such a grcup, it can be supposed that each member would thus experience his or her own authority for a time specified by the group in accordance with the exigencies of group life and survival. The function of each, then, might be to facilitate the development into maturity—and here is meant the development of an individual autonomy and authority which can additionally absorb the circumscribed "responsibility" of the community momentarily—of all the others (all his/her others). Task or goal achievement or crisis resolution could theoretically be managed in this way without the instituting of exclusionist authority and social ideologies of natural superiority. Such would be the nature of transitional and crisis leaderlessness. The suggestion of such a possibility emerges out of the presumption that a critical dynamic for the participation of any individual in a group is dependence on group for identity. Erikson has called this "complementarity."[60] Leadership or dominance, followership or submission are only some forms that dependence may assume, but as such, they should not be taken as the nature of the thing. Relations among group members assume many forms, serving a multiplicity of needs. One social critic observes:

> The most significant positive incentives are probably sociality, the sense of interdependence; followed by emulation, expressed in dominance-patterns of proficiency rather than power, the enjoyment of creative

occupation, the desire for social approval, and the attainment of a secure status. . . . If we wish to find responsible and social attitudes, it is perhaps to the lives of individuals, in the broad current of their various containing cultures and prejudices, that we must look, rather than to the leaders who contain, or float on the surface of, those cultures. The impulse of sociality, distorted by many forms of unreason, and moulded by stress into many destructive and unwelcome patterns, is still the most clearly discernible thread in human cultures.[61]

Sociability, or "sociality" as Alex Comfort would have it, is thus an ambiguous phenomenon—in so far as its formalization is concerned—cementing, potentially, a range of relationships between the individual and the "others." Thus the succession of leader-guides—a succession characterized by the response of individuals with crisis-specific skills, or by availability to technological implements, or by some formal or informal rota—convenes with this understanding of the ontology of the group. The member of the group is in constant arrangement and rearrangement of personal instincts and impulses with self-perceptions and group demands and responsibilities. But as the developments of group and the individual proceed dialectically, the possibility and actual development of new identities is constant, characterized by new and different skills to be demanded and developed, new implements, or implements differently perceived, as well as alternative orderings and/or ordering principles responsive to changing realities.

The second alternative may be considered either as the logical consequence and thus the goal of the first or as a process and end in and of itself. It is to be characterized as true leaderlessness. True leaderlessness as a consequence of "transitional" leaderlessness would follow from the accumulated development of each group member. Growing consciousness of one's own resources and those contained within the group in combination with increasing familiarity with decisions incumbent on the group, could eliminate the role of leader entirely.

As a process, true leaderlessness presupposes the circumstance and occasion for the organic development of a community void of its administrative development. It is in the nature of the evolution and mutually coherent social and economic institutions, styles, interactional patterns, etc., as the demography and technology of the community become increasingly elaborate and complex, which has at its base the interiorization of authority and the consequent absence of external political authority. The leaderless community would thus function and its members co-exist on the basis of alternative authorities to that of power and the variant of the Aristotelian public sphere. The infrastructure, the interior, of the community would be so intricately interwoven as to transcend individualism as a resolution or reconciliation to the humanistic "paradox" of society. That individualism would be relegated to the backwaters of historical society, that is society in alienation as it is presently experienced in political "realities." We should, thus, for programmatic purposes, keep in mind the idea of the thing which Kropotkin presented in his evolutionary reconstruction of human history:

> . . .the primitive man has one quality, elaborated and maintained by the very necessities of his hard struggle for life—he identifies his own existence with that of his tribe; and without that quality mankind never would have attained the level it has attained now.[62]

and as well his observation on the role of belief as ideology:

> Their whole behavior is regulated by an infinite series of unwritten rules of propriety which are the fruit of their common experience as to what is good or bad—that is, beneficial or harmful for their own tribe. Of course, the reasonings upon which their rules of propriety are based sometimes are absurd in the extreme.[63]

The necessary existential extension of community might be accomplished in any of several ways so as to establish alternative metaphysics and necessarily different epistemological processes. Particular historical development results in particular sensibilities and comprehension.[64] The member-parts of the truly leaderless community must perceive, understand and know themselves and their experiences quite differently in order to achieve at one and the same time the sense of personal authority and primacy of the community. In the calculus of the alienated, this would appear paradoxical and contradictory.

The achievement is to arrive at a synthesis of self-consciousness which would characterize the first sense of the ego as a "we." This alternative existential sense might proceed by challenging the temporal and spatial boundaries of the family which have accompanied it as it has evolved in dominant Western experience. For as Wilhelm Reich has observed, ". . .the authoritarian gains an enormous interest in the authoritarian family. *It becomes the factory in which the state's structure and ideology are molded.*"[65]

The transference of authority, as it is recognized in Western social science, from the family to other sociopolitical institutions and roles might be precluded by extending the parameters of the family to include, vertically, those past (ancestors) and those future (posterity) members of the community. Horizontally, the extension would include all of those who produce, share and exchange the means of survival. Of necessity, this implies a rationalization of production, distribution and consumption alternative to the organizing principles of capital and might resemble the kinds of "cottage" and worker self-management industries which are *suggested* by recent efforts in Algeria, Yugoslavia, Poland and Israel.[66] Though these are current examples, the model is historically quite ancient. As such, an integration might be achieved which would be similar enough for comparison as to its functions and consequences to that founding authority *attributed* to the Romans by Arendt, to "savages" by Kropotkin, and to other segmentary societies.[67]

The preeminence of authoritarian parental figures might be rationalized in such a system into the less authoritative roles of consultants, guardians, and/or transmitters—roles which could be performed horizontally. Patriarchy or matriarchy would cease to represent the primordial pool of experience for the developing personality and the referent for the resultant "skills" of conceptualization, interaction and manipulation. In this way, the sources of authority and authorization could be profoundly transformed from those of force or implied force and control to cohesion, integration and "fit." Individualization could be replaced by a stress and celebration of the "whole" personality[68] consistently understood as a construct immersed in, dependent upon and consequent to the social integration of community.

Excellence or achievement would be thus identified, articulated or understood not in terms of proximate or convenient closure with others ("to excell" persistently suggests superiority) but as the occasion of a profound cumulative expression. Instead of laying stress on the exterior or *alter* sense of other, the intent would be to realize its *subject* sense. An obedience or convergence which is a creative event for the community rather than a reassertion of the now sociological-truism that "societies advance through the activities of their dissatis-fied or delinquent members"[69] would be developed.

Such speculation in the long run, however, is premature without settling between us some theory of knowledge, some critique of the ways of knowing. If our social theory is accomplished through paradigms which do not authentically account for themselves, paradigms which build altars to rationality (what Lukacs described as the reifications developed in antinomial bourgeois society), we commit ourselves objectively in a form which profoundly influences our capacity for consciousness. From such a deformed consciousness, one can anticipate persistent, even calculated error. But by continuing our investigation into epistemology, I believe we shall discover the powerful suggestion that the processes of correction are dialectical. That is the suggestion that the processes of epistemological regener-ation and existential rectification are, indeed, synchronic.

CHAPTER III

The Question of Rationality

In pursuing answers as to why the notion of leadership persists, we must go further than we have so far. It is not enough to point out the contradictions in the idea. It is not enough to suggest that the usual analytical supports and justifications for the historically most frequent construction of leadership contain specious or irrational elements. Nor is it totally sufficient to add to this critique alternative rationalizations or institutionalizations around authority. The character of this persistence lies deeper than contradictions or alternatives. We have seen that leadership is less a rational instrument than one which has required rationalization—taking rationalization to mean in this instance presenting "good" reasons for something done for other than those good reasons.[1]

Since the rewards of leadership have been shown to be frequently less than the certainty and persistence of order that some analysts anticipate, the possibility arises that some error occurs in the calculus. This kind of error is a reflection on the analyst. But the phenomenon of leadership is not simply a phantom of academic thinking. Leadership is a manifest social event which exists notwithstanding the historical function of social theorists as its ideologues. What then of the "error" of followers? Is their error the same? When we try to understand what we take to be their surrender are we observing or identifying? Are we seeing what has happened or what it would have meant to ourselves had it happened?

As we pursue Western social scientists in their quest for an understanding (or at least an exposition) of the nature of belief and followership—the error or adherence—we will discover a most interesting phenomenon: the reflexiveness of thought. The unacknowledged absence of critical thought is of a kind with the presumptiveness of ideology. The social scientist shares with the ideologue the need for an architecture of reality. It will become equally apparent, however, that arrogance or ethnocentricism or the seductions of historical distance became formidable barriers to this realization. Instruments of thought, while they were used to probe and characterize other instruments of thought, were used in such a way as to conceal the universality of the relationship between meaning and survival. The metatheoretical implications of this relationship were thus avoided.

The consciousness of the social scientist is not often that of the follower. The analysts of leadership use conceptual tools which seldom have the capacities to trace the contours of the reality comprehended by followers. The despair and defeats which paralyze, the anguish which mobilizes, the promise which points to a salvation, all of these are missing. The analyst sets these aside, recognizing in them no explanatory force. In their stead, there are the logical integrations of his or her paradigm positing their order of things. The analyst, too, is a follower but of a different type, shying away from the immanent realization that it is possible without this paradigmatic order there is no order.

There can be no mistake. We are approaching again a question of paradigms, a question of understanding—to some large measure, a question of metaphysics. If an act cannot be authentically understood, if it cannot be "explained" by what is known of it and its actors when posited in the analytical system or systems to which we attach significance, then we are left with two alternative choices and experiences. The first leads directly to defeat. This choice transgresses against us because in it we acknowledge that what we have seen is unimaginable in that reality which is called "ours" and by our own names of things. Recall Wittgenstein's seventh proposition: "Of those things which one cannot speak, one can say nothing."[2] We withdraw. The event is impossible in any of the terms by which it has been presented.

The second choice is to juxtapose to that which has been demonstrated as the event those whole or partial paradigms *suggested* by the recognizable nature of the event. We may extract and project from the unimaginable a statement of its kind and nature. Taking a clue from I. M. Lewis, we argue, in effect: "My slogan, if one is still necessary, is: let those who believe in spirits and possession speak for themselves."[3] The strategy is to begin with those who have experienced directly the event, borrowing form from their meaning of it.

It is, optimistically, the second alternative that I choose. This is a choice which presupposes the possibility of an understanding which emerges first out of commitment, and second, out of the pursuit of rationality not so much as principle, end or goal, but rather as an instrument of convenience. Rationality is merely a preferred tool. In its first element, this choice precludes objectivity and detachment. The presumption is that the intelligibility of the event is locked into the affect and consciousness of the group. The second element, the peculiar pursuit of rationality, emerges from the recognition that it is possible that the experience of the event may ultimately be incoherent. It may not be the rational coherence of a set of meanings. Therefore in the end rationality may be at best a convenience, the achievement of an experiential transmission into an "alien" person's world and the propulsion back into one's own sphere of sensibilities.

Ultimately, the analyst and the analysis will be richer. The enrichment will be in terms of the awareness of possibilities which results, the suggestions and the range of coherencies from which one extracts reality. The analyst will have more to know and more ways of knowing.

I am suggesting then a rather different bringing together of paradigms than is perceived as possible by Kuhn in any phase of the structuring of scientific knowledge. I am suggesting a dialectic which eludes Kuhn. Or rather, except in those passages[4] where his writing seems to elude his consciousness of thought and takes off independently, he is not a dialectician. I am not arguing for the replacement of one metaphysic by another or the convergence of fundamentally familial constructs whose appearances are antagonistic. Rather I am suggesting that mixture of paradigms is possible in the subjective sphere of the analyst while he maintains the integrity of and consequently the tension between fundamentally different realities and their metaphysics. This integration is at base juxtaposition rather than synthesis. I am suggesting that it is possible to believe, that is, to accord relevance to, one system of knowing and experiencing and then another, while holding onto an awe of the power of each within its boundaries and resisting the temptation and the need to formulate them into a single, articulating, coherent *episteme.*[5]

Furthermore, I am attempting to describe the importance of proceeding in this way especially when one is attempting to achieve an understanding of a people or an event which proceeds from an existential experience whose roots and constructions are quite unsimilar to one's own.

I am insisting that it appears less and less to the point of knowing a thing by identifying it as deviance, an irrationality, or the outgrowth of a subculture, subset, or subsociety. These are strategems characteristic of the dogmatic in Western "objectivity." Such is the usual application of the scientific method and more specifically its application in the attempt at understanding an explanation of followers. Actually, in so doing, one has largely drawn the boundaries of one's own epistemology in a cant, self-service. Such evaluative allocations or depositions contribute little beyond *suggesting* the nature of the truer task which is to discover and identify the terms within which the event takes place or a people know it. Such a suggestion is that the analysts know what they know, who they are, what they are doing and in what kind of reality.

That our own thought, for example, is permeated by a primal economics as calculus where phenomena are weighted, valued or paid attention to according to the accumulation of units of energy, control and power does not make such analytical presumptions or sensibilities encompassing, relevant or attractive to all peoples in their attempts to construct meaning. Our ways of evaluating are objective: making inevitable judgements of things which assume the form of seeing them as relatively important, larger, more powerful, etc. to all other things. Alternatively, it should be realized that the recognition of reality can be brought about quite differently among different peoples. Indeed, a difference may emerge from any systematized thought. The consequence is whole conscious structures with very different capacities and very different incapacities. These are seen, of course, from the perspective of the comparative analyst.[6] This is exactly how what has been achieved in Western philosophies, physical theories and analyses should be understood—a universe of paradigms and evolutions of paradigms different from others.

The growth of knowledge and understanding does not seem to be dependent upon making the unfamiliar familiar. Yet this is often the procedure when the thing confronted is profoundly "different." To the contrary, growth is dependent upon assuming unfamiliar intellectual and experiential postures and positions so as to *approach* the sphere of the thing.

In arguing this, I may have misunderstood the capacities of the human intellect. But it is also possible that the suspicious may have placed too much emphasis and depended too much upon the conservative patterns and impulses of the socialized intellect. Questions of social tolerance (Masterman's sociological paradigms) shade off into the securities of sanity and the dangers presupposed in its loosenings (metaphysical paradigms), but the relationship of this dynamic to the achievement of true understanding by the uncommited, uninvolved, objective analyst of the event of commitment appears spurious. Put simply, that which appears to us as rational may, indeed, be rational but untrue. It may be untrue and invalid to the ontology of the event.[7] According to Arnold Levison, R.G. Collingwood came very close to this position.

> Just as a physical scientist cannot use scientific method in order to understand the content of rival theories, so a social scientist cannot use scientific method in order to understand the intellectual content—the way of life—of a rival social system or a type of human experience involving reflective thought, such as religious experience.[8]

There are good examples of this paradox in the area of followership from which to draw these conclusions. The examples are good ones because they represent the efforts of, at the very least, competent analysts who understood enough about knowing the unfamiliar as to presume the presence of an alternative system. They are also instructive in ways in which they never intended because they tell us something of the limits imposed upon themselves by these radical, unconventional thinkers. In each instance, we will find that the need to recognize some kind of order—manifest as a presumption of the existence of order—interfered with the process of achieving comprehension. Thus the rejection of the order posited by a particular paradigm was concomitant to the introduction of an alternative system. But more of this later.

The Quest for the Intelligibility of Mass Movements

The advent of salvationist social movements—what Anthony Wallace has identified as revitalization movements[9]—has not always posed the dilemma associated in their confrontation with the Cartesian-rational, Newtonian-scientific mind. To put it perhaps too simply, those systems of analysis which came to predominate first the European and then American schools of thought which sought understanding by bringing social phenomena down to their most "physical" elements were accompanied by increasingly awkward insights.[10] These insights possessed explanatory powers which were so slight and whose nature was so approximate to "common sense" that either consciously or unconsciously they were bundled into protective esoterica.

Another characteristic of this *Geist und Wissenschaft* was the supercession of that approach to understanding which one might describe as theological. The roots of this understanding were embedded in an acknowledged metaphysics which served as a "natural" boundary to the things objectively knowable. The significance of this consciousness was that at one and the same time it allowed for the recognition of the rational *to a point* but beyond that point insisted on its integration with the irrational.[11] The irrational was specifically those things which could be understood only through the suspension of the metaphysics and empirical propositions of theological thought.

Certainly, Western peoples did not have to relinquish their beliefs in other than scientific laws but many of their intellectuals did. These intellectuals were intent on the discovery of new "freedoms;" propelled by tradition-old contempts for the masses and a belief in their own superiority; party to their own peculiar rebellion against social disorder; and bound by the terms of mobility and power. Responsible as they were for the development of what has been termed bourgeois social and scientific thought—utilitarianism, logical positivism, scientism, etc.—these intellectuals monopolized and dominated the definition of knowledge.[12] Yet even among the intellectuals the older thought persisted, tempered, perhaps, in men such as J.S. Mill, Durkheim and Marx, but flowering dramatically in others such as William James and Nietzsche—the irrationalists.

Toward the latter third of the nineteenth century, there occurred the "discovery" of the unconscious by neurologists. This was followed by the systematization of that discovery in the theories of Freud and his psychoanalytic successors. These events effected a resurrection of the irrational which slowly matured into a challenge. Just as the eschatologists, for example, found nurturance for their cosmology in their "mission" experiences of colonialisms, so the irrationalists were fed on the historical development of private pathologies among the bourgeoisie and the mass pathologies of the twentieth-century social and political revolutions. Each of these historical processes or developments served to stimulate the growth of a complementary development in social thought and conceptualization. With regard to the mass movements, specifically, they began to make evident that even among "civilized" peoples the residues of a more primitive and irrational "past" were present. Moreoever, not merely were they present among the masses, as it might have been comfortably assumed, but also among their elite.

These were some of the dynamics which tended to emphasize the significance of the irrational in Western culture and thought, but there were other currents as well. There was no linear development in modern Western thought from eschatological thought to rational and constitutive thought ending in a clinical, controlled resurrection of the irrational in thought. But there was change.

As is so dramatically demonstrated in such an intellect as Karl Mannheim,[13] the events of the first thirty-odd years of twentieth-century Western social and political history provoked crises in the West's epistemologies, crises in its meanings, explanations and understandings. In the specific attempt to comprehend the social movements of that period, one reaction was to reach back to the theologians. A very different reaction was to resurrect the nonbehaviorist efforts in psychology.

Rudolph Sohm

The work of Rudolph Sohm is an important example of the first tendency: the reinterpretation of theological thought. It was from Sohm's treatment of the rise of Monasticism within the Catholic Church in the fourth century that Max Weber extracted the outlines of the concept of charisma.

Sohm addressed himself quite matter-of-factly to the problem of understanding obedience. During the course of his writing *Outlines of Church History*, (1892), he had become specifically involved with the rationale from which an episcopal institution and structure had arisen among the *ecclesia*: the people of God. Sohm was concerned because he believed that there was no obvious need for that institution according to the dicta of the Gospel. The people of God were the Church incorporate:

> Where two or three are gathered together in Christ's name, there is the ecclesia, the Church. For Christ has said, 'Where two or three are gathered together in My name, there am I in the midst of them'. . . *There is no need of any human priesthood.* There, in every congregation of believers, is the true Baptism and the true Lord's Supper, the full communion with Christ the High Priest and Mediator of all who believe in Him. *Still less is there any need of a legal constitution.* In fact, every form of legal constitution is excluded.[14]

Thus there was no eminent need for the establishment of the legal authority which had taken place. No eminent need for the "positivity of the Christian religion," in Hegel's phrase.[15] Yet, ultimately, Sohm saw no contradiction in the fact that the Church and its priesthood had become institutionalized. He argued, to the contrary, that the reason for its creation was not difficult to find:

> The reason is not far to seek: Because the natural man is a born enemy of Christianity. . . . The natural man desires to remain under law. He strives against the freedom of the Gospel, and he longs with all his strength for a religion of law and statute. He longs for some legally appointed service, in the performance of which he may exhaust his duty towards God, and so for the rest of his time be free for the service of the world, free from that 'reasonable service,' the presenting of his whole

life as a sacrifice to God. He longs for a legally appointed Church. . .
Before all, he longs for an impressive, authoritative constitution, one
that shall overpower the sense, and rule the upward and reach outward
far and wide. He desires as the key-stone of the whole, a fixed body of
doctrine that shall give certain intelligence concerning all divine
mysteries, presented to him in a literal form, giving an answer to every
possible question. . .Herein lies the secret of the enormous power it has
had over the masses who are 'babes;' it satisfies these cravings.[16]

This argument lay very close to that of Dostoevsky found in his *The
Brothers Karamazov*. According to Sohm and Dostoevsky, natural
man, the being they were confronted with, fled to authority. This
flight was not only from a world without explicit rules, but also a
flight from a world of an overbearing personal responsibility. The
Church constituted definitive, limiting, mundane authority by codi-
fying conduct and human appeal. The Church mediated "the freedom
of the Gospel" and overpowered the senses. It overpowered the existential suspicion of chaos. Within its embrace, "natural man" could
relinquish the fear of the consequences of what he or she might choose
to do, or its inconsequentiality. Confronted with true freedom, it was
in the nature of humans to fathom its foreboding dimensions and
choose against it.

This was for Sohm the "psychology" of the event. And in this
insight we are presented with a psychological sophistication similar to
the content of declarations by such analysts as Freud, Fromm, Reich,
Cassirer, Adorno and Comfort.[17] Though their several works were
written to manage the phenomena of the succeeding century, there
was no existential distinction.

But how, in Sohm's opinion, did the Church transform itself into
legal structures superceding the "communion of believers?" Sohm's
history of the event, too, is quite important and instructive in pursuing
Weber's use and understanding of charisma (as we shall have occasion
to do). This is what Sohm wrote and what Weber obviously read:

This astonishing transformation was completed in the Church's battle
with false doctrine. The Gnostics, on their side, claimed to have pro-
claimed to the Church the truth as it is. . .The Gnostics; also claimed to
be the true Church. The only resource was to fall back upon the ecclesiastical official, namely, the bishop, represents beyond all doubt an un-

broken connection with the earliest times, there, and there alone (so it appeared), is the Church, and there alone her true tradition. . . While the episcopate defended the creed of the Church against Gnosticism, and altered it in defending, it won possession of the Church herself as the reward of its chivalry.[18]

The historical seal of the Church's authority was its successful resistance to "rebellion." The authority of the Church was legitimated by the effectiveness with which it had suppressed theological freedom and the instruments developed to do that.[19]

We have, of course, already referred to a slightly different version of this same period of ecclesiastical history in the works of Arendt and Pitkin.[20] Norman Cohn has, as well, assessed a similar dynamic while replacing the Gnostics and Montanists with the Jews.[21] But the essential point is clearly made: the Church was institutionalized and its structure ratified as the consequence of its believers' need for authority and the historical fact of a struggle over the ultimate location of that authority. But now listen to Sohm's interesting description of the process of that "transformation:"

> With her episcopal constitution the Church put on the armour which gave her power to withstand the storms of the coming ages. What the Christian faith lost in purity of inner substance it gained in power of external organization. Ideas enter not into the world of reality unharmed. The Church had prepared herself to gain possession of the world. By means of her episcopal constitution she was organized after a purely temporal fashion, and set up over the growing multitude of believers a visible, ruling head. . . . The original genuinely apostolic idea of the Church perished that her temporal supremacy might be founded. . .[22]

And so Sohm had stated fairly explicitly that once the participants of a movement, in concern for their survival and continuity, choose the instrument of institutionalization, their survival can only be obtained at the cost of true continuity or authenticity. Though Sohm used the term quite differently (as previously indicated), he stated three essential insights into the understanding of charismatic movements:

1. Natural man is catholic—men desire or require certainty, order

and familiarity and seek it in the establishment of temporal and political authority.

2. Competing systems of metaphysics or systems of meaning have historically been resolved by the establishment of dominance by one or the other by means of institutionalization and structuralization.

3. A frequent concomitant to the process of institutionalization is the decreased emphasis on spontaneity and mass participation in innovative action and ratification. A decrease in the authority of the people of the movement also occurs as allegiance is transferred from a man or an idea to roles and offices.

Sohm thus believed that the root of the event is in the irrational, "the natural man desires to remain under law." Natural man chooses against freedom in an unconscious revolt from freedom. "Salvation" is in order and certainty, they are the satisfactions to the "longings" of the "born enemy of Christianity."

Max Weber, too, believed in the fundamental irrationality of the charismatic event, contrasting it to the legal and economic natures of bureaucracy and patriarchy:

> As in all other respects, charismatic domination is also the opposite of bureaucracy in regard to its economic substructure. Bureaucracy depends on continuous income, at least *a potiori* on a money economy and tax money, but charisma lives in, not off, this world. . .The point is that charisma rejects as undignified all methodological rational acquisition, in fact, all rational economic conduct. This accounts also for its radical difference from the patriarchal structure, which rests upon an orderly household. . .For charisma is by nature not a continuous institution, but in its pure type the very opposite. In order to live up to their mission the master as well as his disciples and immediate following must be free of the ordinary worldly attachments and duties of occupational and family life.[23]

Thus Weber argued that the charismatic phenomenon was represented by the commitment to irrational conduct, to a behavior, to a system of meanings and perceptions whose consequences were to effect a less than clearly functional or rational relationship with objective reality. Charismatic behavior was a moving back into waste and blunder, away from the artifacts of the community which had been constructed with the care and reason of generations:

The mere fact of recognizing the personal mission of a charismatic master establishes his power. Whether it is more active or passive, this recognition derives from the surrender of the faithful to the extraordinary and unheard of, to what is alien to all regulation and tradition and therefore is viewed as divine—surrender which arises from distress or enthusiasm. Because of this mode of legitimation genuine charismatic domination knows no abstract laws and regulations and no formal adjudication. . .Genuine charismatic justice does not refer to rules; in its pure type it is the most extreme contrast to formal and traditional prescription and maintains its autonomy toward the sacredness of tradition as much as toward rationalist deductions from abstract norms . . .charisma, in its most potent forms, disrupts rational rule as well as tradition altogether and over-turns all notions of sanctity. Instead of reverence for customs that are ancient and hence sacred, it enforces the inner subjection to the unprecedented and absolutely unique and therefore Divine. In this purely empirical and value-free sense charisma is indeed the specifically creative revolutionary force of history.[24]

Why do a people forsake the wisdom of their predecessors and patriarchs? Weber had written that the historicity of the event of surrender is when a people are enveloped by "distress" or flush with "enthusiasm." What are the roots of that process which transforms deeply felt emotionality into charismatic action and mobility? That same emotionality which scratches raw the interior of the individual or compels him to shine forth? Weber, like Sohm, seems to be comfortable with the irrational as the final explication:

. . .the power of charisma rests upon the belief in revalation and heroes, upon the conviction that certain manifestations—whether they be of a religious, ethical, artistic, scientific, political or other kind—are important and valuable; it rests upon "heroism" of an ascetic, military, judicial, magical or whichever kind. . . . The decisive difference—and this is important for understanding the meaning of "rationalism"—is not inherent in the creator of ideas or of "works," or in his inner experience; rather the difference is rooted in the manner in which the ruled and led experience and internalize these ideas.[25]

Weber believed, just as Sohm, that the charismatic event was a transitory one:

Every charisma is on the road from a turbulently emotional life that knows no economic rationality to a slow death by suffocation under the weight of material interests: every hour of its existence brings it nearer to this end.[26]

We begin to see the continuity in a contemporary analytical system which is Western yet acknowledges and respects the irrational in human society. On the one hand, one sees Weber's recognition of the significance that the economic possesses for society. But on the other hand and perhaps more importantly, is his realization that those same societies consist too of fundamentally metaphysical forces which are not accessible to understanding through the same procedures. It is slightly paradoxical that though Weber is correct in arguing that charisma as a phenomenon is not restricted to the "religious realm," it was precisely religious scholarship and its intellectual tradition that helped importantly to salvage the element of the irrational as a constituent for a counter-paradigm to that of the materialist-behaviorist.

Perhaps for reasons which are largely no longer a part of our present, Christianity, too, served to dispose of the irrational. There was in early Christian thought an irrationality associated with paganism. This was that European paganism identified as the cult of the horned god by Margaret Murray in her largely ignored anthropological treatise on medieval witchcraft and Christian heresy.[27] As Nietzsche suggested at the end of the nineteenth century, Christiantiy had destroyed the authentic irrational roots of Europe or had at least obscured them beyond recognition in its syncretistic ambitions.

If, as Sohm argued, the Christian church was posited on non-rationality, the paradox was that the Church also attacked irrationality in its older conceptual manifestations. Thus in attacking paganism, the practitioners and hierarchies of the Christian faith chose weapons equally applicable to their own faith. If paganism lacked verifiable, scientific or objective proofs, so did Christianity.

Christianity was protected by its institutional development. The institutional structure, in turn, was protected by the doctrine of revealed truth, the Church's version of objective reality. The irrationality of the Church was screened by its authority. With the identification of paganism with irrationality, the Church sought to destroy the salience of paganism. The notion of the irrational was associated with paganism in the attempt to alientate it. It was presumed that by determining paganism as irrationality, it would limit the significance of its impact. Thus the theologian was an ambivalent force in the role irrationality played in Western thought. At one and the same time he relied upon it as faith and declaimed it as evil.

The Irrational As the Psychologic Subconscious

Again this continuity is demonstrable in the movement of ideas which, among others, matured into psychoanalysis. Contemporary to the writings of Sohm and Weber were the works of Josef Breuer, Pierre Janet, Morton Prince, Binet, Lebon, Freud and others. Though these men were trained primarily as scientists, neurologists and psychiatrists, they found explanation for "aberrations" of the mind, or "alternations of personality" which were nevertheless dependent upon the existence of dramatically nonscientific metaphysics (e.g. those of numerology, cabalism and similitude). Though sometimes within the pale of scientific methodology, they often found it necessary to exceed it. It was, in fact, most of their studies of the "subliminal mind" or the subconscious which William James found so useful in his discussion of religious conversion in the "twice-born sick soul."

James was not concerned with ordinary religious experience. That is, he was not concerned with those experiences which were the product of imitation and socialization. Instead, his attention was drawn to those experiences which were characterized as being creative, innovative, or of "genius." Furthermore his use of the irrational or subconscious was largely restricted to those instances of sudden conversions so total as to be understood as the "surrender of self." He sought to explain conversions which were characterized by the surrendering of the basic presumptions and sentiments of the individual in exchange for their antitheses.

In short, James was concerned most with religious leaders and those who had demonstrated extraordinary talents in other aspects of cultural life. He believed that this had made them sensitive to the anguish of their lack of belief and to the significance of their achievement of belief:

There can be no doubt that as a matter of fact a religious life, exclusively pursued, does tend to make the person exceptional and eccentric. . .We must make search. . .for the original experiences which were the pattern-setters to all this mass of suggested feeling and imitated conduct. These experiences we can only find in individuals for whom religion exists not as a dull habit, but as an acute fever rather. But such individuals are "geniuses" in the religious line; and like many other geniuses who have brought forth fruits effective enough for commemoration in the pages of biography, such religious geniuses have often shown symptoms of nervous instability. . .abnormal psychical visitation. . . exalted emotional sensibility. . .discordant inner life. . .melancholy. . . obsessions and fixed ideas. . .trances, heard voices, seen visions, and presented all sorts of peculiarities which are ordinarily classed as pathological.[28]

Yet in a fashion dissimilar to that of later analysts of religious experience, James saw no ultimate evaluation proceeding out of the attempt to understand these experiences in psychogenic terms. For James the question was still left open as to the value of these experiences to the individual or to the society:

To plead the organic causation of a religious state of mind, then, in refutation of its claim to possess superior spiritual value, is quite illogical and arbitrary, unless one has already worked out in advance some psycho-physical theory connecting spiritual values in general with determinate sorts of physiological change. Otherwise none of our thought and feelings, not even our scientific doctrines, not even our *dis*beliefs, could retain any value as revalations of the truth, for every one of them without exception flows from the state of its possessor's body at the time.[29]

This was a fundamental element of what James called his "piecemeal supernaturalism." He could assert that meanings in life were not simply constructed from objects and epiphenomena but were finally dependent upon and determined by ". . .a set of memories, thoughts, and feelings which are extra-marginal and outside of the primary consciousness altogether. . ."[30] A new commitment by these sick-souls as total as that of religious conversion came about by making the choice subconsciously for a new order of things. The mind reordered reality after suffering deep humiliation, depression and anxiety—the symptoms of a sick soul. By this new order, the formerly sick soul approximated the perceptual version of the world of the healthy-minded.

> At our last lecture, I explained the shifting of men's centers of personal energy within them and the lighting up of new crises of emotion. I explained the phenomena as partly due to explicitly conscious processes of thought and will, but as due largely also to the subconscious incubation and maturing of motives deposited by the experiences of life. . .I have now to speak of the subconscious region. . .[31]
>
> Interpreting the unknown after the analogy of the known, it seems to me that hereafter, wherever we meet with a phenomenon of automatism, be it motor impulses, or obsessive idea, or unaccountable caprice, or delusion, or hallucination, we are bound first of all to make search whether it be not an explosion, into the fields of ordinary consciousness, of ideas elaborated outside of those fields in subliminal regions of the mind. . .If. . .we take them on their psychological side exclusively. . .[we] suspect. . .that in the recipient of the more instantaneous grace we have one of those Subjects who are in possession of a large region in which mental work can go on subliminally, and from which invasive experiences, abruptly upsetting the equilibrium of the primary consciousness, may come.[32]

At this edge of the twentieth century, James was fighting for a recognition that the mind has the capacity for its own defense independent of institutions, social systems and other objective phenomena. He was arguing that the mind could transcend rationality or divorce itself from those orders of things presented to it by an external set in order to salvage its integrity. In terms more directly attributable to the imagery of James, the mind could draw upon the subsconscious for instruments and a new locus for "personal energy." The traumatized setting for the deposition of identity was replaced by a new 'universe' within which the organism could survive nurturing a new identity. Rather than the leap of faith conceptualized by Husserl, Sartre, and Camus, the mechanism that James understood was a propulsion into faith:

> But beyond all question there are persons in whom, quite independently of any exhaustion in the Subject's capacity for feeling, or even in the

absence of any acute previous feeling, the higher condition, having reached the due degree of energy, bursts through all barriers and sweeps in like a sudden flood.[33]

The more profound the crises, the less likely the effort would be conscious, voluntary or deliberate. The more profound the injury, the more acute the sense of "present wrongness." the more likely that the event (or events) of redemption would be beyond the instruments and mechanisms of rationality and, ultimately, the charting of a rational analyst.

Yet, though it was irrational, James continuously believed the phenomenon would be no less real or actual to those who experienced it. And in many instances, such an experience might be more real than anything produced by reason. "The axis of reality runs solely through the egoistic places—they are strung upon it like so many beads."[34] Most importantly, though irrational, the phenomenon might be no less true as a reconciliation of the destructive and disintegrative forces encompassed in the individual.

> . . .we belong in the most intimate sense wherever our ideals belong. Yet the unseen region in question is not merely ideal, for it produces effects in this world. When we commune with it, work is actually done upon our finite personality, for we are turned into new men, and consequences in the way of conduct follow in the natural world upon our regenerative change. But that which produces effects within another reality must be termed a reality itself, so I feel as if we had no philosophic excuse for calling the unseen or mystical world unreal.[35]

Yet one other comment by James seems important to what I will later describe under the rubic of the myth of leadership. That comment has to do with his understanding of the metaphysics of asceticism:

> [Asceticism] symbolizes, lamely enough no doubt, but sincerely, the belief that there is an element of real wrongness in this world, which is neither to be ignored nor evaded, but which must be squarely met and overcome by an appeal to the soul's heroic resources, and neutralized and cleansed away by suffering. . . . I am leaning only upon mankind's common instinct for reality, which in point of fact has always held the

world to be essentially a theatre for heroism. In heroism, we feel, life's supreme mystery is hidden. . . . The metaphysical mystery, thus recognized by common sense, that he who feeds on death that feeds on men possesses life supereminently and excellently, and meets best the secret demands of the universe, is the truth of which asceticism has been the faithful champion.[36]

Let me somewhat anticipate the later discussion in this essay on leadership as myth. Whether one accepts it as myth or not, the notion of leadership does not have to do with the confrontation between the powerful forces which are reality and some "pseudo-species," or community of mankind emboldened or empowered by the possession of a new mystery, a divulged secret, a revolutionary technology. The leader is presumed to play a critical role at a point in time when historical forces converge on some society, group or community. Through leadership, that group absorbs the trauma of having to become something quite different in the face of alien demands.

Leadership and asceticism, then, are counter phenomena, alternative options to the use of this new knowledge, this new revelation or machinery. In leadership, the thrust of social vision is turned outside, it breaks out to confront history and to mangle it. In the ascetic, the force of social vision encapsulates the individual, guarding him from the voracious, gnashing jaws of an inviolate history and historical forces. Leadership is a form of objective activism while asceticism involves subjective activism.

James, of course, was not dealing with obedience or followership. He was not concerned with religious movements or social movements any more than he was concerned with the "ordinary religious belief" which he explained in terms of habit, tradition and imitation.[37] Yet his concern was with an element which is thought by most analysts to be the crucial event in the development of social and political movements whatever their ideological matrix. He was concerned with an element made crucial in the accounts of most participants of such movements. That element is the phenomenon of total conversion.

Let us recall further, that it did not matter to James whether one was observing a fundamental religious phenomenon or one which might be understood as "political" (remember James' "other geniuses''), it was an irrational constituent of the mind out of which resolution and explanation proceeded.

Thus James' work is unquestionably relevant to us, whatever its supposed validity or isolation since he sought to treat with that event which characterizes or explains the fundamental nature of the act of commitment. He reached into the irrational processes—in their extreme, subconscious "life motives" and "racial instincts"—to distinguish at the most elemental level, in its most simple unity accessible to articulation, the acquisition of a faith posited in a new construction of reality.

The Irrational As the Psychoanalytic Subconscious

With religious experience as a subject for psychological analysis, James makes for an appropriate synapse between those chambers of irrationalist perseverance represented by the ecclesiasticism of Sohm and the nonbehaviorist psychology which matured into psychoanalysis. There exists, expectedly, a remarkable coincidence between the theories of Freud and James. This coincidence concerned, respectively, the psychology of the group or crowd and the psychology of individual religious experience.

Despite the fact that in Freud's work one finds the familial praxis writ large—a framework largely absent from James' analyses which were in their turn dependent upon a more private, more momentary developmental framework—a dominant metaphysical root brought some convergence to his and James' insights. This was that metaphysics did not merely consist of the subconscious. Nor did it merely consist of the belief that the subconscious, in injury or the addressing of injury, somehow had the force to break through and dominate the conscious and its rational processes. Most importantly, that metaphysics consisted of the existence of a subconscious that was *in its very nature* a racial memory.[38]

To James whose own life was dominated by illness, physical and psychological weakness, and an overwhelming but benevolent paternal authority, that memory was a redemptive reserve in the psychic matrix of the species.[39] But for Freud, whose understanding of his own will as something proceeding out of the compulsion to destroy, revolutionize or ignore Judaic and European tradition, that memory was a monstrous, frightening phenomenon poised against civilization.[40]

For example, Freud in partially agreeing with Lebon's analysis and description of the psychological group as "led almost exclusively by the unconscious" was to describe that force as "imperious."[41] The collective unconscious identified with the leader was a response to the overwhelming primeval need for authority among the now uninhibited individuals who made up the group:

> The uncanny and coercive characteristics of group formations, which are shown in the phenomena of suggestion that accompany them, may therefore with justice be traced back to the fact of their origin from the primal horde. The leader of the group is still the dreaded primal father; the group still wishes to be governed by unrestricted force; it has an extreme passion for authority. . . . [42]

> What it demands of its heroes is strength, or even violence. It wants to be ruled and oppressed and to fear its masters. Fundamentally it is entirely conservative, and it has a deep aversion to all innovations and advances and an unbounded respect for tradition.[43]

Yet as Freud's thought converged with that of James (and Lebon) in subscribing to the psychological group's need for heroic action and myth, Freud went further by developing an analytical and anthropological formulation which supported Lebon's notion that the group would *prefer* myth to incoherence:

> *A primary group of this kind is a number of individuals who have put one and the same object in the place of their ego ideal and have consequently identified themselves with one another in their ego.*[44]

The "object" is, of course, the group ideal as represented in the leader or an idea as ideology.

Freud was corroborating James' notion about the human mind's extraordinary capacity to weld reconciliation. The difference, as already mentioned, was that Freud, here, was identifying that process within the context of a group. He was arguing that the construction and secondary experiencing of a primary group was an alternative resolution of the fragmentation of the ego, or of that hysteria described by James as an element in the process of religious conversion.

There is no question that Freud located the critical phenomenon, the explanatory event, in the unconscious: "The libido attaches itself to the satisfaction of the great vital needs, and chooses as its first objects the people who have a share in the process."[45] However, Freud's theory of group cohesion, unlike James', Weber's and Sohm's, did not rely on the occasion of extraordinary stress—the situational prelude for the charismatic event or the religious conversion. Instead, Freud envisioned a comprehensive approach in attempting to explain the identification processes which drew individuals together in the most ordinary institutions, e.g. the Christian Church and the army. This was the affectual matrix of those groups which Weber had categorized as traditional and patriarchal.

Freud was arguing that the psychological group's matrix would always consist of libidinal forces. The obvious differences between groups—whether they be large or small, transient or enduring, politically reactionary or revolutionary—would depend on factors essentially distinct from those forces which were at the base of those processes of integration. Yet when Freud understood the psychological group ties to be fundamentally erotic, he also saw them as regressive and, as such, therapeutic:

> There are abundant indications that being in love only made its appearance late on in the sexual relations between men and women; so that the opposition between sexual love and group ties is also a late development.[46]

> It may be said that a neurosis has the same disintegrating effect upon a group as being in love. . . . Justifiable attempts have also been made to turn this antagonism between neuroses and group formation to therapeutic account. Even those who do not regret the disappearance of religious illusions from the civilized world of today will admit that so long as they were in force they offered those who were bound by them the most powerful protection against the danger of neurosis.[47]

Freud thus came to a very different understanding of that religious conversion described by James:

94

If he is left to himself, a neurotic is obliged to replace by his own symp-
tom formations the great group formations from which he is excluded.
He creates his own world of imagination for himself, his own religion,
his own system of delusions, and thus recapitulates the institutions of
humanity in a distorted way which is clear evidence of the dominating
part played by the directly sexual impulsions.[48]

Yet, essentially, Freud, too, sought explanation in the irrational components of man's experience and capacities. An assertion, it is true,
which is quite unremarkable:

*Hypnosis. . .*is based entirely on sexual impulses that are inhibited in
their aims and puts the object in the place of the ego ideal.
The group multiplies this process; it agrees with hypnosis in the nature
of the instincts which hold it together, and in the replacement of the ego
ideal by the object; but to this it adds identification with other individuals, which was perhaps originally made possible by their having
the same relation to the object.[49]

For Freud, the explanation of followership had as its critical constituent the separation and degree of separation effected between the
ego and the ego ideal. The critical constituent was the separation
between identity realization and that identity, partially conscious and
partially unconscious, which we had "promised" and were supposed
to be. The greater the disparity, the more unstable would be the
relationship and resolutions between these two psychic concentrates.
The larger the gulf between ego and ego ideal, the more desperate and
reckless would be the choice of the instruments of reconciliation.

One such desperate choice entailed the replacement, or more
accurately in terms of Freudian theory, displacement of the ego ideal
by an object. The leader was an object which contained those
particular characteristics which would facilitate the closure with the
ego or what is known as identification. In leadership was contained
the enormity of the illusion of being lived equally and the exaggeration
in the presumption of a superhuman power to discern truth and pre-
scribe correct action. This identification of ego with object accomplished the suspension of the ego ideal and its complex of proscriptions. It also achieved the tempering and rerouting of the anxious
tensions accompanying the separation of ego and ego ideal.[50]

The Historicization of the Analyses of the Subconscious

The irrationalists who succeeded Freud were quite evidently directly impressed by his formulations. Especially impressed were those who sought to explain followership in social and political movements by the agency of some form of psychoanalysis.

Wilhelm Reich, for instance, in his analysis of German fascism relied heavily for explanatory purposes on sexual repression and consequent authoritarian familial patterns. Reich identified fascism as a "middle class" movement in its mass basis. For Reich it was a movement built upon a "class" whose socioeconomic and status position had been variously undermined by a strange war, industrial capitalism and depression.

Reich argued that one critical response by members of this class to the increasing lack of material and social substantiation to their "normative" location in German society was to affirm their existence by the assumption of a "superior" sexual morality. This reaction was specifically in reference to the threat of disappearing into the bottomless well of the urban lower classes. In Reich's perception, this defensive morality consisted of "the strictest sexual suppression of the women and the children."

The agency of this "differentiating code" was, of course, the authoritarian (patriarchal) family:

> In the figure of the father the authoritarian state has its representative in every family, so that the family becomes its most important instrument of power. The authoritarian position of the father reflects his political role and discloses the relation of the family to the authoritarian state. Within the family the father holds the same position that his boss holds toward him in the production process. And he reproduces his subservient attitude toward authority in his children, particularly in his sons. Lower middle-class man's passive and servile attitude toward the Führer-figure issues from these conditions.[51]

It is important, though, to realize that Reich was not merely reiterating Freudian theory but had, at once, simplified and supplemented Freud's analysis. For one, Reich was not concerned with the broader notion of sexuality that was Freud's mature[52] interest, but rather with the "function of the orgasm."[53] If for Freud, according to Norman O.

Brown, genital sexuality was a perversion, a fixating limitation of the polymorphic perversity natural to human beings, Reich was specifically committed to transforming society through that perversion.[54] Secondly, Reich was a student of Marx, Engels, and Lenin and, as such, in his early career, concerned with integrating the theories of the various Marxist analysts with psychoanalytic theory.

One important effect of this analytical mix was that Reich managed to avoid the pessimism evidenced by Freud most systematically in his work, *Civilization and Its Discontents.*

There, Freud had argued that a fundamental conflict between man's "natural instincts" and civilization was inevitable. This struggle would result either in the destruction of civilization or the development of neuroses within the whole of the species. Naturally some psychoses or dysfunctional alienation would occur, being *sui generis* to the successful defense of civilization. Yet at its foundation, Freud was persuaded, civilization was to be understood as always repressive.

> Since civilization obeys an internal erotic impulsion which causes human beings to unite in a closely-knit group, it can only achieve this aim through an ever-increasing reinforcement of the sense of guilt. . .If civilization is a necessary course of development from the family to humanity as a whole, then. . .there is inextricably bound up with it an increase of the sense of guilt; which will perhaps reach heights that the individual finds hard to tolerate.[55]

At the point of choosing between civilization and repression, Freud claimed impartiality and the innocence of objectivity:

> For a wide variety of reasons, it is very far from my intention to express an opinion upon the value of human civilization. I have endeavoured to guard myself against the enthusiastic prejudice which holds that our civilization is the most precious thing that we possess or could acquire and that its path will necessarily lead to heights of unimagined perfection.[56]

Reich contradicted Freud in both instances: the relationship between sexuality and civilization; and the value of Western civilization. Reich, infected somewhat paradoxically with a vision of

97

the perfectability of man, believed that the struggle was between a culture, the European Christian-feudal-capitalist set, and man's sexual nature. Marxism had not only presented to Reich a critique of early twentieth-century German capitalist society but had, as well, promised perfectability through the rationalization of society's institutions, structures and social relations. It was this bourgeois capitalist culture and its social conditions which had precipitated irrationality. Fascism was only one variant of the irrationality resultant from that culture's sexual repression and oppression:

> After social conditions and changes have transmuted man's original biologic demands and made them a part of his character structure, the latter reproduces the social structure of society in the form of ideologies.[57]

> Fascist mentality is the mentality of the "little man," who is enslaved and craves authority and is at the same time rebellious. It is no coincidence that all fascist dictators stem from the reactionary milieu of the little man. The industrial magnate and the feudal militarist exploit this social fact for their own purposes, after it has evolved within the framework of the general suppression of life-impulses.[58]

In his most direct contradiction to Freud, Reich argued that man's "natural biologic core" was the fount of creative, rational and democratic society:

> Since the breakdown of the primitive work-democratic form of social organization, the biologic code of man has been without social representation. The "natural" and "sublime" in man, that which links him to his cosmos, has found genuine expression only in great works of art, especially in music and painting. . .Everything that is genuinely revolutionary, every genuine art and science, stems from man's natural biologic core.[59]

Not surprisingly in this synthesis of Freudian and Marxian thoughts, Reich resurrected the earlier Marx in intent and sentiment and produced, subsequently, in his *Mass Psychology of Fascism,* what must be considered as one of the most powerful and contemporary pseudo-anarchistic "manifestos."

The work of Freud, Weber and Marx in the area of group

psychology on the subject of obedience and followership has been the basis of explanatory systems contemporary and subsequent to that of Reich. Erich Fromm is one example.

Fromm to some degree parallels Reich in being more sensitive to history, social conditions and institutions than Freud.

> The first point of difference [is that I] look upon human nature as essentially historically conditioned, although we do not minimize the significance of biological factors and do not believe that the question can be put correctly in terms of cultural *versus* biological factors. In the second place, Freud's essential principle is to look upon man as an entity, a closed system. . .whereas, in our opinion, the fundamental approach to human personality is the understanding of man's relation to the world. . . . We believe that man is *primarily* a social being, and not, as Freud assumes, primarily self-sufficient and only secondarily in need of others in order to satisfy his instinctual needs.[60]

He, too, has written of the escape from the (negative) freedom of bourgeois-capitalist society:

> The mechanisms we shall discuss in this chapter are mechanisms of escape, which result from the insecurity of the isolated individual.
> Once the primary bonds which gave security to the individual are severed, once the individual faces the world outside of himself as a completely separate entity, two courses are open to him since he has to overcome the unbearable state of powerlessness and aloneness. By one course he can progress to "positive freedom"; he can relate himself spontaneously to the world in love and work, in the genuine expression of his emotional, sensuous, and intellectual capacities. . . . The other course open to him is to fall back, to give up his freedom, and to try to overcome his aloneness by eliminating the gap that has arisen between his individual self and the world.[61]

Like Reich, again, Fromm has chosen Nazi Germany as the phenomenon with which to demonstrate his conceptualization. But perhaps "chosen" is a weak representation since Reich and Fromm had this choice thrust upon them by their biographic-historical conditions.

Fromm believed that the atomization and deracination which happened to the individual as a consequence of the breakdown of pre-capitalist society by its bourgeois successor settled, as well, upon the individual intolerable feelings of powerlessness and aloneness. These feelings had to be repressed and the institutions and structures lost had to be substituted and compensated for.

The compulsive psychic mechanisms which redressed this existential injury were masochism-sadism, hostile and aggressive destruction, and automaton-conformity. The social mechanism which evolved was the construction of a society or a movement which consisted of an ideology and the organizational structures which articulated with these ego-defense reconciliations.

> The increasing social frustration led to a projection which became an important source for National Socialism: instead of being aware of the economic and social fate of the old middle class, its members consciously thought of their fate in terms of the nation.[62]

> Those psychological conditions were not the "cause" of Nazism. They constituted its human basis without which it could not have developed, but any analysis of the whole phenomenon of the rise and victory of Nazism must deal with the strictly economic and political, as well as with the psychological, conditions.[63]

> We have seen, then, that certain socioeconomic changes, notably the decline of the middle class and the rising power of monopolistic capital, had a deep psychological effect. These effects were increased or systematized by a political ideology. . .Nazism resurrected the lower middle class psychologically while participating in the destruction of its old socioeconomic position. It mobilized its emotional energies to become an important force in the struggle for the economic and political aims of German imperialism.[64]

From Fromm, capitalist pseudo-democracy with its suppressive monopolies and submissive worker-consciousness, and fascism with its dramatic state authoritarianism, were the most appropriate social structures for encompassing this peculiarly neurotic mass. These societies were thus the product of, and produced as their impact, universal pathologies. Harry K. Wells has put it this way:

> Modern history, Fromm asserts, will swing uneasily like a pendulum between capitalist pseudo-democracy and fascism just so long as the two psychic mechanisms of masochism-sadism and automaton-conformity

alternate in ascendency. The mechanisms give rise to capitalism and its forms of political hegemony, and the latter give rise to the neurotic mechanisms. The circle appears hopelessly vicious.[65]

Fromm's sensibilities, of course, led him to an architectonic vanguard.

> The chief agency of social change is not historical forces but, according to Fromm, "humanistic psychoanalysis." The agent that can lay bare the unconscious mechanisms and repressions is the reformed psycho-analyst, and it is he upon whom the responsibility for social change, the transformation of capitalism into socialism, rests.[66]

History As The Subconscious

The work of Norman Cohn is also concerned with the development of totalitarian movements of modern times. Cohn has written on the continuity of millenarian movements in the Christian period of European history with the sociopolitical movements of the twentieth century. Particularly, he has sought to establish the patterns of panic and hysteria which functioned as root and models for the "modern"[67] mass movements of Soviet Communism and Italian and German fascisms.

> When, finally, one comes to consider the anarcho-communistic millen-arian groups which flourished around the close of the Middle Ages. . . .
> In each of these instances the mass insurrection itself was directed towards limited and realistic aims—yet in each instance the climate of mass insurrection fostered a special kind of millenarian group. As social tensions mounted and the revolt became nation-wide, there would appear, somewhere on the radical fringe, a *propheta* with his following of paupers, intent on turning this one particular upheaval into the apocalyptic battle, the final purification of the world.
> Like the millenarian movements themselves, the *propheta* evolved over the centuries.[68]

Thus not only in his analysis of what he describes as the demoni-zation of the Jews, but in the more general millenarian pursuit, Cohn has identified a process which is encompassed by what he terms a theory of collective psychopathology. A theory which hypothesizes a process consisting of psychological projections, transferences, repressions, regressions and infantilizations.

It is true, then, that Cohn, like Reich, Fromm and Herbert Marcuse, has attempted a syncretism between the dialectical materialism of Marx and the psychic dualisms and antagonisms of Freud.[68] Cohn's social stress theory is addended to those Freudian metaphors and that paradigm which profers a system of skills, capacities and resources in the psyche. His theory is a familiar one including the progressive deterioration of institutions interacting with economic and environmental crises.

> It can happen that a mystic emerges from his or her experience of introversion—like a patient from a successful psychoanalysis—as a more integrated personality, with a widened range of sympathy and freer from illusions about himself and his fellow human beings. But it can also happen that the mystic introjects the gigantic parental images in their omnipotent, most aggressive and wanton aspects and emerges as a nihilistic megalomaniac. This last was the case with many adepts of the Free Spirit.[70]

> In the Middle Ages the people for whom it had most appeal were neither peasants firmly integrated in the life of village and manor nor artisans firmly integrated in their guilds. . . . These *prophetae* found their following, rather, where there existed an unorganized, atomized population, rural or urban or both.[71]

But Cohn, as was his express intention, significantly extended the historical data base of the phenomenon.

Unconcerned as he was with the parameters inherited from the late nineteenth century's historians and social analysts[72] who were dominated by the immediate emergence of the modern, industrial world, and 'shadowed' by the presumption of it as a critical parameter, he has produced an historical record which suggests that the *id*, as a theoretical assertion, is something more than a metaphor. He has argued that certain properties, certain characteristics, certain responses of primitive Christian and medieval peoples have had an enduring, a paradigmatic continuity. Of course, these responses have matured among different peoples at different times and different places. But they have matured in significantly similar pathologies—resembling, thus, a "racial memory."[73]

. . .for all their exploitation of the most modern technology, Communism and Nazism have been inspired by phantasies which are downright archaic. And such is in fact the case. It can be shown (though to do so in detail would require another volume) that the ideologies of Communism and Nazism, dissimilar though they are in many respects, are both heavily endebted to that very ancient body of beliefs which constituted the popular apocalyptic lore of Europe.[74]

Cohn traces the variants and elaborations of the dark side of Christian and Christian-syncretic cosmologies. He lays particular stress on the development and evolution of messianic and anti-Christ beliefs. He concerns himself with their artifacts, notes their supercessions, suppressions and reemergences. His analysis concentrates on the lower orders, the "masses" of pre-capitalist society. In this way he differs from Reich, Freud, or Fromm whose immediate foci were on the bourgeoisie and petit-bourgeoisie.

In agreement with Freud and especially the latter's *Civilization and Its Discontents,* Cohn concludes that certain primitive, i.e. total, mechanisms for the suspension of anxiety and the withdrawal from traumatic reality have been retained by Western, Christianized people. These mechanisms, however, obtain their most brilliant exposition in group behavior and in mass movements. They are furthermore directly correlated in their strength with the size of the group massed and the successful development of organizational structures which facilitate and predicate collectivities.

First, in the medieval period:

Almost as much as to the Church, supernatural authority pertained to the national monarchy. Medieval kingship was still to a large extent a sacred kingship; the monarch was the representative of the powers that govern the cosmos, an incarnation of the moral law and the divine intention, a guarantor of the order and rightness of the world. And here again it was the poor who most needed such a figure.[75]

And then, the modern period:

. . .during the half-century since 1917 there has been a constant repetition, and on an ever-increasing scale, of the socio-psychological process which once joined the Taborite priests or Thomas Muntzer with the most disoriented and desperate of the poor, in phantasies of a final,

103

exterminatory struggle against 'the great ones': and of a perfect world from which self-seeking would be for ever banished.[76]

Once again we are confronted with the hold that a fantasy possesses over the human mind. Just as Sohm had indicated, Cohn agrees, that the human mind is trapped in authority as a response to the uncertainty which is crisis. But Cohn has gone no farther. In many ways, we have traced a circle back to Sohm's "natural man." Cohn has added onto those of his other colleagues an etiology for the appearance of that natural man but he has not forwarded a true explanation. He has counterposed "revolutionary millenarianism" to the rational efforts at change of peasantry bounded by custom and kinship and of workers brought together in "trade-unions, co-operatives and parliamentry parties." Like Eric Wolf, another student of peasant movements, Cohn has located his explanatory phenomena in the conventional crises of medieval feudalism and capitalist dislocations: demographic crises; crises produced by the integration of subsistence peasantry into capitalist market economies; and crises of traditional power and authority.[77]

But departing from Wolf, a neo-Marxist scholar, Cohn has substituted madmen for the revolutionary party (or class). The end result, however, is the same. The obedience of the follower, the participation of men and women in mass, "spontaneous" movements, is convened with the phenomenon of leadership. One is instructed to again look to the leader or the vanguard for the clues to the peculiar formation of the movement. Whatever be the nature of the leadership, so, too, the nature of the movement.

Disappointingly, even those most coherent among the "irrationalists" have failed to broaden to a full satisfaction the insights of Sohm, James, Marx or Freud concerning the phenomenon of authority-submission, self-surrender or obedience. An architecture of the act or experience of followership has not been achieved in so far as one means an understanding independent of metaphors, reductionisms, and determinisms. These strategies merely compromise understanding by either changing the phenomenon into something else or redirecting attention away from it.

Just as with the sociologies and scientisms of obedience and followership attended to in the previous two chapters, the metaphysicians have not achieved an explanatory paradigm authentic at each tier, in each nuance, to each suggestion to the follower as an event. Proceeding as they did from the presumption of the possibility of and necessity for such a paradigm, they have perhaps helped us to realize its non-existence.

Yet one important strategy has been demonstrated. That strategy is the potential capacity for sensitively integrating paradigms constituting different sources, namely the ecclesiastical, the clinical and the philosophical costumed as historical materialism. The energies or motive forces of each of these realities as paradigms are fundamentally different, resulting in different projections of human behavior and different mechanisms through which closure is achieved.

The ecclesiastical asserts that the individual must converge with the infinite to accomplish the completion of the species— the divinely destined fulfillment of mankind. It offers the chiliastic and messianic visions as the framework of reconciliation. The empirical or temporal manifestation is the charismatic leader.

The clinical designates the anguish of experience as consequent to the primordial magnificence of the individual and the paradox of his proximation to others who are similarly natured. The individual possesses a potential greater than that which can be obtained in society. The clinical paradigm thus projects a tempered madness at 'best,' but as well the presumption that the injury will not always be tolerable. In point of fact, psychosis is *the* logical consequence, the solution, and not merely an aberration. It is the subjective closure which ultimately expels what Kierkegaard had termed dread and Freud basic anxiety—the inevitable existential injury.

Historical materialism is somewhat more ambiguous since on the one hand it asserts that the nature of the individual is unidentifiable in that it is a product of an infinite process, but on the other hand asserts that this particular species is uniquely affected by reflection both as a social optic and as introspection, i.e. feeling. As a consequence, historical materialism embraces a dialectical historicism—the progressive reconciliation of contradiction until the deliberate elimination of material distinctions is achieved—as a 'natural' stopping point and the end of time. But it retains, as well, the suggestion of circularity in its incorporation of a classical sense of revolution.

In these three paradigms, mankind is understood as a contrary: In the first, mankind is contrary to infinity; in the second, mankind is contrary to society in being infinite; and in the third, mankind is contrary to itself by being subject and sympathetic to the infinite. And in each, reconciliation is achieved by the dissolution of the species in conformity with those several, disparate presumptions: by becoming infinite; by becoming finite; by being subject to an infinite dialectic. So if we do attribute some explanatory power to each of these paradigms, we must too acknowledge that what explanation has passed as an integration of these must more appropriately be understood as either a distortive syncretism or a deceptive mix. If we grant to these paradigms some aesthetic fit, or some conceptual authenticity, or some closing onto experienced-reality, we must also recognize the conflicts between the realities they enclose.

Expectedly, critical controversy has suggested that both phenomena —that is, mixture and contradiction—have been the case. The alternatives appear to be to presume either a more profound truth exists which will ultimately subvert all reasonable allegiance to these paradigms or to attempt to achieve a more authentic mixture of them. And such a mixture might actually consist in putting these paradigms in sequence. The ethos of scientific thought, that is the methodological paradigm associated with Karl Popper, would seem to dictate the first alternative as a resolution. My own predilection, as indicated at the beginning of this chapter, is for the latter: the mixture. The reasons for this will be demonstrated in the following section which concludes the remarks on irrationality.

The Subconscious and Analytic Terror

Perhaps we now have a clue to the extraordinary persistence of the paradigm of social order understood as political order. We had every reason to believe that it would have a vitality among the conventional rationalists of social organization, but now we have discovered its survival even in that branch of Western thought which orbited about the irrational and the subconscious. Searching for social coherence in mass movements, they, too, presumed that it would be consequent to what lay on top. Being out of sympathy with the "mass" consciousness of itself, they ignored the base beyond their establishment of its "readiness:" its structural dislocation.

Just as the idea of social coherence was analytically related to the idea of leadership, it bent back on the analyst's approach in a dialectical fashion. The analyst having seen a thing, understands what is possible in the way the thing is seen. He then amends the structure of reality so that the thing seen might be possible.

As well, these analysts have chosen the more "economic" approach in avoiding an investigation of the formulations of reality experienced by the mass element of movements before they become followers. In lieu of the peculiar epistemologies located there, these analysts have imposed the phenomenological paradigm of the thing: social coherence. But it is more than a question of choosing the cheaper approach. Most importantly they have chosen to avoid the inevitable paradoxes emergent in social reality. Instead they have chosen for the certainty posited in the logical order of the words they use.

If one can extract a simple design for truth from the works of Berger and Luckmann, Wittgenstein, Polanyi, Louch, Levi-Strauss and Foucault, it is that words are at once the evidence and instruments of our understandings. They are in their very fundament the representation of our environs, our experience, whichever the several means by which they enter and simultaneously extend our consciousness. Though one cannot deny that there seems to be more, other elements if you will, in subjective, objective or environmental realities, it cannot be reached and encompassed by words. It can only be indicated.

Words are then that order of things which serves the conjunctive aspects of life, that order of things which makes possible a relationship of the human organism to itself. We must then anticipate and affirm a continuous interaction between the rational and the irrational, between words whose meaning begins and ends with other words and therefore have no singular integrity for they are merely elements of bounded semantic experience. Such fundamentally different classes of words will and do interpenetrate for that is their nature as authentic representations: that which they represent has the very same pattern at the same points.

Knowing this, or presuming this as a certainty, we may then proceed

to extract from the concept political authority and from the phenomenon of followership, the root words order and terror. These are words
which in and of themselves portray the interrelatedness possible
between that which follows (recalling Louch's use of the term entitle-
ness), and that which preceded. Such are the characteristics,
respectively, of the rational and the irrational as meanings.

As we have already presented a set of explanations in an attempt to
expose the sympathy of the organism for order and in the present
chapter concerned ourselves with a record of mechanisms responsive
to terror, so we may now ratify the claims of those who would know
order through terror and realize terror in order.

Terror must be understood as the absence of order and bearing no
other relationship to order. Terror is neither the presence of too much
order, regardless of its administration, nor order's midwife.[78] If, as
Camus suggested, decency is the resolve to know what one knows,
then the decency of order—what one knows—is always potentially
terror. The intuition that there is no true existential order is constantly
available to the human being. Pocock has stated:

> To rebel against existing paradigms is indeed to go in search of new
> ones; but it is also to assert what it is like to be without them, to
> experience the terror and freedom of existential creativity. Paradigms
> do not define this condition for us. We may think of them as serving to
> conceal it from us or as the output of the creativity it isolates—
> according as we think of the mask as that which we hid behind or that
> through which we speak—but it is not their function to express the
> nakedness of the existential freedom or dereliction.[79]

And this is an intuition which is terrible in the extreme. If we
remember this, R.D. Laing's characterization of the schizophrenic
individual as "suffering" from "ontological insecurity" becomes a
remark on a psychosocial process by which human society reproduces
the human condition in microcosm: the absence of order.

Interestingly enough, a parallel insight exists in the presumably
distinct field of physics. F.S.C. Northrop has suggested that quantum
mechanics has had a singular effect on the mechanics of Einstein and
Newton. Quantum mechanics has identified the ordering principles of
the latter as consequence of observing *gross* phenomena. According to

Werner Heisenberg, both Einstein's and Newton's general theories were really special theories. These "general" theories projected a determinable order which was, in truth, an epistemological impression. It was not the nature of the physical world that Einstein and Newton were describing but the impression of that nature on them. Thus Einstein's reputed response to Heisenberg's principle of uncertainty was appropriately axiological: "God does not play dice."[80]

It is in this same fashion that terror and order may be said to articulate. Order results from the observation of terror at the level of gross phenomena. And it is this insight which propels the follower and the phenomenon of followership, as a device to avoid the experience of terror, into preeminence. There are, of course, important differences to be perceived between different order from the various vantage points of observation. But their true richness—true as an authenticity to their participants—is the capacity for integrating the elements, the facts, of experience. All else is historical, that is superfluous.

CHAPTER IV

The Messiah And the Metaphor

In pursuing the question of the mixed paradigm and its epistemological role in the study of political society, this chapter will be concerned with just such a mixed paradigm: charismatic leadership, its forms, characteristics and functions. It is intended here that what one discovers in the relationship between the event and concept of charisma, its phenomenology, and the development of an explanatory paradigm for leadership in political science, will reveal the degree of coherence possible in an epistemological system founded on contradiction.

What is to be discovered is an epistemological system which is historical and syncretic rather than ideological; that is, a system which is *at base* not a system but a juxtaposition of elements related by dialectical processes but themselves the result of phenomenological and ontological practices and experiences. Such a discovery will as well underline an awareness of the potential force, even among social scientists, of explanatory systems which are at base disjointed.

Furthermore, just as discomforting perhaps, charismatic leadership will be treated initially as a mythic phenomenon. It will be treated as an historical and *conceptual event* in human societies and cultures. The genesis of charisma is a social response to the discovery of empirical insolubles and objective crises experienced by those societies through the use, in this instance, of theogony.

This strategy rests on a number of rationales and conclusions, some of which have already been explored in this essay, others still to be suggested. Some of these presumptive rationales and conclusions deal with the importance of charisma as an analytical tool in what is in its broadest terms political science, while others are concerned with the justification of the use of myth. But for convenience these arguments are here summarized together, momentarily suspending a consideration of the quite specific purpose of their more deliberate presentations in the paper. Here quite succinctly is the problem presented in a series of propositions.

A first proposition is that charisma as a conceptualization represents a holdover from a prescientific past in Western thought; specifically, those traditions of thought concerned with the understanding of social organization and social movements.[1]

A second contributory insight is that charisma, as it has taken its place in social science and analysis from Weber's formulations on authority and its legitimizations, is considered an actual variant of leadership forms, a classification and description under which some historical phenomena may be deposited.

A third consideration is that in the intellectual history of the West, I believe that the notion of charismatic leadership has an identifiable genealogy, one which will contain important information and insights about the larger question posed in this essay concerning political society and political order, notably its metaphysical and epistemological parameters.

A fourth rationale is that the charismatic phenomenon is epistemologically, rather than chronologically or historically, the root, the metaphysical base, for those who think about or experience society in political terms.

The final consideration is that the explanatory role of charisma in Cartesian scientific thought conforms with one of Freud's reactions to the prospect of using genius as explanation. He argued: "We know that genius is incomprehensible and unaccountable and it should therefore not be called upon as an explanation until every other solution has failed."[2] Charisma has been the court of last resort, useful after all other explanatory devices have been found to be unsatisfactory, and sometimes used before. Yet it is quite likely more powerful than either of these procedures would immediately suggest.

As for the term myth, let it suffice merely for the moment to remind ourselves that it possesses an etymological ambiguity, between the actual and the imaginary. Myth has in the past been used to designate a story; perhaps a history, perhaps not. So just as myth has, in our times, come to be associated with the fictional, recall too that fiction has meant, somewhat problematically, that which is contrary to fact, and fact is a product of the conduct of inquiry.

Here a caution would appear appropriate. A distinction needs to be made between an objective phenomenon and the response which has arisen consequent to its appearance. Nothing in the foregoing paragraphs should be understood to imply that the charismatic event is insubstantial, that is to say that charismatic leadership as the subject of countless, creative analytical and descriptive treatments has had no historical basis. To the contrary, the intent is to assure that the charismatic event is real but that it has had a character which has largely been ignored or muted in scientific thought because that character was understood to be archaic, primitive or pre-scientific.

Thus some difficulties with charisma can be understood in epistemological terms. On the one hand, it will be argued that one finds human groups whose political cultures contain some charismatic model mobilized in times of perceived crisis as a means of restoring coherence, but on the other that the coherence achieved or "restored" will be necessarily delusional precisely because of the social instrument utilized. And furthermore, this significance—the recognition of the peculiar nature of the equilibrium obtained—has not been perceived because of a misunderstanding. The apparent social transfiguration—specifically and historically the emergence or reconstruction of a different political system—has been understood by students of society as a fundamental transformation of values, social and cultural norms and institutions: an admittedly important, significant institutional exchange.[3] It is misunderstandings such as these which have made the concept of charisma an ambiguous contribution to the fields of social science.

Concepts of Time

In the previous chapter, some attention was given to the immediate source through which charisma was introduced into Max Weber's work, namely the work of Rudolf Sohm. In that chapter, the metaphysics of time was also treated briefly but primarily as an enigmatic element in some modern social theories. At this point, however, the concept of time will be reconsidered, but differently, for it is more important that the consideration of Time be used as an instrument by which the antiquity and ambiguity of the charismatic construct is traced. This approach is predicated on the presumption that the construct—charisma—is a means of dealing with Time as History and that it is as well a particular expression of the process of that identification.

Time, as a concept, may be and has been assembled in a variety of ways, each way discrete from the others but also related to them. In the following, three ways of looking at time will be reviewed so that some attention may be subsequently given to the integration of Time with variations of political authority and political society.

For example, Time has been considered to be linear in its nature, that is possessing an additive unity which is experienced by the individual as a present which proceeds to the past by the penetration of the future. The future is constantly in imminent danger from incorporation by the present as the present is, in turn, itself continuously encroached upon by its deposition into the past.

> There is no punctual present: either it is already past or still future. When we say it is nine thirty, it is no longer nine thirty, and the telephone operator's voice announcing the time does not speak of time at all, but only of the clock. . .But there is no fixed point; we are carried along by time as though by a torrent. We are temporal—that is to say, we can neither grasp nor hold fast a point in time, can neither grasp nor hold fast our own existence. The man of nine thirty is not the same as the man of nine twenty-five. We *are* time.[4]

This linear temporal order is thus successive or serial in its character. And, consequently, it is actually only a matter of emphasis and attention whether the process is perceived as an advance into the future or a progression of events into the past (which would be called history). Events, as such, are distinguished by temporal parameters and may be thus enumerated and, subsequently, themselves become the means of quantifying and calibrating the spaces between themselves, i.e., Time. For example, the phrase "revolutionary period" has a meaning based upon several presuppositions concerning the nature of events, a "revolution," and Time. It is presupposed that revolutions can be periodized, having beginnings and ends and that between these temporal brackets, the "system" which is the revolutionary event can be identified in its process from conception to actualization. As such, all remarkable events "contained" within the revolutionary period refer to that system and are comprehensible by their spatio-temporal place and context. Thus the lineality of time, history, etc., penetrates the consciousness of events and their "structures."

Alternatively, Time may be described and experienced as fundamentally cyclical in nature. The past, present and future are collapsed on one another in this view, so the present, the most marked impression, is actually a realization rather than an objective phenomenon. It is more a face of Time, or perhaps a mask, which is exchangeable only momentarily for the human mind with the true aspect of Time, its boundless, unitary aspect which confirms the identity of events to be experience with those which already have been experienced. What is attributable to past and future in the linear temporal order are in the cyclical temporal order more illusory than definite. The *convenience* of a past and a future is recognized in lieu of a commitment to believe that there is a past and a future.

> . . .primordial time is not a beginning in the strict sense. It is just as much alive today as it was yesterday; it begins each day anew. Consequently there is no end corresponding to it. Primitive myth has little if anything to say of final time. The myth finds no conclusion: according to it, time turns round and round. "What happens now is what happened long ago." Primitive man—that is, the man who still lives close to the womb, in an unsplit world, who has objectified neither his own life nor that of the world—lives in circles, in an eternal today. The patriarchs and what they did are today as much alive as they were then. A real past exists no more than a real future.[5]

This cyclical past and future may then be of varying duration, depending as they do on the perceived nature and character of events.

For example, in monistic mystical thought, the life of a spirit and the life-time of a man—the incorporate or encapsulated spirit—represent the presence of very different senses of Time's duration. On the one hand the present is unremarkable in its persistence since the spirit exists in an arena of infinite continuance, while on the other hand it may be the past which is relatively insignificant as the period of alienation or apartness is compared to those of the conjoining (the present) and identity (the future) of the spirit with God or universe.

Yet such a conceptual system might still incorporate the analytical insight that the idea of a past, present and future was an inevitable folk-myth or history, responsive to the finite and particularistic (limited) nature of the spirit condemned for the moment to a mortal experience of the universe. And so the tension between conflictual perceptions of Time are not allowed to generate into contradiction. Reality is conceived of as containing two elements, one structural and the other constructural, one real and the other merely apparent.[6]

A third alternative conceptualization of Time has been called eschatological time. Contrary to the epistemologies of the two previously noted temporal orders, in eschatological order, the metaphysics consists of an end to Time, a point at which a future analogous to that found in linear order interdicts with the present bringing an entirely new age. And this age is characterized by equilibrium, permanence and staticism—the immutable damming of the temporal flow. In the eschatological vision, the present is merely a transitory, auspicious phase, remarkable only to the extent that events in it symbolize and signify the approach of this end to all time, that is the final historical event.

Thus eschatological time can be understood as a mix of linear and cyclical orders combined by the eschatological premise. Though present events relate to the last (or literally "furtherest") event in linear terms, the future and the past manifest a cycle wherein the last event recapitulates the critical relatedness extant in the past. The new age, the new world, are the fulfillment of a promise given in the beginning to a people (usually in literal, spatial and spiritual terms) with such a Being.

. . .the doctrine that the world was created from nothingness establishes an absolute beginning and so puts an end to the image of the cosmic cycle. The great year makes place for a linear chronology which has its source in a divine plan and provides the framework for history. . . The Savior is a man. Hence this fusion of aeonic-cyclical and historical-chronological time reckoning has come down to us as the story of salvation, in which myth and history form an undifferentiable whole, running from the beginning of creation through the Old and New Testaments down to the end of time. . . .

The *creatio ex nihilo* implies the possibility of dissolution into nothingness. . .[7]

And so eschatological time, combining in this way linear and cyclical temporal orderings issues in as well a last "alternative" to the conceptualization of Time and that is of a supratemporal order, a time when there is no longer Time. This is infinity.

As this brief exploration of the concepts of Time concludes, attention returns to Weber, for it is through his work that the subject concept, charisma, enters social science. The immediate task is to identify how he saw Time and political society articulating and which Time he reserved for the charismatic phenomenon, for it is his treatment which has dominated the meaning of charisma.

Time and Authority in Weber

It becomes somewhat obvious that in describing his ideal types of legitimacies for social authority, Weber was as well tracing the consequence of, in political and social institutions, forms and structures, a culture presuming one or the other of these concepts of Time.[8] In analytical terms, those processes by which particular political organizations and societies arose from metaphysics might be explicated in the following ways.

For those societies whose temporal metaphysics was linear, there first arose the problem of characterizing that infinite series of successive events; yet, what character or value that history would be ascribed would not prove critical in the instrumentation of social authority. This is suggested by recalling that European social thought has swung between the cynicism of Plato, the nihilism of Nietzsche and the sanguinariness of a Marx or Passmore, no less its theocratic traditions. But once Time had been deciphered, it became appropriate to tamper with or temper its character, to rationalize it to the degree that it might be lived with or lived through. As such bureaucracy was an apparent instrument for the purpose. Apparent, certainly, if for no other reason than by its very structure, it was a model for the most economic organization of resources in the mammoth task of fulfilling history, or staving it off.

Once it is fully established, bureaucracy is among those social structures which are the hardest to destroy. Bureaucracy is *the* means of carrying "community action" over into rationally ordered "social action." . . .this bureaucracy rests upon expert training, a functional specialization of work, and an attitude set for habitual and virtuoso-like mastery of single yet methodically integrated functions.[9]

In Weber's rational, legal and applied institutional authority, each time, each episode was a message unit to be decodified and its secrets formulated for succeeding generations. In the past was the origin of the present just as in the present were the patterns which would emerge to determine the nature of the future. The culture within which authority was bureaucratized accepted the imminence of the future and made deliberate preparations for it. This protoscience of society was the paradigmatic foundation for what is currently called empirical theory, or the process analysis of the instrumentation of the political society; and behavioral science, or the analysis of the social and cultural matrix of political societies and their interaction with political structures. Leszek Kolakowski captures the spirit and commitment of this epistemology when he recounts August Comte's rationalization for his "sociology:"

. . .the distinction between spiritual and secular authority is not a medieval invention, but an essential feature of all collective life. The division of authority between Pope and Emperor is to be replaced with a division of power between scientists and industrialists. The fact that society has yet to be rationally organized is accounted for by the short-comings of public instruction and the lack of a scientific knowledge. . . sociology does not just include "statics," that is, the science dealing with the permanent structural features of society, but also "dynamics," that is, the science of progress. But once the positive spirit has been victorious, progress will no longer face obstacles created by prejudice, ignorance, and myth.[10]

The cyclical temporal order was in its turn a critical element in the epistemological base for those groups whose authority was legitimized, according to Weber, by tradition. Here was required the demonstration of an unbroken line of authorization from the originating authoritative source to the contemporary elites. In this circumstance, G. van der Leeuw states:

Culture, in a manner of speaking, is the fixation and confirmation of the given, the establishment of the cosmos as opposed to chaos.

The confirmation of the act, whether we call it rite or act of culture, is always myth. It "points," as Preuss says, "into the past where the sacral action was first undertaken; in fact, it can sometimes be shown that the primitive does not merely repeat the initial event, but consciously represents its first performance with all the beings who then participated in it." Hence myth is a "necessary ingredient in the cult (and in culture) insofar as a beginning in primordial time is regarded as requisite to its validity. . . ."

The circular course of time impresses itself upon us more and more. There are no new times, no moment that has not yet been attained. There is only primordial time, today as in the past and in the most distant future.[11]

The omnipresence of the past was a benign presence, for it brought with it the commitment and promise that the integrity of the group was without menace regardless of apparent difficulties. The life of the community was warranted by its past. And the remembrance of the past was kept near by the repetition of the deeds and names of ancestral heroes and in so doing the rhythm and order of occasion was reviewed, sacralized by time, the lauded wisdom of the ancestral superman and its more than apparent good sense. It was incumbent upon the members of the community merely to renew the understandably fading awareness peculiar to men and to intensify ritually the prescribed cohesion in order to insure the community's health.

What is actually new is thus claimed to have always been in force but only recently to have become known through the wisdom of the promulgator. The only documents which can play a part in the orientation of legal administration are the documents of tradition; namely precedents.[12]

Just as Time itself was closed, conserved and forever, so was the peoplehood of the community closed to any final injury though given to unevenly periodized disjunctions. But these disjunctions were really understood to be exemplaries, occasions to spur the memory, to prick the waning consciousness.

Thus, whatever the institutions in which authority was deposited, their primary function and legitimacy lay in their integrative aspect, the extent to which social cohesion was obtained. These were not new integrations which might be administrative in the locus of their motive or, possibly, structurally innovative or crises-adaptive, yet fundamentally organizational, but traditional integrations: organic in substance, customary in style, and resistant to the recognition or acknowledgment of crises hitherto unknown.

It is to this type of political, moral and religious organization of society that Weber applied the term "primitive formalistic irrationalism" signifying scale, organizational principles (e.g. kinship), inviolable sacred norms (custom) and, in this instance, systems grounded in religious and magical authority.[13] "Traditional authority is bound to the precedents handed down from the past and to this extent is also oriented to rules."[14] Collingwood identified a variant of this strategy for dealing with Time in his analysis of Greco-Roman historiography, a historiography which he characterized as substantialism:

> . . .a substantialistic metaphysics implies a theory of knowledge according to which only what is unchanging is knowable. But what is unchanging is not historical. What is historical is the transitory event. The substance to which an event happens, or from whose nature it proceeds, is nothing to the historian. Hence the attempt to think historically and the attempt to think in terms of substance were incompatible. . .It is taken for granted that the historian's proper business is with acts, which come into being in time, develop in time through their phases, and terminate in time. The agent from which they flow, being a substance, is eternal and unchanging and consequently stands outside history. In order that acts may flow from it, the agent itself must exist unchanged throughout the series of its acts: for it has to exist before this series begins and nothing that happens as the series goes on can add anything to it or take away anything from it. History cannot explain how any agent came into being or underwent any change of nature; for it is metaphysically axiomatic that an agent, being a substance, can never have come into being and can never undergo any change of nature.[15]

Eschatological time unlike the other two senses of Time emerges necessarily from theology, that is to say that it arises from a tradition in which man was identified as the actualization of a divine will and authority. Eschatology by emphasizing the significance of one species over the others and as well over its physical environment thus represents a separation of man from nature, the abandoning of a relationship which had previously dominated man's perception of his own kind as well as its circumstance which, of course, included Time. The periodicity peculiar to what could conscientiously be identified as earlier conceptualizations of Time—passing through Christian and post-Christian thought from Egyptian, Babylonian and Judaic thought—and which was a response influenced by the presumption that man was inextricably subject to the rhythms of nature, was challenged by eschatological thought. Here man was preeminently a divine instrument with a fate and interest which was supernatural in its origins and locus. The cyclical rhythm of nature within which a consciousness of history could be accomodated could no longer command a primary attention since history was teleological and purposive and subsequently closed.

Yet, in truth, eschatology had developed out of just such a periodicity rooted in the observation of nature's regularities. It arose out of cosmic mythology as the mythology was, following Rudolf Bultmann, "rationalized" and "historicized":

> The course of the world-year was originally conceived as purely natural process in which the periods followed each other like the seasons. But later the periods were distinguished by the character of the human generations living in them. The idea of the withering and passing away of every natural growth was transmuted into the idea of degeneration, of the permanent deterioration of humanity. . .Still greater importance must be ascribed to another modification of the myth which is also a historicizing of it. This variation abandons the idea of the eternal cyclical movement of world-years but retains the idea of the periodicity of the course of time. The new beginning which is to follow the end of the old world-era is understood as the beginning of a time of unending welfare. Here the cosmic world-year is reduced to the history of the world.[16]

From the Stoic tradition, "the defeatist philosophies" as Collingwood described them, with their recognition of the unresponsiveness of an essentially evil world to the efforts of good men who attempt to alter its nature; with their argument that all of mankind was caught up in the same processes in a shared world (a presumption which was an important pre-condition for a world history) and consequently the anticipation of the destruction of mankind from time to time; there arose the anguish and harmony in periodicity characterized in eschatology. Some Stoics argued that if man in spite of his beautiful reason could make no final historical imprint, then, this: the ironical bounding of what was the most beautiful experience in the universe to impotence, indicated the existence of a higher order of reason, and thus the necessity for the achievement of a more profound recognition.[17] The true order of relationships was not to be found in the society or the political community with its moral chasms and existential injuries but in the recurrent renaissance of nature, the changing changelessness which secured what *Was* to what *Is* to what *Will Be.* And for eschatology to emerge from this Stoicism it was merely required that the episodic be inflated to cosmic dimensions.

Hegel wrote of this dialectic of closure in two different but not distinct contexts, one metaphysical, the other, historical. In the first context, concerning himself with "the *Unhappy Consciousness*, the Alienated Soul which is the consciousness of self as a divided Nature, a doubled and merely contradictory being,"[18] Hegel reasoned that in the struggle against itself (a struggle which was its nature) to abolish the particularity of its experience of its existence (consciousness of "the conflicting contradictory process;" i.e., the dialectic) Stoic consciousness is defeated by its victory. The temporality of consciousness is continuously rediscovered in its experience of the eternal ("the unchangeable"). Reality ("the immutable essence"), to the Stoic, is realizable only through the particular constructs of experienced reality. Closure is achieved, according to Hegel in three ways:

> In one form it comes before itself as opposed to the unchangeable essence, and is thrown back to the beginning of that struggle, which is, from first to last, the principle constituting the entire situation (God as Judge). At another time it finds the unchangeable appearing in the form of particularity; so that the latter is an embodiment of unchangeableness, into which, in consequence, the entire form of existence passes Christ. In the third case, it discovers *itself* to be this particular fact in the unchangeable. The religious communion.[19]

But Hegel went further, ratifying by his use of the historical his belief in the State. Along the way, *mutatis mutandis,* he reiterated the Stoic momentum:

> It is quite otherwise the comprehensive relations that History has to do with. In this sphere are presented those momentous collisions between existing, acknowledged duties, laws, and rights, and those contingencies which are adverse to this fixed system; which assail and even destroy its foundations and existence; whose tenor may nevertheless seem good—on the large scale advantageous—yes, even indispensable and necessary. These contingencies realize themselves in History: they involve a general principle of a different order from that on which depends the *permanence* of a people or a State. This principle is an essential phase in the development of the *creating* Idea, of Truth striving and urging towards consciousness of itself. Historical men—World-Historical Individuals—are those in whose aims such a general principle lies.[20]

For the Stoics, if human society was inevitably disintegrative, the recurrent pattern of disorder followed by order in turn succeeded by disorder, could only be precluded by the interdiction of a superhuman element. For Hegel, too, though the orders of anguish were only the experience of the thing, the superhuman were there, as actualization of the Spirit in process of Being.

Divine intervention, too, would represent a form of closure for what was otherwise an infinite series. And it was this closure which was accomplished by Judaic thought which had inherited, importantly, from its immediate east the notion that each age was marked and signified by the appearance of a great leader-king. Extending this concept, the Jews accomplished the construction of the prototype for the charismatic figure in the Messiah, a convening hypothesized by Bultmann[21] of Greek astrology, Iranian speculative thought and Roman religio-mythology:

> The conception of God as creator prevented the idea of the cyclic movement of world-ages from being accepted by Israel, although the imagery of this mythology was to some extent adopted.
> This imagery appears in such themes as the prophetic portrayals of the tribulations which precede the change in Israel's fortunes, tribulations which later in the apocalyptic writings are signs of the coming end, the 'birth-pangs of the Messiah'.[22]

Thus, according to Weber, eschatological thought arose in that Jewish thought subsequent to the Old Testament in the apocalyptic literature which was itself the consequence of Jewish historical, social and political crises in the break-up and submission of Israel by foreign states.[23] These disolutions in scale and duration extended beyond Judaic orthodoxy's capacity to explain and interpret; yet there were other traditions extant which might be useful. So eschatological thought and time proper emerged, being the product of the penetration of orthodox rabbinical thought and tradition (as manifest in the Old Testament) by a mysticism which revitalized earlier Mediterranean and Levantine mythologies.

> The poetry of the Psalms has also taken over some themes from this cosmology. This appears to be so in the case of the New Year Festival as the festival of God's accession to the throne. And indeed, this originally cosmological festival was already historicized in Babylon in that the renewal of the world and the beginning of the world were both celebrated as the king's accession to the throne.[24]

Yet as the eschatological aspiration continued unfulfilled, it became incumbent upon the Christian ecclesiastes, as one line of the direct heirs of Jewish messianism, to rationalize that disappointment. This rationalization was accomplished, in part, by the formulation of the teleological nature of history associated with Augustine. At this point, human history became purposive and ordained. It was this conceptualization which emerged much later in Hegelian and Marxist thought as historicism: Hegelian historical consciousness and Marxist historical materialism respectively. And it was in the opposition to this tradition and some of its epistemological constituents that Weber reached back into the history of the Church and the sociology of religion for the phenomenological basis for historical relativism, positivism and the sociology of knowledge. As he did so, this meant that Weber closed the circle of the consciousness concerned with the historical meaning of the superman, as Nietzsche[25] had called him, as had been done innumerable times before.[26] As history was particular and synthetic in nature, and with no permanence except the record of the decline of man, the charismatic phenomenon assumed less the scale and significance of the messiah and more the recognition of the roles (other than negative deviance) that merely extraordinary figures (as opposed to divine) can play in the reintegration-through-action of social groups.

Yet, objectively, in Weber's thought, the messianic scale was the hidden ideal type, seen not from the orthodoxy of the eschatologist but from the vantage point of the student of eschatological social movements concerned with the continuity and transmission of the concept. And, additionally, in some ways, Time and history had exchanged natures in the Weberian system, returning to their earlier juxtaposition: suspended spheres proximate, but uninvolved with each other. For Weber, the historical relativist, Time was unencumbered with a character or with a general meaning. History, on the other hand, was meaning-filled, more emphatically it was the source and arena of all meaning. Yet because history was for Weber specific and particular to a people in a time and at a place, it was also varied and its meaning existentially myriad and diverse. In transposing the messianic ideal into the pattern of the charismatic phenomenon, Weber achieved a new synthesis between eschatology and history. By reversing eschatology and putting the "furthest ends" in the past rather than in the future; by making history posteschatological rather than pre-eschatological, all history could bee seen as the record of foundings followed by progressive deteriorations.

The paradox in Weber was that it is in the irrational, charismatic beginnings of history rather than at its rational, bureaucratic dissolution that reason and thus freedom articulate most highly with political organization.[27] The charismatic relationship whose conceptual roots are in the mysticism of the messiah is the most complete expression of the will of the community, the most effective integration of interests and benefits, yet it falls, historically, outside the process of rational calculi:

> . . .the validity of charismatic authority rests entirely on recognition by those subject to it, conditioned as this is by "proof" of its genuineness. This is true in spite of the fact that this recognition of a charismatically qualified, and hence legitimate, person is treated as a duty. . .The leader whose legitimacy rested on his personal charisma then becomes leader by the grace of those who follow him since the latter are formally free to elect and elevate to power as they please and even to dispose. For

the loss of charisma and its proof involves the loss of genuine legitimacy. The chief now becomes the freely elected leader.[28]

Charismatic authority then becomes at once the most total of authorities and the least authoritarian. Expectedly, one recognizes in this characterization integrations and meanings taken directly by Weber from messianic thought to construct the charismatic ideal type.

In short, then, Weber borrows from the eschatological tradition the notion of the messiah and seeks to rationalize (systematize) it in the concept of charisma by reversing and as well particularizing the eschatological sequence. The accompaniment of eschatological time in Weber's analysis is thus reserved for the irrational while cyclical and linear senses of Time are, in their institutional expressions, characterized by calculi of formalism and rationality, respectively.

The Meaning of Myth

If the recognition can be made of the uses of Time as a litmus for determining the particular class of *episteme* from which conceptual elements are taken in mixed paradigms, then we can proceed. We can proceed, that is, toward confirming the mixture which constitutes the paradigm in question and discover the reasons for its "explanatory" powers. But, first, before continuing with the characterization of this paradigm, we must rediscover something about myth which has been obscured by the development of modern thought. Again, keep in mind that we are concerned with that paradigm which presupposes a seminal relationship between political leadership and political society where political society is equated with order. Recall, further, that we have here proposed that charismatic authority has been suggested, and to some degree accepted, as the foundation for political authority regardless of the subsequent transformations in structure and legitimation of that authority. (This latter presupposition is certainly recognizable as a tradition in Western thought, in its histories, its political theories and analysis, its sociologies, in short, in the studies of its own culture and its history. One finds this tradition associated with thinkers as far back as Herodotus, Thucydides, Plato, Livy and Tacitus with their dependencies on those oral traditions of their subject communities which celebrated that relationship in which they

125

identified their beginnings. One finds it in Machiavelli as certainly as in his Christological predecessors and successors. From Carlyle to Nietzsche, Weber and Freud, the tradition has been brought forward by many of those concerned with the foundation of political authority in the antecedent stages of development of their own society.)[29] Through various forms of biography, intellectual history, political movements, this particular construction of the ontogenesis of social authority, so suspiciously similar to what Joseph Campbell has called the "monomyth," has persisted:

> The composite hero of the monomyth is a personage of exceptional gifts. Frequently he is honored by his society, frequently unrecognized or disdained. He and / or the world in which he finds himself suffers from a symbolical deficiency. In fairy tales this may be as slight as the lack of a certain golden ring, whereas in apocalyptic vision the physical and spiritual life of the whole earth can be represented as fallen, or on the point of falling, into ruin.
>
> Typically, the hero of the fairy tale achieves a domestic, microcosmic triumph, and the hero of myth a world-historical macrocosmic triumph.[30]

Questions then force themselves on our attention. Is it coincidence that what we now instruct ourselves to know about human society, in particular its structures (its political systems, its orderings) and its vital systemic principle (its *sine qua non,* political authority), is very much like what we have been told to know through the archaicisms of cosmogonic myths, theogonic fables, folk-stories, oral and literary traditions? I think not. Is it that regardless of the changing natures of heroes or principal actors, we have compulsively come to associate them with authorships? That is, whether these figures are in nature divine, mortal or something in between, that when we think about them, ritually or reasonably, in myth or in analysis, we are celebrating them—celebrating their authority over life and death.

In contradiction to the presumption of synthesis found in Western history of ideas, can it be anticipated that the distinctions between what is now recognized as scientific knowledge and that "knowing" which proceeded from mythologies and mysticisms as they both relate to society, are at base subsidiary in their mutual criticality? That is that the distinctions, rather than being of themselves antithetic to each other, if looked at structurally, proceed from the conflict between deeper paradigmatic systems of knowing.

Continuing with the suggestion of antithesis, is it an important realization that political society is no less a salvationist or redemptionist paradigm than those theologic paradigms out of which it emerged and with which it has had a most constant existential and historical simultaneity?[31] What must we make of this relatedness? Is it as well significant to remind ourselves that the State as a paradigm evolved from the fact of the city which was itself an historic expression of the community, the tribe, the familial group?

The implications of these questions for determining whether the base of political science rests on a mixed paradigm would best be revealed by coming to some true understanding—of myth—that is, an understanding unprejudiced by the presumption that myth is primitive and thus anachronistic: that myth is to be associated with the species through its spokesmen and spokeswomen at a primitive level of social organization and thought and that myth no longer penetrates modern thought. Such a presumption clearly and somewhat abortively designates myth as unacceptable to scientific knowledge and history. It furthermore characterizes the latter as modern and post-mythical by definition.

This position, associated with the cultural evolutionist theory of society most popular in 19th-century myth scholarship, has long been superceded. It was superceded first by functionalist, then by behavioralist and psychological frameworks and finally by psychoanalytic and semiological theoretical presumptions. (These currents could be represented by the writings of such scholars as Malinowski and Radcliffe-Brown, Murdock, Kluckhohn, Freud and Levi-Strauss, respectively.)

Alternatively, if the myth is, objectively, a "lie," a fabrication, it has, too, been revealed to possess subjective and social capacities which make its objective nature a trivial consideration. For even when it is recognized as fiction, the myth necessarily and deliberately reflects social facts through borrowings, and thus portrays truths.

Myths then, have ideological capabilities and epistemological natures. They contain a construction of reality in a larger knowing system of some form. But more pointedly, it must be understood that myths take on the peculiar artifacts of the society out of which they emerge. As a class of phenomena, they are not made recognizable only by their structure or their appearance but by their function. Myths are not merely the "oral narratives" of Robert Georges[32] nor the literate "raw material" of Harry Levin[33] to span conventional parameters.

Setting aside the question of the significance of the almost universally acknowledged polarity between literate and non-literate peoples, myths continue to signify a structural primitiveness of cognitive, technical aspect. Rather than continue to delineate what myths are not, it might be more economic to address ourselves to the literature of the most influential contemporary schools of myth scholarship. I will, then, begin to explore what myths are by enlisting the insights into myths of two quite different trainings; different, yet each literary in its presumptions and its artifact, the one functional and the other structural.

Functional Mythologists

The work of Mark Shorer, whose thoughts on myth are contained in his treatment of William Blake, has been recommended to us by the self-styled "rank amateur" Henry Murray in the following way: "It provides, so far as we know, as complete and concise a view of current usage of the term as recent literature affords."[34] Now here is what Shorer interpreted the myth as being:

> Myths are the instruments by which we continually struggle to make our experience intelligible to ourselves. A myth is a large, controlling image that gives philosophical meaning to the facts of ordinary life; that is, which has organizing value for experience. A mythology is a more or less articulated body of such images, a pantheon. Without such images, experience is chaotic, fragmentary and merely phenomenal. It is the chaos of experience that creates them, and they are intended to rectify it.[35]

Though Shorer writes of "ordinary life," does his description of the necessity fulfilled by myth differ qualitatively from the truism that Hobsbawm repeats in his analysis of millenarian movements?

> It is especially difficult, but necessary, to understand that utopianism, or "impossibilism" which the most primitive revolutionaries share with

128

all but the most sophisticated, and which makes even very modern ones feel a sense of almost physical pain at the realization that the coming of Socialism will not eliminate *all* grief and sadness, unhappy love affairs or mourning, and will not solve or make soluble *all* problems; a feeling reflected in the ample literature of revolutionary disillusionment.

First, utopianism is probably a necessary social device for generating the superhuman efforts without which no major revolution is achieved. . . .

Second, utopianism can become such a social device because *revolutionary movements and revolutions appear to prove that almost no change is beyond their reach.*[36]

There would seem to be no significant distinction between the operation of myth as integrator and as action-precipitant. This universal function of myth is as well retained in Clifford Geertz's formulation:

It is a loss of orientation that most directly gives rise to ideological activity, an inability, for lack of usable models, to comprehend the universe of civic rights and responsibilities in which one finds oneself located. . . . It is a confluence of socio-psychological strain and an absence of cultural resources by means of which to make (political, moral or economic) sense of that strain, each exacerbating the other, that sets the stage for the rise of systematic (political, moral, economic) ideologies. . . . Whatever else ideologies may be—projections of acknowledged fears, disguises for ulterior motives, phatic expression of group solidarity—they are, most distinctively, maps of problematic social reality and matrices for the creation of collective conscience.[37]

Mythical functions are thus recognizable in ideology, or, on the other hand, in what is called ideology. Such functions are found in that ideology which Erikson has termed "the social institution which is the guardian of identity" and whose process of dissemination is described by him in the following terms:

For it is through their ideology that social systems enter into the fiber of the next generation and attempt to absorb into their lifeblood the rejuvenative power of youth. Adolescence is thus a vital regenerator in the process of social evolution, for youth can offer its loyalties and energies both to the conservation of that which continues to feel true and to the revolutionary correction of that which has lost its regenerative significance.[38]

These terms would do as well for that ideology which Werner Stark has typified as "a mode of thinking which is thrown off its proper course." Again Geertz with remarkable precision, in his critique of the most influential conception of ideology in the social sciences, the "evaluative (that is, pejorative) one,"[39] has indicated that though myth and ideology differ artifactually, they retain an identity of function and share phenomenology.

Indeed it is the analyst himself who is thus responsible for reconciling his taste for "ideology," or "myth," or "operational code," or "belief system," or "paradigm" or "domain assumptions." This assertion is admittedly quite different from the implications emerging from the processes of application of these terms. Too often, for the analyst, the use of these categories rest on that particular particle of social integration under study and not on analytical distinctions.

Conventionally, for example, the beliefs of primitives have been contrasted to those of sophisticates; those deposited in oral traditions have been distinguished from those of literate, historical societies; those of hysterics with those of rational people; those of totalitarian societies with those of democratic ones; those of peasant workers with those of industrial proletariats, etc. This is an analytical framework which reminds one of nothing so much as the predilection for "dualisms" mentioned in connection with Freud by Norman O. Brown and the "binary oppositions" in Levi-Strauss' structural approach to the study of myth.

Setting aside for the moment this latter correspondence, the identifications of relevant empirical propositions have proceeded arbitrarily rather than at random, that is, they have proceeded consequent to the cognitive peculiarities of the analyst and the representations of reality sympathetic to his or her understanding rather than to the presentation of reality as natural fact. Just as myth most frequently appears in those literatures which treat primitive groups, that is, groups whose thought is characterized as prescientific, so ideology is associated with neo-primitives, or those groups whose thought suggests to the observer that they have located their ontological security in institutions and dynamics which the progressive element of the species has left behind.[40] Such a supposition is persistent, I am suggesting, in the treatment of major (mass) and minor (sect) 20th-century social movements. These movements are understood to be total rather than coherent in as much as they demand of the participant the forging of his life into an instrument, and to the degree that they are, they are referent to the closed society, the dark age which preceded liberal and scientific thought and social praxis. The total institution is seen as a reversion back to a tribal period rather than a reflection of the analyst's sense of being in his own world.[41]

Even Gouldner's "background assumptions" and "domain assumptions," Nathan Leite's "operational code" and Kuhn's "paradigm" reveal a bias since they emerge from the systematic study of not merely Western but "rational" para-scientific, if not truly scientific, systems.[42] The total institutions of Western society: disciplines, modern political parties, State bureaucracies and the scientific establishment, are not merely the germinal arenas for these metaphysics but their reference as well—the analogy of their subsequent application. Their use would be properly understood to be confined to phenomena which evidence a basic similarity to those observed systems from which they originate. Instead, the practice of employing them beyond these boundaries would very often appear to be an attempt to dramatize how far a group whose familiarity was anticipated has transgressed—eschewing what is "appropriate" for the bizarre, denying to itself the authentic in exchange for the twisted or the perverted.

Traversing these dangers with a concept such as myth, one has reason to believe that the functionalist approach, though simplistic, is a minimal, expedient safeguard for the moment. The meaning of myth will rest in the hands of Shorer while we pursue a slightly different signification.

Structural Mythologists

To be succinct and abusive in one movement, in pursuing the structuralist declaration, the works of Claude Levi-Strauss and Michel Foucault may be conveniently converged under the term semiology, an analytical framework which serves our concern with myth. We will take (quite literally) from Foucault the meaning of semiology as that study of the symbols produced by men to represent reality and more specifically the nature of reality. Both Levi Strauss and Foucault are concerned with the development of a theory of human behavior (behavior is for them thought) through the study of the signs, literary symbols and meaning integration which emerge from the social imagination.[43] To use Foucault's term, they both have glimpsed or revealed through this process an "archaeology" of the human mind, an imprint of its structural stratigraphy, which may or may not have a historical character. More specifically, for Levi-Strauss, the historical is trivial,[44] but for Foucault, it is the curious, paradoxical feature of the human record which reveals through its strata the underlying organization of the human mind.

Notwithstanding this disagreement of a secondary or methodological importance, their thoughts are focused eventually on the same object: the pattern of intelligence the human mind constructs, whether it be "savage" or "civilized." But let us take them one at a time, paying close attention to the contributions each has made toward justifying our supposition as to the meaning and significance of myth in contemporary thought.

In the work of Levi-Strauss, there emerges a formal signification of myth which may yet result in the most proximate representation of myth yet achieved. This, perhaps, strange, convoluted way of analyzing and describing his work in its own way demonstrates some of the difficulty in addressing Levi-Strauss' insights. This difficulty is inevitable when it is realized that in dismissing the absoluteness of truth, one assumes that the explication of myth is accomplished in its translation from one language to another language: one which is the setting and product of a dialectic between myth and its grammar in the context of the universal opposition of nature and culture; while the other is itself setting and product for a similar but different dialectic. This is how Levi-Strauss, himself, puts it in the introduction to his theoretical work, *Les Mythologiques*:

> I therefore claim to show, not how men think in myths, but how myths operate in men's minds without their being aware of the fact.
> . . .For what I am concerned to clarify is not so much what there is *in* myths (without, incidentally, being in man's consciousness) as the

system of axioms and postulates defining the best possible code, capable of conferring a common significance on unconscious formulations which are the work of minds, societies, and civilizations chosen from among those most remote from each other.[45]

There is too, the additional difficulty that notwithstanding the terrible complexity that Levi-Strauss attempts to reveal in his subject, he himself is complex and elusive. Intellectually, he has flowed from a mathematical calculus, through a philosophic philology, into his own particular "musico-dialectic." He is convinced that he has torn from his thought a representation of Marxist determinism, struggled back to Hegelian dialectics to assume finally a Kantian, categorical epistemology, all the while eloquently challenging the need and even further the authenticity of representing his thought in serial, linear expressions coherent with acceptable analytical thought. He has pursued the explication of analogical thought through the use of analogy. In all of this, universals are deceptive. Those which seem to emerge from an earlier work are transcended, contradicted or ridiculed in later ones. They are indeed structural, that is, data and methodology. Yet there are appropriately, two such universals around which and through which Levi-Strauss addresses himself in his voyage to human truths. One is the dialectic, the pattern of interchange.

> In my view dialectical reason is always constitutive: it is the bridge, forever extended and improved, which analytical reason throws out over an abyss; it is unable to see the further shore but it knows that it is there, even should it be constantly receding. The term dialectical reason thus covers the perpetual efforts analytical reason must make to reform itself if it aspires to account for language, society and thought; and the distinction between the two forms of reason in my view rests only on the temporary gap separating analytical reason from the understanding of life.[46]

The second universal is consequent to the first for it is a precise formulation of the metaphysics of the dialectic as an epistemology. This second universal is the concept of binary oppositions, the assertion that the human mind, regardless of its historical or cultural base, receives, responds to and constructs reality by opposing the truth of affirmation to the truth of negation:

By taking its raw material from nature, mythic thought proceeds in the same way as language, which chooses phonemes from among the natural sounds of which a practically unlimited range is to be found in childish babbling. For, as in the case of language, the empirical material is too abundant to be all accepted indiscriminately or to be all used on the same level. Here again, it must be accepted as a fact that the material is the instrument of meaning, not its object. For it to play this part, it must be whittled down. Only a few of its elements are retained—those suitable for the expression of contrasts or forming pairs of opposites.[47]

For Levi-Strauss, the human mind at its source, its roots and its foundation, is ambivalent, recognizing the universe in the context of paired contrasts. The most important of these paired contrasts is the opposition between nature and culture, between the continuous and the intermittent. And this nature of the mind leaves its imprint, its dualistic character in every statement of cosmography.

Proceeding from this terse, psychographic introduction to Levi-Strauss, we move to the specificity of Levi-Strauss on myth, anticipating some contradiction and fluidity.

In the context of his (early) analysis of several Tshimian myths, reflecting on the "myth of Asdiwal," Levi-Strauss had this to say about the *function* of myth:

All the paradoxes conceived by the native mind, on the most diverse planes: geographic, economic, sociological, and even cosmological, are, when all is said and done, assimilated to that less obvious yet so real paradox which marriage with the matrilateral cousin attempts but fails to resolve. But the failure is *admitted* in our myths, and there precisely lies their function.[48]

Antecedent to a further comment on this formulation, let us continue with Levi-Strauss' analytical presentation of this myth, as to its *structure*:

The myth is certainly related to given (empirical) facts, but not as a *representation* of them. The relationship is of a dialectic kind, and the institutions described in the myths can be the very opposite of the real institutions. This will in fact always be the case when the myth is trying to express a negative truth.[49]

and finally to its *process:*

Such speculations, in the last analysis, do not seek to depict what is real, but to justify the shortcoming of reality, since the extreme positions are only *imagined* in order to show that they are *untenable*. This step, which is fitting for mythical thought, implies an admission (but in the veiled language of the myth) that the social facts when thus examined are marred by an insurmountable contradiction.[50]

In his later work, *The Raw and the Cooked,* subtitled an "Introduction to a Science of Mythology," he went further towards ratifying this interpretation of the myth, but now understood as a "system of truth," a system counterposing the attainable with the untenable, opposing culture and nature, the discrete with the continuous, the cooked with the raw.[51]

What finally seems to have emerged from Levi-Strauss' work is an understanding of the function of myth as the systematic presentation of limits. The myth is a statement of the paradox of human action and institution, but a statement which does not merely explore paradox but also deliberately signifies, in the layer upon layer of its stratigraphy, what man through culture cannot achieve. The myth is then a dialogue and a memory of the species, whatever the location, the historical, cultural or social condition of its members. It is a dialogue between its knowing and its unlearned, between its wise and its foolish; and a memory of a set of infinite alternatives irretrievably forsaken, chosen against. Man in his development, in the very process of his becoming himself has naively but not unknowingly conceded the capacity for alternative existence. Otherwise trite, the consciousness of this concession remains unattended to—thus myth survives in one lexicon or another, from one group to another:

Myths are constructed on the basis of a certain logicality of tangible qualities which makes no clear-cut distinction between subjective states and the properties of the cosmos. Nevertheless it must not be forgotten that such a distinction has corresponded, and to a lesser extent still corresponds, to a particular stage in the development of scientific knowledge—a stage that in theory, if not in actual fact, is doomed to disappear. In this respect, mythological thought is not prescientific; it should be seen rather as an anticipation of the future state of science, whose past development and present trend show that it has always been progressing in the same direction.[52]

Despite his nominal antagonism to structuralism,[53] there are in the work of Michel Foucault some basic similarities to Levi-Strauss, especially to the later work of Levi-Strauss. This later work proceeds from structuralism as a methodology to a record of the "convertibility" of systems of truth. Foucault, in the context of French "thought" (and we shall discover in a moment why thought must be qualified so as not to suggest in archaeology an exercise in intellectual history), more specifically in the context of what he terms the classical period and the subsequent modern age, has applied an "archaeology" which seeks to identify the cause and dynamic of the "silence" between the modern age and the classical period. That silence is consequent but not attributable to the appearance of Man in human thought. The nature of this silence is the same as that incommensurability of paradigms or language described by Kuhn:

> In the transition from one theory to the next words change their meanings or conditions of applicability in subtle ways. Though most of the same signs are used before and after a revolution—e.g., force, mass, element, compound, cell—the ways in which some of them attach to nature has somehow changed. Successive theories are thus, we say, incommensurable. . .
>
> Why is translation, whether between theories or languages, so difficult? Because, as has often been remarked, languages cut up the world in different ways, and we have no access to a neutral sublinguistic means of reporting.[54]

However, as Foucault understands it, the historical process which results in a critical change of knowledge is quite different from the dialectic of Kuhn indicated much earlier (Chapter One). What is of interest to Foucault, the critical dynamic that he realized in his work, results in the diminution of the history of science to epiphenomena. Even Kuhn's attempt at an explanation for the exchange of paradigms: cumbersomeness, anomalies, impatience, etc., which at first appeared radical becomes sophmoric and unnecessary in the light of Foucault's interest. For Foucault is not concerned with what he calls "the unconscious of science" (Masterman's metaphysical paradigms) but the epistemological root out of which convergence arose:

> This unconscious is always the negative side of science—that which resists it, deflects it, or disturbs it. What I would like to do, however, is

to reveal a *positive unconscious* of knowledge: a level that eludes the consciousness of the scientist and yet is part of scientific discourse, instead of disputing its validity and seeking to diminish its scientific nature.[55]

What Foucault wishes to reveal is a mechanism somewhat parallel to that movement characteristic of Levi-Strauss' "systems of truth." More particularly, Foucault intends to explicate the movement of one system of truth: that of what he terms the classical period, which emerges into that of another: that of the modern age. Foucault calls his "system" "conditions of possibility" of knowledge which is to be unearthed by an "archaeology." But what is the process? Here is Foucault's (somewhat extended) vision:

> Order is, at one and the same time, that which is given in things as their inner law, the hidden network that determines the way they confront one another, and also that which has no existence except in the grid created by a glance, an examination, a language; and it is only in the bland spaces of this grid that order manifests itself in depth as though already there, waiting in silence for the moment of its expression.
>
> The fundamental codes of a culture—those governing its language, its schemas of perception, its exchanges, its techniques, its values, the hierarchy of its practices—establish for every man, from the very first, the empirical orders with which he will be dealing and within which he will be at home. At the other extremity of thought, there are the scientific theories or the philosophical interpretations which explain why order exists in general, what universal law it obeys, what principle can account for it, and why this particular order has been established and not some other. But between these two regions, so distant from one another, lies a domain which, even though its role is mainly an intermediary one, is nonetheless fundamental: it is more confused, more obscure, and probably less easy to analyse. It is here that a culture, imperceptibly deviating from the empirical orders prescribed for it by its primary codes, instituting an initial separation from them, causes them to lose their original powers, frees itself sufficiently to discover that these orders are perhaps not the only possible ones or the best ones; this culture then finds itself faced with the fact that there exists, below the level of its spontaneous orders, things that are in themselves capable of being ordered, that belong to a certain unspoken order; the fact, in short, that order *exists*.[56]

Foucault thus seeks to articulate for an objective culture, in this instance a cultural, historical period, what Levi-Strauss has sought to achieve for the human mind. He intends not to reveal the structure of thought but, in the manner of Levi-Strauss, its procedure:

> As the myths themselves are based on secondary codes (the primary codes being those that provide the substance of language), the present work is put forward as a tentative draft of a tertiary code, which is intended to ensure the reciprocal translatability of several myths. This is why it would not be wrong to consider this book itself as a myth: it is, as it were, the myth of mythology.[57]

This last is Levi-Strauss' assertion yet it might well substitute for Foucault's "conditions of possibility." In the human sciences which are Foucault's primary dependent variables, that is in economics, biology, and philology as they emerge in the 19th century from their earlier counterparts, the analysis of wealth and exchange, natural history and general grammar, the crucial phenomenon is the transition in representation, that is in the language which sought to mark the nature of reality.

Foucault argues that the classical period was characterized by a representation of the Same, signified by convenience, emulation, sympathy and the special analogy of similitude. However, in the 19th century, that period which marks the beginning of the modern age, the human sciences escape from the *episteme* of the Same to that of analogical organic structures and successive identities and differences. In the 19th century, the language of representation instead of manifesting the Same becomes reflexive and presumes consciousness. This new language has, as a concomitant, transcendental philosophy, a philosophy which asserts at one and the same time that it is man who bequeaths meaning, signs and significance to the world but he is not the center, the reason for the universe. Yet it is man who achieves the Archimedian point for the arrangement and truth of the universe, and it is man who is the self-dependent phenomenon from which ideas emerge, but it is man who is finally the consequence of the new *episteme*. An *episteme* which unfortunately has emerged for vaguely understood reasons:

> The end of Classical thought—and of the *episteme* that made general grammar, natural history, and the science of wealth possible—will

coincide with the decline of representation, or rather with the emancipation of language, of the living being, and of need, with regard to representation. The obscure but stubborn spirit of a people who talk, the violence and the endless effort of life, the hidden energy of needs, were all to escape from the mode of being of representation. And representation itself was to be paralleled, limited, circumscribed, mocked perhaps, but in any case regulated from the outside, by the enormous thrust of a freedom, a desire, or a will, posited as the metaphysical converse of consciousness.[58]

Yet in Foucault's perception of this new concept of man as that "being whose nature. . .is to know nature, and itself, in consequence, as a natural being,"[59] that self reflexive character of the *episteme* presents itself in the fundamental conditions of possibility and as well as its organizing principle. Consequently, the concept of man achieved by the modern age in its own founding is the reflection and empirical proposition which impacts modern thought, culture and human science:

> This is to say that each of these positive forms in which man can learn that he is finite is given to him only against the background of its own finitude. Moreover, the latter is not the most completely purified essence of positivity, but that upon the basis of which it is possible for positivity to arise. . . . Thus, in the very heart of empiricity, there is indicated the obligation to work backwards—or downwards—to an analytic of finitude, in which man's being will be able to provide a foundation in their own positivity for all those forms that indicate to him that he is not infinite. And the first characteristic with which this analytic will mark man's mode of being, or rather the space in which that mode of being will be deployed in its entirety, will be that of repetition—of the identity and the difference between the positive and the fundamental. . . .[60]

It is here that the most basic similarity between Foucault and Levi-Strauss reveals itself. Not surprisingly that similarity is the centralness in each of their thought of the dialectic. Yet again it is not an unambiguous or true similarity, for what is found is that one understanding (Foucault) of the dialectic proceeds from Hegel's unity of opposition while the other (Levi-Strauss) understands the dialectic as it has been extracted from Marxist dialogue: the identities of opposites. The first interpretation encompasses a dynamic of history while the second, as was previously indicated, requires no history.[61]

What this means for this present work is that Foucault's thought is relevant in a very different way from that of Levi-Strauss. The critical articulation in Foucault's thought of myth, paradigm and the human sciences, is presented in the following way:

> Modern thought, then, will contest even its own metaphysical impulses, and show that reflections upon life, labour, and language, in so far as they have value as analysis of finitude, express the end of metaphysics: the philosophy of life denounces metaphysics as a veil of illusion, that of labour denounces it as an alienated form of thought and an ideology, that of language as a cultural episode.[62]

Thus Levi-Strauss can be interpreted as theorizing that "savage thought" as revealed by myth is not formally or structurally distinguishable from that of men in other historical circumstances, that, as Maurice Godelier writes,

> Thought in the savage state and scientific thought are thus not 'two unequal stages of development of the human mind', since thought in the savage state, the mind in its formal structure, has no development and operates in all periods and on all the materials provided it by history. There is no progress of the Mind, but there is a progress of knowledge. But once this has been said, it would be wrong to identify the thought of savages and savage thought completely, or to reduce the one entirely to the other.[63]

And Foucault has demonstrated this "progress of knowledge" using the instance of the movement of representation and knowledge in the 16th, 17th, 18th and 19th centuries in France. It is more than interesting to note that this is precisely what Zevedei Barbu sought to accomplish but, unfortunately, did not with his attention focused on the same empirical proposition:

> I wanted to investigate as thoroughly as possible what I believe to be a constitutive element of mental life: its historicity. Mind in all its manifestations is never only what it is, but also what it was; it is a system which has depth.[64]

The difference between the historicity of the Mind (Barbu), with its background presumption of some constant, the Mind, and the Mind through history (Foucault) is a subtle one. The difference all but disappears when we compare Foucault's achievement with what Barbu had assumed, that is, what Barbu had "concluded:"

> This enterprise led me to the following conclusions: a) the individual's perceptual field can be regarded as a historical phenomenon, i.e., it changes in some of its main aspects with the historical development of his community; b) the change in the perceptual field can be understood in terms of the change taking place in the system of beliefs, values and the general ideas; c) it is, therefore, reasonable to assume that the historical character of man's perceptual field is dependent upon the historical character of his basic beliefs, values and ideas.[65]

This, then, is the intellectual direction with which Foucault's accomplishment closed and with some completeness brought to closure.[66]

Yet, of more immediate importance, Levi-Strauss and Foucault complement each other and, as well, our concern as we return to Shorer's identification of a controlling, organizing, rectifying instrument: the myth. But now in addition to Shorer's suggestion of its significance we have as well an understanding of its process in integration and exchange. Drawing from the tradition of Marx and the writings of Levi-Strauss, Godelier puts it quite well:

> Thought in its spontaneous or savage state is able by means of analogy to compare with one another all levels of Nature and Culture, and it is therefore immediately and simultaneously *analytical* and *synthetic,* able both to *totalize* all the aspects of the real in mythical representations, and to *move* from one level of the real to another by reciprocal *transformations* of its analogies.[67]

It is important to sustain these sensibilities as we turn, finally, to political society as the mixed paradigm in question.

The Mythology of Political Thought

Myth, we have been recently advised by Godelier, proceeds by determining reality by analogy. Analogical thought, that is a *form* or a *structure* of thought, has its own impact on the content of thought, transforming and totalizing thought. Thought, through analogical patterning, becomes synthetic and analytical.

The contemporary paradigm of political society proceeds by analogy. The paradigm itself presupposes the actuality of the *polis* represented in the thought of Socrates and the writing of Plato, and through that presupposition reifies. And it is this reification on which political order rests—by analogy. However, it is not just one analogy but two inequivalent and complex analogies.

The first analogy—to *physis* (Nature)—resides in the midst of the controversy which arose in Greek thought during the Sophistic movement: the controversy between *nomos* and *physis*. Dodds argues that this movement was the conjunction of the "Inherited Conglomerate" (Gilbert Murray's term) of the Archaic Age whose end was marked approximately by Aeschylus,[68] and the Greek Enlightenment; "its roots are in sixth-century Ionia; it is at work in Hecataeus, Xenophanes, and Heraclitus, and in a later generation is carried further by speculative scientists like Anaxagoras and Democritus."[69] That is, it was a conjunction between a cultural history and a rationalism which resulted in "the revival of incubation, the taste for orgiastic religion, the prevalence of magical attack. . . ."[70] With this transgression against tradition, and as an expression of it, arose the question of what basis did human society rest upon: on tradition (and if so, on which aspects of what had become a complex and contradictory tradition), or on human nature (the *physis* which Dodds describes as "human psychology")?

In addressing themselves to this dispute, the rationalists sought their answer in the critical investigation of Virtue (*arete*), an investigation which for many of them would end in trials for heresy.[71] Specifically, for Socrates, *arete* was identified with *episteme*, as Dodds puts it:

> For to Socrates *arete* was something which proceeded from within outward; it was not a set of behavior-patterns to be acquired through habituation, but a consistent attitude of mind springing from a steady insight into the nature and meaning of human life. In its self-consistency it resembled a science.[72]

Bruno Snell makes the same point:

> The model which Socrates required for his teleological knowledge had to come from another quarter. He found it—another innovation—in

the craftsmen. As a carpenter must know a good table before he is able to construct it, so must a man know in advance what is good before he can act properly. Anyone who possesses a mechanical knowledge of some sort will also, as a matter of course, turn out something good.

And further:

The direction of Socrates' thinking is, for that reason, given with his language from the first. The nature of his vocabulary enforces a close relation between knowledge and practical interest, between knowledge and ethical thought; and this is in fact the special achievement of Socrates in the history of Greek philosophy.[73]

Thus in the sixth and fifth centuries, while not distinguishing between physical nature and society, Greek philosophers, Sophists as well as Socrates and Plato, began to presume that *physis* was coherent with human intellect.[74]

On the one hand, *physis* was represented, according to Vernant and subsequently Godelier, by a mathematicized, isonomic, symmetrical universe—a universe in which the order of things, the very nature of the cosmos was accessible by rational calculus revealing "a mathematized space constituted by purely geometrical relations."[75] Thus, a dominant stream of Greek political philosophy was to become, indeed, by the fourth and third centuries, a branch of mathematics and geometry, i.e., learning concerned with the discovery and articulation of the precise, exact measure of the universe. It was to such a universe that the *polis* and politics, "the art of living in a polis"[76] as Isaiah Berlin has termed it, was to be analogous.

But by analogy (recall in Foucault's *The Order of Things,* the treatment of the French Classical period's analysis of resemblance: emulations, convenience, analogy and sympathy) another signification of *physis* emerged: the Nature that was of the human organism. The human body was also *physis*, that is in its consciousness and its physiology. So just as the cosmology of *physis* as a metaphysics would result in a mathematical and geometric political philosophy when applied to the affairs of men, so too that same metaphysics when conceived in a different set of analogies would manifest itself in an aesthetic anatomy and a concern with psychic harmony, balance and symmetry. Dodds states:

I do not propose to say much about this celebrated antithesis *Nomos* versus *Physis*. . .But it may not be superfluous to point out that thinking in these terms could lead to widely different conclusions according to the meaning you assigned to the terms themselves. . . *Physis* could represent an unwritten, unconditionally valid "natural law," against the particularism of local custom; or it could represent the "natural rights" of the individual, against the arbitrary requirements of the State; and this in turn could pass—as always happens when rights are asserted without corresponding recognition of duties—into a pure anarchic immoralism, the "natural right of the stronger. . . ."[77]

Thus one could conceptualize a semblance in the deterioration of the *polis* reflected in the deterioration of the body or the mind.

But the Archaic Age which preceeded the Classical Age, according to Dodds, was a guilt-culture. As such, it would be expected to evidence the denials, repressions, and the cathartic cycle associated with such a concept.

. . .it was the Archaic Age that recast the tales of Oedipus and Orestes as horror-stories of bloodguilt; that made purification a main concern of its greatest religious institution, the Oracle of Delphi; that magnified the importance of *phthonos* until it became for Herodotus the underlying pattern of all history.[78]

The preoccupations of the Classical period with order and the ordering of things as described above would suggest, possibly, the very reaction-formations expected of such a legacy:

Pindar piously reconciles this popular fatalism with the will of God: "the great purpose of Zeus *directs* the daemon of the men he loves." Eventually Plato picked up and completely transformed the idea, as he did with so many elements of popular belief: the daemon becomes a sort of lofty spirit-guide, or Freudian Super-ego, who in the Timaeus is identified with the element of pure reason in man. In that glorified dress, made morally and philosophically respectable, he enjoyed a renewed lease of life in the pages of stoics and Neo-platonists, and even of medieval Christian writers.[79]

And further:

. . .The cultural inheritance which Archaic Greece shared with Italy and India included a set of ideas about ritual impurity which provided a natural explanation for guilt-feelings generated by repressed desires. An archaic Greek who suffered from such feelings was able to give them concrete form. . .was able to relieve them by undergoing a cathartic ritual. Have we not here a possible clue to the part played in Greek culture by the idea of *catharsis,* and the gradual development from it, on the one hand of the notions of sin and atonement, on the other of Aristotle's psychological purgation, which relieves us of unwanted feelings through contemplating their projection in a work of art?[80]

In other words, following Dodds, these societies produced a culture which overlay what he termed a "puritan psychology."[81] A psychology he sees represented in the Orphic and Pythagorean movements and their traditions concerning the soul:

What is the original root of all this wickedness? How comes it that a divine self sins and suffers in mortal bodies?. . .To this unescapable question Orphic poetry, at any rate later Orphic poetry, provided a mythological answer. It all began with the wicked Titans. . . .
The Titan myth neatly explained to the Greek puritan why he felt himself to be at once a god and a criminal; the "Apolline" sentiment of remoteness from the divine and the "Dionysiac" sentiment of identity with it were both of them accounted for and both of them justified. That was something that went deeper than any logic.[82]

As such, in the discovery of irrational numbers, itself a reflection of the turmoil into which Greek society had degenerated, came the revelation of the possibility for a conceptual disorder to juxtapose to the perception of social disorder; that is physical disorder presented paradigmatic closure with societal disintegration; the transformation of the set of symmetrical laws and equilibrium into twisted, tangled and perhaps fatal disequilibrium. Like the universe, the *polis,* the mind and the body contained the capacity for chaos, the possibility for the disintegration of order.

What is certain is that these beliefs promoted in their adherents a horror of the body and a revulsion against the life of the senses which were quite new in Greece. Any guilt-culture will, I suppose, provide a soil favourable to the growth of puritanism, since it creates an unconscious need for self-punishment which puritanism gratifies.[83]

It became, then, incumbent upon Greek classical thought, for the purpose of reintegration, to converge this *episteme* with another, prior analogy; one associated with prepolitical Greek history: *kratos*, that is rule or leadership (arche). This was that ordering of things which pervades the later logic, mathematics, philosophies and sciences of Greek and Western culture, that analogy which would prove so accessible to the messianic *episteme* closing with it historically in the beginnings of the Western Judeo-Christian era, that *episteme* whose spatial sensibility would penetrate the Western mind directing it to acceleration, pursuit, triumph and disfigurement.

However, it should be made clear that this reintegration, that is the accomplishment of a holistic salvationist myth, synthesizing *physis, kratos,* and *arche,* Nature, rule and leadership, was subsequent to the period of classical Greek thought, occurring during the period of Hellenistic civilization and of Roman authority over the Mediterranean area.

Eschewing eschatological mysticisms (such as Orphism), the Greek rationalists chose another ploy consisting of several maneuvers which allowed them to avoid that primitivization of their intellectual tradition which a stress on rule and leadership might lead to. Instead, they chose means by which *physis* as cosmology would maintain its apparent integrity.

First, as the discovery of the irrational number (the squareroot of 2) was referred to by Plato as the "unmentionable mystery," Popper conjectures that there was a conspiracy of silence among the Greek scholars. Though Democritus had written of the "noncommensurable" or the "illogical lines," recognizing that in the Pythagorean tradition the irrational could not be numbers and were therefore not things, the initial reaction of the Platonic academy was to dismiss its relevance, making a secret of it.

The second reaction was the transference from Pythagorean (arithmetic) cosmology by Greek scholarship to a Euclidean one, the proposal of a geometric cosmology to replace the doctrine of things as numbers and moral ideas as the ratios of numbers. Popper, to whose hypothesis this sequence is owed, argues that this was an attempt at the synthesis of "the atomistic character of Pythagoreanism" with the incommensurable by introducing the no-longer avoidable realization of the illogical. Evidently as a part of this strategy, Euclid proposed that the incommensurable numbers were in fact "commensurable by their squares!"

The third reaction was like the first in that although it accepted the fact of irrational numbers, it chose to ignore their consequence for the Pythagorean doctrine of cosmology. Thus for all intents and purposes, Foucault though factually in error, states the case when he writes in *Madness and Civilization:*

> The Greeks had a relation to something that they called   *hubris.* This relation was not merely one of condemnation; the existence of Thrasymachus or of Callicles suffices to prove it, even if their language has reached us already enveloped in the reassuring dialectic of Socrates. But the Greek Logos had no contrary.[84]

And Karl Popper puts it more plainly:

> . . .one generation later, the Academy could return to the Pythagorean doctrine. Once the shock caused by the discovery of irrationality had worn off, mathematicians began to get used to the idea that the *irrationals must be numbers,* in spite of everything, since they stand in the elementary relations of greater or less to other (rational) numbers. This stage reached, the reasons against Pythagoreanism disappeared, although the theory that shapes are numbers of ratios of numbers meant, after the admission of irrationals, something different from what it had meant before (a point which possibly was not fully appreciated by the adherents of the new theory.[85]

This represents, then, part of the intellectual development and integument which was associated with the *polis* as that concept became a part of early Western political thought. It contained an ordering of things whose irrational basis was denied, that is, suppressed in both its psychohistorical and conceptual contents. This denial deposited a fault in the Western understanding of political order.

Messianism and Charisma

When the mytho-scholastic tradition of the Greeks coalesced with the mytho-theocratic tradition of the Jews, during the early Christian era, political society became the syncretic of geometric order and salvation. Jewish historical experience crystallized from its conditions of possibility the messianic paradigm which in mix with the penetration of Greek thought brought forth the *Christian* expression of political society as the instrumentation through which men could achieve experiential and transcendental order.

The messianic myth had opposed Time to History. It was the device by which historical consciousness—finitude—could be reconciled to the sense of interminability. It was the myth which revealed that mortality was the acknowledgement that men had failed to recognize in their development of an historical consciousness. That having achieved the conceptualization of Time as a space given a substance by specific, discrete, death-filled organisms in interaction, the dialectic of knowledge presented an awareness, a knowing of the infinite. The messianic myth subdued the consciousness of histories as series of pointless deaths.

The patriarchal Jew by making in his mythology the human species analogous to the son and its existential authority analogous to the father, constructed a myth of reconciliation, a system of deliverance which demanded death in exchange for eternal life. If the Jew was oppressed, it was because he was the Elect; if he was scattered, it was because he was indivisible from his people; if he was impotent, it was because he possessed in his history the power to condemn or salvage the whole of mankind; if he was to die, defeated, degraded, scorned, forgotten, it was because he would be resurrected in a glorious eternal life. The Father that he had so often forgotten or blasphemed was inseperable from His son, His children. The Father would send the anointed one, the Messiah, as the deliverer. (As the messianic tradition was brought to the Greek cities, the Jews rejected the particular claims of the "Nazarean party" as their counterparts had done in Israel, but some of the gentiles did not; translating the messianic figure into the terms of their own tongue, these Hellenic pagans embraced this legend as *christ*.) Thus the messianic signification developed from the tribal ritual of anointing priests and kings to mark their birth from the womb of the monotheistic Semite's god, achieving in time a synthesis with the Greek scholastic expression of cosmology and the Roman imperial cult.[86]

From this point on, the political society would be tantamount to the good order and it would merely fall to Weber after the thoughts of Augustine, Aquinas, Machiavelli, the social contractists, the encyclopedists and the Romantics, to close once again with the materials of history and suggest that the generic messiah in its particular form, charisma, was the foundation of political organization, not its destroyer.

Weber's was then a secularization of a mystery, the rationalization of a myth which had long ago settled in the root and branch of Western conception of human integration and organization in political terms. Most certainly it was Weber's intention to settle on the charismatic figure as the explanation of revolutionary change, to mark extraordinary change as the consequence of extraordinary men. This was no more than what Jewish thought had begun with before, germinating into, among others, the messianic tradition.

Yet in closing with the tradition of the political order as *physis*, the messianic, the charismatic, had alternative and qualitatively different possibilities. One of these possibilities was the revelation of an antithesis to the isonomy of the mind which had been conceived by the Greeks.

As the Greeks had bequeathed to the notion of *polis* a spatial symmetry, a realization of proportion, so the mind was conceived by them in similar terms. Weber, however, reversed the order of things by identifying chaos with salvation, revolution with deliverance. It is of course true that he was simply conforming with the ancient Jewish texts, but in so doing, order, harmony, etc., had become identifiable with the oppressive authority of Roman rule and subsequently the founding charismatic figure became as well the instrument and symbol for fundamental change—the embodiment of that disorder which necessarily preceded the more just society. It was in this way that the charismatic figure could come to be perceived as extraordinary *because* the things of his mind were no longer in balance, no longer in harmony. Paradoxically, Weber was employing the Roman paradigm of authority (the foundation) to explain the nature of rebellion to authority.

In his own treatment of charisma, in both his historical and analytical studies, Weber had arbitrarily confined himself to a description of individual, collective or transmitted charisma in relation to ecstasy. Thus prophetic or warrior ecstasy, manifest in visions and total disregard of personal safety, were understood to be the concomitants of severe deprivation, asceticism or intense indulgence (orgiastic rituals). Holding to the texts of ancient Judism, Weber understood the relationship between ecstasy and the charismatic figures to be episodic, discontinuous with other aspects of their lives. For Weber, charisma was not explained by ecstasy but was often accompanied by it, either induced by collective ritual, the "ecstatic community" as he described the emotive phenomena of warriors, some prophets and the Christian congregation; or by the "pathos of solitude," characterized by "oppressive brooding" and a "constant state of tension"[87] Notwithstanding his disavowal of interest in such explanation, Weber did manage to strongly suggest that the charismatic leader, whether king, prophet or warrior, behaved in bizarre fashion. He thus contributed to the concern of modern psychology, psychohistory and psychoanalysis in treating charismatic figures as psychopathic. This analytical procedure ignored at least two other interpretations of the charismatic figure which would require for their fruition a very different understanding of the charismatic leader's relationship to political order.

One analytical framework emerges from the procedure of taking, for example, the charismatic prophetic tradition quite literally. This is the framework which convenes with the perception of the event shared by most of its prophetic participants: the charismatic prophetic figure is, indeed, influenced by some superhuman, divine authority. He or she is precisely what the followers believe and the leader declares: the anointed one. According to this interpretation, the force and authority of the charismatic figure would be consequent to the inter-cession of a people's affairs by some force more powerful than, and qualitatively different from, what is thought rationally or objectively possible. It is to such an interpretation some attention has been given in an earlier chapter.[88]

A second possible interpretation somewhat anticipates one of the subject matters of another chapter. That subject matter is anarchism. One of the obvious difficulties in the treatment of anarchism as a serious theory and machinery for revolution or rebellion is the role of leadership. If the members of an anarchist movement are to be consistent with their theoretical sympathies and beliefs, the movement itself must avoid the generation of authority vested in particular individuals to whom the others refer choice and responsibility. Petr Kropotkin, a quite significant contributor to the anarchist tradition, reflects that concern in the following:

> What struck me most was that Bakunin's influence was felt much less as the influence of an intellectual authority than as the influence of a moral personality. In conversations about anarchism, or about the attitude of the federation, I never heard it said, "Bakunin says so," or "Bakunin thinks so," as if it settled the question. His writings and his sayings were not regarded as laws,—as is unfortunately often the case in political parties. In all such matters, in which intellect is the supreme judge, every one in discussion used his own arguments.[89]

Yet, historically, as a movement, anarchism does precipitate an opposition which seeks to suppress it. As a consequence, the anarchist movement as an organization is vulnerable to the machinations of the political societies it seeks to oppose, mobilizing a repressive instrument on whose terms it cannot effectively respond. In many ways the charismatic figure is the resolution of that leadership dilemma if charisma is understood in terms which do not depend for their meaning on the presumptions which follow from the acceptance of political order as the paradigm for communal integration.[90]

There has inevitably been a tension in anarchism between anarchism as a doctrine of individualistic liberation (e.g., Max Stirner), and anarchism as communal liberation (e.g., Kropotkin). The tension has crystallized into contradiction, precipitated by the concept of the individual current in 19th- and 20th-century Western thought. However, if one conceives of the charismatic figure in terms of the expression of a people focused onto one of their members; if, indeed, the charismatic figure is understood as the responsive instrument of a people, then contrary to Weber's view that charismatic authority is the most total dominance of a people by a single individual, it becomes the most pure form of a people's authority over themselves.

In this latter view, the charismatic relationship between leader and followers becomes the submission of one identity to the demand that it become the vehicle of a collective, and thus embodied, identity. At the temporal and spatial center of the charismatic phenomenon, an identification between "leader" and "followers" becomes so complete, so total, as to warrant no authentic differentiation between the led and the leader. Thus in analytical terms, a very different meaning comes to mind when we recall the Freudian explanation of the demagogue's authority over his mass as the replacement of follower by ego ideal. The ego ideal is now understood as the collective projection of the charismatic mass, a projection out of its anguish, its myths, its visions, its history and its culture, in short its tradition and its oppression.

> The ego-ideal is of great importance for the understanding of group psychology. Besides its individual side, this ideal has a social side; it is also the common ideal of a family, a class, or a nation." [Freud]
> It would seem that here the terms superego and ego ideal have come to be distinguished by their different relation to the ontogenetic and the phylogenetic history of the race. The superego is conceived as a more archaic, more thoroughly internalized and more unconscious representative of man's inborn proclivity toward the development of a primitive, categorical conscience. . . . The ego ideal, however, seems to be more flexibly and consciously bound to the ideals of the particular historical era as absorbed in childhood.[91]

It becomes, then, no longer necessary to explain why a people are willing to surrender their own authority when in fact not only do they not perceive the event in those terms, but it does not appear to this writer that this is what they are doing. Instead, in the charismatic phenomenon, the followers may be now understood as having, through an irrational process, succeeded in the fusing of themselves into an organic instrument—an instrument occasioned by their objective and conscious need to escape a circumstance which has brought a final threat to the existential being.

Despite the appearance of the phenomenon, given it in much of the literature, the charismatic leader becomes the charismaticized follower, the element most totally subordinate, to the extent that his every action is charged with not merely an obligation but as well a detailed instruction. It is, in truth, the charismatic figure who has been selected by social circumstance, psychodynamic peculiarities and tradition, and not his followers by him.[92] The spatial extent and temporal duration of his authorization will acutely depend on the degree to which he is finally willing and capable of precise conformity to the substance of his authorization. In psychographic terms, such an individual is a finely tuned, sensitive instrument, not only sympathetic to the most extraordinary degree, to the anguish and plight of his own people, but as well convinced that he is the very instrument which has been conceptualized out of their "war psychosis" and expressed in their folk-myth.[93]

Yet this relationship is an extraordinarily sensitive one, vulnerable to a range of phenomena which might result in its perversion or distortion. For example, the leader himself may be incapable of maintaining the relationship, subject as he quite likely is to excessive anxieties and insecurities; he may falter under the enormity of the projection by the elements of his time.[94] Again, the folk-myth, itself as prescription for the nature of the charismatic relationship, may have temporal limits built into its vision thus precluding the fructification or deterioration of the relationship into a political one.[95] Yet it may deteriorate into just such a political relationship if the forces which it opposes and/or its own internal dynamic succeeds in penetrating the fusion, making of the movement a collection of individuals with competing interests and insecurities, or competing groups, rather than a collectivity sharing the same identifications of themselves and reality. As a political relationship it will then conform to the expectations of demagoguery, that is an ideology propagated by one individual and a subordinate cadre for the purpose of achieving authoritarian mastery over a people.

> There obviously can be illegitimate, albeit humanly meaningful, authority. Without the setting and limits imposed by tradition, shared values and experience, institutions, and philosophical reason, humanly meaningful leadership can be as pathological and dangerous, and as illegitimate, as the processes of power-without-authority characteristic of modern states.[96]

Still it must be understood that the charismatic phenomenon is, at base, one of liberation rather than one of totalitarianism. Though archaic (and questions as to whether it is "prepolitical" as Hobsbawm might call it are irrelevant) and fragile, there is no question as to the power of the charismatic phenomenon. It has been the means to survival, more often entailing an heroic effort rather than a routine one, of the oppressed for millennia. It may in fact be the only instrument of survival and liberation organic, that is, authentic, to the circumstance, tradition and psychic nature of the bulk of human beings living in oppression.[97]

Yet when we recall Weber's placement of the charismatic phenomenon, at the root of the various forms of authority-legitimation, those forms, in turn, being traditional or rational terms, the routinization of charismatic authority, a very different specter emerges. This specter is that these subsequent forms are consequent to a dynamic of authorization from which they separate. Traditional and rational authorities become legitimate only if they call upon a very different reference, which they seem to do only in part. To the degree that their significance rests on ethics of economy and efficiency, they are in large measure mythologies though I do not intend to deny that there are as such useful elements about them. Tradition does preserve energies; rationalized institutions do accomplish integrations of data and action on a massive scale, yet are they in the end qualitatively more effective mechanisms for survival? Not apparently, for tradition as a political strategy, in its relative inadaptability, is almost perennially overwhelmed by the exigencies in the contemporary world to the degree that this world is different from that which generated the tradition; and rational institutionalization has proven as cumbersome as myth or mysticism or intuition in developing integral, effective choices.

But more importantly, if the charismatic phenomenon is understood in those terms most recently discussed, i.e., as a fusion of identities between leader and community consequent to event, tradition and psychography, then to extract from this a different authority, viz. that of tradition or reason, requires a qualitatively different resource. The process and substance of the identification between mass and leader which characterized the charismatic event can not be substituted for organization or structure, i.e., by traditional leadership or bureaucratic authority. Such a deposition results in the positioning of one or several autonomous opinions, interests, etc. *over* that of the mass of individuals who make up the community. Certainly some of those who occupy such roles at certain times may emerge as charismatic figures but does their structurally convenient accessibility to the possibility of such fulfillment justify their predecessors and successors who will remain, at best, imposed authority? And, if Weber was correct in identifying charisma as the primal legitimation for these, subsequent authorities, then is it not so that charisma, an almost tribal bonding between leader and followers, legitimates kinds of relationships to authority which are in every way antithetic to it? These subsequent authorities, regardless of historical contradictions, can only continue to rationalize their legitimacy in terms of leader-follower mutual interests, identities, etc. But outside the accident of charisma, they continue to encompass distinctively different contradictory and antagonistic consciousnesses which empirically and logically results in the abdication of authority or the resort to deception, coercion, terrorization and brutalization as concomitants to authority.

So Weber notwithstanding, political society and political order can not logically locate their foundations, structurally, in the charismatic phenomenon for the substance of that relationship is fundamentally different from what can be achieved in a rationally related society. The charismatic phenomenon is an irrational one which means in consequence that it can only be conceptualized from within the political order paradigm as sociopathic or psychopathic. One recent interpreter, Jean Cohen, argues that Weber understood the antagonism not merely in analytical terms but programmatic ones as well:

Weber's answer to the deadening effect of bureaucracy is individualistic opposition. . . . The self-responsible individual. . .never conforms to the set role, but brings his individuality to it, thus enriching his acts. Thus, Weber opposes the political leader to the bureaucratic official (who symbolizes impersonal selfless rule). The political leader takes a stand, he is passionate in his activity. His honor lies precisely in an exclusive *personal responsibility* for what he does. . . to Marx, the human hero of Weber probably would have seemed a "conjuration of the dead," an isolated second edition of the heroic age of the bourgeoisie whose "sober reality" is "unheroic" and merely the ghost of its once great past.[98]

And precisely because there is a conceptual residue of the charismatic phenomenon in the political order paradigm, in the rationalization of the role of leader as authority, the charismatic relationship becomes less accessible perceptually and analytically. Charismatic authority is understood as leadership *par excellence,* having thus a paternal, historical relationship to political society and its various instrumentations. But to the degree that political order as an arrangement makes a mass, a people, a community *subject* to authority, it is antithetic to the charismatic relationship, or, in organic terms, a pathology of it. The leader-follower relationship that exists in various forms in politically conceptualized, perceived and institutionalized society can be seen thusly as pathological in as much as it is a subversion of the charismatic relationship wherein authority rests elsewhere. Submission and obedience which result from the former should not be confused descriptively or analytically with what results from the integration which is the latter. Yet, ultimately, the charismatic and the politcal must be related, that is to say that they must be brought into an analytical framework which allows for the exploration of the significance of one for the other.

What is being suggested here is that this might best be accomplished at this point by reversing polarities, by presuming the antiquity and primitiveness of charisma as a reason for it becoming the framework in which other resolutions for the integration of human society can be evaluated. One assumes for charisma a primal integration in which is recognized a psychohistorical authenticity which becomes referent to other systems of integration.

In the following chapter, one such "system," anarchism, will be critically reviewed; that is, its theory will be explored for the paradigm from which it emerges and, contrarily, the experience in which it might have located authenticity.

But in this chapter, I have attempted to locate charisma in the development of the *episteme* which presupposes that political society is order. I have argued that charisma was Weber's rationalization of the messianic myth, a rationalization which took place within the context of an increasingly bureaucratic and capitalistic organization of Western society. Weber was attempting to reconstruct history in such as way as to extort from the past a process and an instrument for human (individual) freedom.

In doing so, Weber recognized the primitive and irrational elements associated with eschatological ideologies, whether Christian or Marxist, but in reversing these historicisms his theory of history remained no less primitive and irrational. His charismatic legitimation of authority was no less mythological than the traditions upon which it too rested. The mixed paradigm of charisma was ideological, epistemological and archaic.

It was ideological in its prescription that the reemergence of a (German) people in crisis would come as the result of the appearance of a (German) charismatic leader. It was epistemological as heir to an historiography (in Hegel, Burckhardt and others) rooted in eschatology. It was archaic in its debt to a concept of Time held constant in traditions going back as far as Babylonian and Sumerian mythologies, a concept of Time antagonistic to History.

In terms of the sociology of knowledge, Weber's general theory of charisma evolved out of the particularity of the immediate German problematic, but it was not merely German history generalized. In universalizing that experience, Weber followed the order of things of the parent epistemology. His reconstruction followed the structure of myths in the repetition of older themes and an older ontology. It was proscriptive as well as prescriptive. In speaking of myths, Edmund Leach succinctly described the point: "It is common to all mythological systems that all important stories recur in several different versions."[99]

Despite its metaphysical and epistemological inconsistencies, its subjectiveness, Weber's notion of charisma remains powerful and vital to many social scientists, for like Weber, they are inevitably peculiar mixes of sociological empiricist and historiological idealist. Charisma remains a powerful concept, for as myth, to paraphrase Shorer, it is a system lending coherence to the ordinary facts of life. Again, Leach is concise:

> To such a man [the believer] the redundancy of myth is a very reassuring fact. Any particular myth in isolation is like a coded message badly snarled up with noisy interference. Even the most confident devotee

might feel a little uncertain as to what precisely is being said. But, as a result of redundancy, the believer can feel that, even when the details vary, each alternative version of a myth confirms his understanding and reinforces the essential meaning of all the others.[100]

In challenging Weber's interpretation of charisma, I have made it possible to relate charisma to political authority in a way which contradicts his discussion of that relationship. Political authority is the perversion of charisma. Political authority is the alienation of the mass authority of charisma. When the internal relationships of the charismatic movement become politicized, the charismatic figure is no longer instructed by the mass and its consciousness but becomes its leader. The identity is shattered into a problematic of mastery. As I have stated above, the causes of this alienation may be complex.

The analyst, however, must not identify charmismatic authenticity with rationality or social benevolence. Charisma is a psychosocial force constructed by a people who have undergone an extended period of traumatizing stress. The significance of the movement is to end that stress, either by destroying its actual or presumptive causes or circumventing its dynamics. . . . The movement will conform to a construct of reality contained in elements of group consciousness produced in the dialectic of oppression and survival. Thus the social or historical effect of such a movement has an indeterminant relationship to any particular set of values the analyst might possess. It is the ambiguity of charismatic movements in this particular context which has lent to the concept's use much controversy. However, reaction is in the nature of the confrontation between the ideological and the persistently ambiguous.

In Western social thought, charisma is as theory of the most extreme symbolic functions of leadership. The analysis of charismatic theory, then, provides clues to the epistemological and metaphysical bases to the concepts of political society, political order and political authority.

What that analysis has revealed is that the theory of charisma is a rationalization of prescientific mythology; and following the procedures associated with Levi-Strauss and Foucault, we have discovered the ordering function of myths. Charisma is a rational version of the messiah, a paradigm mixed with mystifying notions of rational (geometric) social order and apocalyptic salvation. It is a coalescence of pre-Classical (Babylonian, Sumerian, Egyptian), Classical (Greek, Roman) and Judaic thought systems. In its persistence, charisma demonstrates the effective power of metaphysical elements (order, authority). It demonstrates the intellectual and psychic authority of speciously conceived notions of social and political order.

CHAPTER V

On Anarchism

Human experience, deposited as "historical" knowledge, has left as its bequest several alternative models of authority. These alternative "prototypes" are, of course, in contrast to the currently much-applied model which prescribes authority[1] in the form of political leadership. This is not to say that authority itself—that is, final, ultimate authorship and sanction of a group's social and evaluation patterns and its role in the process of institutionalization—has been somehow circumvented, but rather, that the bequest at different times has been fundamentally distinct from that of the political.

Political authority has been replaced[2] at some points in human development by economic authority, kinship authority, and the authority of presumed and presupposed ideological sameness as found in religion and communalism. Simplified, most certainly, these are the fundaments of what have been named communal or social anarchy, "stateless" or acephalic tribe societies ("tribes without rulers") and those communalisms characterized by the doctrine of election. The outlines of these forms of authority are less clearly etched in our consciousness than political authority for perhaps two reasons, both of which are also basic to our larger epistemological concern.

Firstly, at some point, all human groups to which the term society can be applied appropriately (current usage suggesting strongly an element of "continuity through generations") contain systems of familial projection and introjection (kinship) which *intersect* with systems of objective survival (economics) and those of perceived survival and continuity (ideology and theology). This intersection challenges, as it were, assumed analytical or conceptual distinctions since it bombards the particular senses accompanying these systems with the *totality* of its integration rather than its elementary multiplicity.

Secondly, the acknowledged analysts of these alternative forms have been most conspicuously committed to and influenced by paradigmatic frameworks emerging from a social reality characterized by some form of political authority. That is, they have been trained and socialized away from the recognition of alternative continuities, they have labored through systems of thought which have at their centers the element of power, both in its private and public natures. Thus, the blurring of these systems has been, on the one hand, authentic to the sensed nature of these phenomena, and on the other, a question of the absence of the skills, capacities and finally access of the observer.

Yet there does seem to be some authentic justification for suspending these other forms of authority analytically and conceptually and examining them as discrete phenomena. Presumably, that justification ultimately relates to a concern with clearly identifying the structural criticality of each form which is itself dependent upon and a construct of the emphasis (conscious) and direction of (unconscious) activity of the system participants themselves. The justification rests on the attempt to see what the participants have done whether they have done it consciously or unconsciously. It is they who have erected social systems which stand or fall upon the integrity and maintenance of their theology, their economics, their kinship or their epistemological systems. They have elaborated full and sophisticated rationalities which solemnize and demonstrate the fundamental sensitivity through which their society relates to its universe (whether it be a divine universe, History, the cosmos or reason) serviced by an ambivalent or neutral agent or instrument such as revelation, blood ties or shared needs.

These authorities, then, each in its own systemic context, bear the weight of full, integrated meaning systems. Each is a reference to a social reality the true understanding of which requires the epistemological analyst to maintain the tension between its proper matrix and his own.

Because our concern, in this essay, is with the political, we will confine ourselves here to exploring the paradox of a social authority most intimate, analytically and now historically, with that phenomenon. We will look at anarchism as an expression of economic authority, as promised earlier, since Western anarchism is in a real sense the residue of a dialectic with the most familiar of "authorities," the political.

But true to our methodology, we will attempt to go beyond the development of anarchism within the Western political environment—the attempt to develop an alternative authority within the social, cultural and historical matrix of political authority. There is a more positive tradition of anarchism in the stateless societies of the anthropological literature. Through the latter, we will be in the position of contrasting the results of the history of anarchism in the West to the evolution of a culture of anarchism of a non-Western people.[3]

In the West, anarchism developed as a specific negation to the evolution of a political authority—the State—which served to orchestrate and to some degree mystify the structure of economic relations. In our non-Western example, we will find that kinship was the ordering principle of what were social and psychological rather than economic relations.[4] To put it in a general way, we will be contrasting an anarchism rooted in a politically ordered society to an anarchism rooted in a traditionally nonpolitical community.

Anarchy and Anarchism

It has been argued that anarchy has had two fundamental meanings, each the obverse of the other, one the negation of the human animal and the other, an affirmation. The first seems linked with popular or "public" thought, the second appropriately linked to the intellectual market of scientific analysts.

The public mind, generously prejudiced by historical misassociation and fear-inciting imagery, understands anarchy as one of a kind with cancerous, Dionysian terror. In anarchy, human beings have become beasts, shocked into desperate unruliness by some transcendent threat to their survival. Mad men, mad women, have taken to the streets forming mobs whose kinship rests on the most primitive of all social bases: the pack security. It is their sense of the need for collective strength which has brought these maddened creatures together; they are bound by fears and desperate hatreds, destined only to destroy whatever stands, for those things which stand in such times are mute testaments of their individual weaknesses. The behavior of these individuals is compulsive, unstructured and unspecifically destructive. Such human animals are often the deposits left in the devastating wake of wars, famine and other social disruption. The breakdown of rule signals the eruption of the no longer controlled passions of men and women, and the loss, no matter how momentary, of security.

One interesting example of the persistence of this attitude toward the meaning of anarchy is provided by the experience of the Russian anarchist, Peter (Petr) Kropotkin. James Joll writes that:

> It is typical of the gulf between anarchist theory and terrorist practice that when the enterprising editor of the tenth edition of the *Encyclopaedia Britannica* invited Kropotkin to write the article on anarchism, it was the editor who felt obliged to append a footnote saying: 'It is important to remember that the term "Anarchist" is inevitably rather loosely used in public, in connexion with the authors of a certain class of murderous outrage', and added a resume of 'the chief modern so-called "Anarchist" incidents', since Kropotkin had wholly omitted to mention them.[5]

This "editor,"[6] of whom Joll reminds us, would appear to have been less convinced of the relationship between anarchism and terror than Joll, since the bulk of Joll's essay is an attempt to construct a relationship between the two. This follows from his particular conception of history on which more will be said momentarily.

The second interpretation of anarchy is the one attributable to those less hysterical (or more complacent?) social scientists and analysts. Questioned here is the preeminent presumption that rules and social order presuppose rulers. Instead, it is argued that for some groups of men and women, appearing at particular points in the development of social organization, rulers are redundant. Rulers become superfluous since the matrix of reciprocal interaction and relations which is society has been internalized through the processes of socialization and rationality. Men and women are left to their own private authorities. Reason rules not as their distinctively singular achievement but as the consummation of their birthright—human consciousness. Such groups have reached a stage in their existential communion where their differences are no longer the basis for faction but rather complementarity. Relations between them are fixed and in the fixity justice, the highest good, is achieved and order is warranted. This interpretation is to be found in differing degrees in the modern traditions and literature of Socialism, Communism and Anarchism.

That these two senses of anarchy represent directly contrasting interpretations does not, however, mean to imply that they possess equal strength, vitality or relevance in human affairs. The first seems to be rather more frequently vindicated by human history than its opposite, even to the proponents of the latter interpretation. Anarchy has been associated in many of its historical appearances with terror—violence and disorder—at least in its periphery—since its inception and formulation as a discrete phenomenon. Yet as a purely conceptual phenomenon, it must be remembered anarchy means literally and simply "without rulers (authorities)." It is thus something of a dependent clause with potentially several bases which, though important to this discussion, have been peripheral or marginal to anarchist thought. The anarchistic clause might be preceded by either or a combination of the terms "the individual," "groups," "societies," or "communities". . ."without rulers."

In the anthropology of Rousseau and Hobbes, for example, theory proceeded with some strain from the first root: the unbound, autonomous human, to the construction of political authority! This was because each theorist had at the base of his theoretical imagination a third variable between the idea and its social or pre-social unity: order. To both men, order was coexistent with some form of political authority.

Rousseau could deliberately pretend otherwise but the deception was intended to be for only a short duration. Ernst Cassirer instructs us that Rousseau had created the vision of the noble savage in the state of nature so that he might justify a new form of political organization. Cassirer notes what Rousseau had written in the *Confessions:*

> I denied myself all the easy deceits to which men are prone. I dared to
> unveil human nature and to look upon it in its nakedness, to trace the

course of times and of events which have disfigured human nature. And while comparing conventional man (*l'homme de l'homme*) with natural man, I pointed out the true source of our misery in our pretended perfection.[7]

But in daring to become the first "truthful 'historian of human nature,' "[8] Rousseau created a myth with the intention of using it to follow a logic similar to Plato's earlier theory of historical degeneration. Rousseau's "Noble Savage, a figure dear to all anarchists' hearts,"[9] was to serve as the moral and anthropological justification for a *new* political society.

> He explains [writes Cassirer] that it had never been his intention, even in his earliest writings, to try to turn back the wheel of history and to restore man once more to that starting-point from which he had set forth. "Human nature does not go back": man cannot at will reverse the direction he has once taken—he cannot go back, only ahead. The wounds the existing structure of society has inflicted on mankind cannot be healed by destroying the instrument that caused them. We must look further; we must attack not the instrument but the hand that guided it. It is not the form of the social contract as such that is at fault; it is rather the will that inspires the contract.[10]

Hobbes in this instance was much the more consummate propagandist. The tension and lack of fit between Rousseau's existential vision and his sociology concluded in—and in some part contributed to—his destruction. Lester Crocker observes:

> It is enough to say, according to contemporary psychological and sociological studies, he was a perfect model of what we now refer to as "the authoritarian personality." The roots of his personality deformation lay in his obsessionality and his paranoid tendencies. An alienated "outsider," tormented by feelings of inferiority, worthlessness, and guilt, he condemned a world that to him seemed unreceptive and hostile. . . . In his intellectual fantasies his own moral and personal weaknesses were redeemed by a need for rigid moral values and puritanical discipline, his own disorder by a vision of rigidly stable order.[11]

A force of a very different kind but similarly brutal resulted in Hobbes becoming for himself and others a merchant of purposively healing State authoritarianism.

Hobbes' seventeenth-century England was a society which had achieved for many (to use Wolin's terms) "the condition of political nothingness:"

> So dramatic had been the suddenness with which England had been plunged into war and revolution, so great had been the devastation, and so bitter had been the enmities that for the next three centuries and more English politics was conducted on the unwritten premise that history ought not be allowed to repeat itself.[12]

Hobbes' terror was a consequence of the dissolution of the institutional arrangements between the forms of English social authority (the monarchy, the Church, the army, and the parliament) by the shock of the revival of Scot and Irish resistance movements and the structurally more significant rise of the English gentry as a class. Hobbes' abhorence of the state of nature was thus formed by a chaos punctuated by regicide, genocidal wars of pacification and conquest, and regimes of military rule.[13] He found it expedient, then, to surrender to the "alien presence" of political order:[14] ". . .in the act of our *submission*, consisteth both our *obligation*, and our *liberty*."[15]

Rousseau's Hell, as we have seen, was of a different making: a guilt-inducing childhood enveloped in a Calvinist Geneva; and an adulthood characterized by a spiritual and physical prostitution to the ruling class of eighteenth-century Paris society permanently marked his intellect.[16] In the end, however, both Rousseau and Hobbes, each in his own way, betrayed the embryonic logic of anarchy in his philosophy because distrust of solitary free individuals (for Hobbes, the rebel; for Rousseau, the amoralist) was more primal and thus natural for him. Yet, consideration of those contradictions has been largely by-passed because the character of scholarship and its paradigms have diverted our attentions to other directions.

For example, in this treatment of anarchist development, I am certainly much closer to George Woodcock than to James Joll. Both are historians of anarchism, but the subject assumes very different properties in each of their hands. Joll's perceptions of anarchism are much less sensitively organized than Woodcock's. Joll tends to rely on rather crudely constructed historical dynamics. In his characterization of Rousseau as "the true eighteenth-century ancestor of anarchism" ("Man was born free. . .," "Man is by nature neither good nor bad. . .," ". . .institutions corrupt him. . ."), there is something of the interminable search for "fatherhood" (surely the authority of the ontogenetic paradigm) characteristic of much of modern European historical thought, historical scholarship and historical sense. With similar analytical machinations (that is employing selective and ultimately specious interpretations) one could designate Jesus of Nazareth and John the Baptist as seminal contributors to this particular vision, anarchy, and as well exorcise William Godwin, Michael Bakunin and Malatesta from the stream.

Joll cannot consistently sustain a recognition and interest in the contradictions present in Rousseau for as an *historian of ideas*, presuming an idealist stance, he understands ". . .it is Rousseau who created the climate of ideas in which anarchism was possible." In other words, for Joll, anarchism is an idea or a system of ideas which is generated outside of historical and social time and space—in the mind. As such, for him, Rousseau's literal contradictions are reconciled ultimately by the argument "In some degree, what he said is less important than the way he said it. . . ."[17] My criticism is thus directed at the arbitration and arbitrariness of an art *cum* science. Joll's history is more artful than analytical.

There is some sense of fluidity in Joll's history of anarchism when he nods in quick passage at the Waldensian, Albigensian, Gnostic and Anabaptist sects and heresies mentioned in more authentic historical detail by Norman Cohn, yet his intent is to delimit and bound an event, a stilled, sectioned, sample of a dynamic (that is, human) phenomenon.

Though his historical sense is fundamentally the same as Joll's, Woodcock is more sensitive to this compulsion for origins. He acknowledges the varied quantities and experiences out of which the European anarchistic vision emerged. His scenario is made up of the convergencies between diverse ideational and social experiences. It also speaks of the dynamic between ideas and the social contexts from which they emerge and to which they contribute definition. It is made clear by Woodcock that (just as our own time attests) the anarchist vision has been experienced in adumbration and renaissance—eclipse and rebirth. Anarchism has not had a linear or orthogenetic history proceeding from some father-figure to maturity and subsequent decline. To the contrary, since anarchism describes diverse theories as well as social movements, it has developed in many places and at several points in time as a complex exchange and interchange between historical processes and cultures of ideas. Unfortunately, the biographical historiography to which Joll, and to some degree, Woodcock are committed does not lead to a consistent consciousness of the sometimes spontaneous developments which they attach to the "anarchist tradition."

William Godwin and the Authority of Reason

However that may be, both Woodcock and Joll have agreed that it is in the mind of the 18th-century English philosopher, William Godwin, that those peculiar elements coalesce which make up that rationalist anarchism most approximate to our time. It is Godwin's thought and systematic theorizing—as contained in his work, *Enquiry Concerning Political Justice*—which initially reflects a true anarchist vision. It is here that individual responsibility, order, architectonicism, community, economic organization without property, egalitarianism (whose dangers are there suspended by a sense of inherent good, human value and justice), perfectibility, and the antipolitical demand are first merged.

Godwin is significant further because of the timing and systematic nature of his conception. It was formulated in the very midst of what Popper has called the "open society:" the industrialized, demographically mobilized, classed, Cartesian, contractual, multi-ethnicized, ideologically competitive and politicized social environment of England's late 18th and early 19th centuries. Godwin, in his thought, was, of course, responding to the very nature of that society with its human waste and its social and psychological dislocations. But in so doing, he was also theorizing from an empirical base similar enough to some contemporary Western societies (similar in both the progenetic and analytical senses) as to be engaged in managing social and analytical tensions, real and presumed, analogous to those confronted by contemporary normative theorists.

It seems that for anarchist theorists too, the questions have always been, among others, ones of history, relevance and pragmatic workability. Are the descriptive elements of the analyst authentic, is society truly fragmented and indeed fracturing to the individual? If so, can one really do something about this condition through some form of deliberate social engineering whether using sweeping or incremental gestures? Have not the processes of society gone beyond "reversibility" without the intervention of some historic-scaled *deus ex machina* to necessitate the reconstruction? Might not such a "revolutionary" event occasion even more suffering for all of us and additionally incur the loss of the most pedestrian gains already acquired?

Godwin could rely upon the example of the early phase of the French Revolution to allay the fears of his near-converts and the incredulity of his critics. For the moment his timing was fortunate since the violence of the subsequent phases of the Revolution (or perhaps more accurately of the subsequent revolutions) betrayed many of Godwin's responses and served to diffuse the impact of his theoretical contributions. Yet, on the other hand, because of his systematic treatment of anarchy as an actualizable alternative to political authority, Godwin's analyses revealed, though most certainly unintentionally, most of the contradictions and weaknesses in his own social prescription and in anarchy *in totus*. These failings may be made more concrete by the following challenges: Is not the individual force of anarchy inevitably weaker than the collectivized force of social authority? How could a movement against the state succeed without creating, in the very imprint of its coming into opposition, counter-responsive political associations or counter-revolutions? In short, how can anarchy succeed without creating power and organs of power, and how can power assume a non-politicized or depoliticized form? Is not the anarchistic movement in such a form inevitably committed to a revolutionary vision which in its very realization is either self-destructive, self-contradictory or a mockery?

Campaigning against power, Godwin could or would not distinguish between power which had at its base irrationality and power which was consequent to rationality—the distinction between mystery and the adaptation to fear. Though he, like most anarchists, gave the highest honor to intelligence and reason, he chose a metaphorical and somewhat mystical conceptualization of force to serve as its conduit. He maintained through this circumlocution his perception of power as inherently subversive to individual integrity. Rationality though recognized as a social authority was denied the organizational rudiments required for its ascendancy by quite avoidable analytical timidities.[18] Yet Godwin did understand the distinction between a familiar, signified, authoritarian turbulence and essential order.[19] He sought to rationalize the replacement of the former by the latter incorporating Rousseau-like arguments of the corrupting and subversive force of authoritarian institutions on the "free soul of man."

Godwin's theory would appear to have proceeded from an outrage welling out of an individual made sensitive by his familial background and personal biography to English (Calvinist) dissent.

> Godwin's childhood was dominated by the gloomy Calvinist atmosphere of the home. His father was strict and scrupulous in the details of pietistic austerity.[20]
> The resentment bred of religious servitude in childhood produced eventually a stubborn independence and a passionate desire for freedom. Having been in youth the victim of physical austerity and of the tyranny of ideas enforced by others, William Godwin took as his life's work the liberation of man from the slavery of the mind and thence from the bondage of material coercion. Above all, he struggled for the freedom of children from the dominant opinions of their parents and masters, and sought to evolve an attitude towards education based on the natural development of inherent capacities rather than the coercive imposition of a mental pattern designed to turn the child into what his parents would like him to be.[21]

The critical intellectual influences on Godwin which would be reflected in his later political theory were the teachings of Robert Sandeman and the 16th-century Italian theologian, Socinius. A brief description of these theological traditions and the manner in which Godwin came to be acquainted with them should suffice to indicate the impacts they would have on his political and social thought.

In his eleventh year, Godwin became the sole pupil of Samuel Newton, a self-taught cleric and religious instructor who was a disciple of Sandeman. Woodcock describes Newton as "a religious bigot," and Godwin's characterization of the man would appear to be the source:

". . .a celebrated north country apostle, who, after Calvin had damned
ninety-nine in a hundred of mankind, has contrived a scheme for
damning ninety-nine in a hundred of the followers of Calvin."[22]

It was through Newton that Godwin learned of doctrines which
questioned a range of Calvinist practices and beliefs, from the civil
establishment of the Church to the divinity of Christ. The
Sandemanians also rejected the accumulation of wealth, believing the
property of any member of their sect to be at the disposal of any one
of them needing it. Calvinists, of course, looked upon the Sandemanians (or Glassites as they were known in Scotland their place of
origin) as heretics. Following his four years of pupilage under
Newton, Sandemanian beliefs would cost Godwin admission into at
least one dissenting college (Homerton Academy).

Eventually Godwin was admitted into a dissenting college, Hoxton,
in 1773 at the age of seventeen. Here he continued the heretical
inquiries which had been stimulated by Newton and to some degree by
the hostility he maintained towards his now-deceased father. But now
his Christological doubts had developed to the point of questioning
and debating the existence of God. Godwin later described his
youthful debates as purely academic, but they went far beyond the
boundaries of acceptable Calvinist dispute. He was on his way to the
scepticism which Woodcock maintains characterized his mature years.

> During my academical life, and from this time forward, I was inde-
> fatigable in my search after truth. I read all the authors of greatest
> repute, for and against the Trinity, original sin, and the most disputed
> doctrines, but I was not yet of an understanding sufficiently ripe for
> impartial decision, and all my enquiries terminated in Calvinism.[23]

Finishing at Hoxton in 1778, Godwin entered the ministry. For the
next five years, he struggled with the tenets of orthodox and non-
orthodox Calvinism, ultimately commiting himself to Socinianism.
During the five years which followed, he accepted the beliefs of this
Christian heresy which rejected, through the instrument of reason,
original sin, the divinity of Christ, the "mysteries" of the Gospels,
Hell, and the Trinity. He was by now, the true sceptic, committed to
the belief in the preeminent role of reason presented to him by Sande-
manianism and Socinianism. "The last traces of Calvinism were

purged away, and the development of a libertarian philosopher now began,"[24] according to Woodcock.

Godwin was convinced of the immanence of human reason and individual judgement but he was just as certain of the sanguinary character of government in principle and actuality:

> But government [Woodcock paraphrases Godwin] "lays its hand upon the spring that is in society and puts a stop to its motion." It gives substance and permanence to our errors. It reverses the genuine propensities of mind, and instead of suffering us to look forward, teaches us to look backward for perfection. It prompts us to seek the public welfare, not in innovation and improvement, but in a timid reverence for the decisions of our ancestors, as if it were the nature of mind always to degenerate and never to advance.[25]
>
> Above all, we should not forget that government is an evil, an usurpation upon the private judgement and individual conscience of mankind; and that, *however we may be obliged to admit it as a necessary evil for the present,* it behoves us, as the friends of reason and the human species, to admit as little of it as possible, and carefully to observe whether, in consequence of the gradual illumination of the human mind, that little may not hereafter be diminished.[26]

Godwin's programmatic development in his major treatise was sparse in comparison to the time spent in intellectual, social, philosophical and historical criticism.[27] In addition, some of the strategies he employed in his far-reaching critiques led to ambiguities in his utopian and programmatic suggestions. Godwin's discussion of democracy gives us some idea of the problems contained in his political theory.

Having been obliged to admit the necessary evil of government for the present, Godwin was somewhat explicit as to its transitory functions:

> All that is to be asked on the part of government in behalf of morality and virtue is a clear stage upon which for them to exert their own energies, and perhaps some restraint for the present upon the violent disturbers of the peace of society that the efforts of these principles may be allowed to go on uninterrupted to their natural conclusion.[28]

Of the forms of government that he recognized, monarchy, aristocracy and democracy, Godwin believed the least objectionable was democracy. But when he used the term democracy, he meant different things at different points in his argument.

In defending democracy against the advocates of monarchy and aristocracy, Godwin chose as his rebuttal the historical example of Athens, "with all these errors on its head, it is incontrovertible that Athens exhibited a more illustrious and enviable spectacle than all the monarchies and aristocracies that ever existed."[29] Admitting to the "errors" of "turbulence and instability" of Athenian society, its lapses of social and moral virtues, Godwin argued that Athens as an example of "democratical society" could never "be brought down to the level of monstrous institutions" extant in monarchy and aristocracy:

> Shall we compare a people of such incredible achievements, such exquisite refinement, gay without insensibility and splendid without intemperance, in the midst of whom grew up the greatest poets, the noblest artists, the most finished orators and political writers, and the most disinterested philosophers the world ever saw—shall we compare this chosen seat of patriotism, independence and generous virtue with the torpid and selfish realms of monarchy and aristocracy? All is not happiness that looks tranquility. Better were a portion of turbulence and fluctuation than that unwholesome calm which is a stranger to virtue.[30]

However, Athens was not what Godwin had in mind when he used the term democracy in a programmatic or utopian sense.[31] His program called for the creation of "parishes"—small, autonomous communities—and the reduction of the national government to infrequently-called national assemblies. The national assemblies would have "the purpose of adjusting the differences between district and district and of consulting respecting the best mode of repelling foreign invasion. . ."[32] Godwin believed it was possible that they would never be assembled. In the off-chance that the assemblies were convened in extreme emergency, he presumed their business could be concluded within "a certain limit" of time—he had in mind one day. As for the parishes, the only administrative organization Godwin mentions is a jury to decide upon "offences of individuals within the community and upon the questions and controversies respecting property which may chance to arise."[33] But, of course, as the perfectability of man proceeded to develop, the presence of offences or disputes (or property) in communities would be precluded by the instrument of human reason.

In short, Godwin's democracy would be characterized by no government, no property, no crime, no classes, no dispute of opinion, "in the end what he calls *democracy* becomes nothing short of what his modern spiritual descendants call *anarchy.*"[34] Kropotkin would appear to have agreed with the preceding assessment of Godwin. Woodcock remarks that:

> . . .it was not until comparatively late in Kropotkin's life, after his own theories were fully formed, that the latter encountered *Political Justice* and realized the deep affinity between his own thought and Godwin's. After Kropotkin, Godwin became recognized by the more intellectual anarchists as one of their predecessors. . . .[35]

But there is a third meaning given to the term democracy in Godwin's programmatic counsel. It is a meaning which Woodcock has found unsettling. At one point, Godwin had talked about "loose discussion groups" anticipating the stage of developing and organizing society into parishes. In the former, the pursuit of truth, the use of reason and inquiry would prevail. Godwin believed that these groups might eventually form a universal movement, a revolutionary movement of social change characterized by gradual transformations rather than violence. But as parishes and their administrative juries came into existence, a rather different kind of democracy would emerge. Woodcock states:

> At first, in the extreme democracy which Godwin envisages, both assemblies and juries may have to issue commands.[36]
>
> Godwin contends that in all these respects the small social group has the advantage over the extensive political institution. But the way he talks of the operations of such groups arouses one's deepest misgivings. In circles of this kind, he says, "opinion would be all sufficient; the inspection of every man over the conduct of his neighbors, when un- stained by caprice, would constitute a censorship of the most irresistible nature. But the force of this censorship would depend upon its freedom, not following the positive dictates of law, but the spontaneous decisions

of the understanding." Even Godwin's assurance that such a process would be free and spontaneous does not entirely erase the distasteful picture of a future where mutual inspection and censorship will be the order of the day and public opinion will reign triumphant.[37]

Thus, democracy in Godwin's deliberation is no more democracy than Rousseau's General Will resembles a general will.[38] Godwin calls democracy that which might be associated *mutatis mutandis* with what Popper argues Plato would identify as timocracy—the rule of the noble. Under the guise of a rudimentary form of democracy, Godwin postulates a coercive, dictatorial rule of reasonable men, "timocracy," which processes subjects into "pure" self-rulers through the agency of education.[39] To the degree that Godwin's philosophy depended upon political authority in its service, it was dominated by the logic of irrational forms of power and persuasion. Godwin's use of the term administration was a (self-) deceptive ploy implying an aesthetically clinical element to circumvent the fundamentally manipulative nature of his vision.

His propositions, then, issue out of that very political authority which he wished to abrogate. He could not sustain the tension between reason as authority and political authority.[40] Neither was Godwin a naive idealist in his understanding of the inevitable self-serving nature of the relationship when government penetrates education. One text summarizes Godwin's position on that relationship:

> Government will not fail to employ it [a national education system] to strengthen its hands and perpetuate its institutions. If we could even suppose the agents of government not to propose themselves an object which will be apt to appear in their eyes not merely innocent but meritorious, the evil would not the less happen. Their view as institutors of a system of education will not fail to be analogous to their views in their political capacity; the data on which their conduct as statesmen is vindicated will be the data upon which their instructions are founded.[41]

Yet he could presumably see no way around coercion in the beginning despite his declared antipathy to "violence."

Godwin's refusal or failure to acknowledge the violence which characterized his prescription—the totalitarian and coercive aspects of educational structures and opinion—does not set him apart from most anarchist theorists. Woodcock had summarized from his various works on anarchists:

> The anarchists accept much too uncritically the idea of an active public opinion as an easy way out of the problem of dealing with antisocial tendencies. Few of them have given sufficient thought to the danger of a moral tyranny replacing a physical one, and the frown of the man next door becoming as much a thing to fear as the sentence of the judge. And some of them have undoubtedly been positively attracted by the idea of radiating moral authority; anarchism has had its Pharisees like every other movement for human regeneration.[42]

Again the failure to distinguish between rational and irrational power in the attempt to assassinate political authority results in confusion, deception and delusion. At this point it seems no mean observation to recall that Mary Shelley, née Godwin, succeeded with *Dr. Frankenstein* in creating in English literature a singularly powerful image of the Machiavellian rationalist driven mad by the enormity of the scope of his invention. And the anguish expressed to his creator by the self-awakened monster, his suffering and his needs, would have certainly been too well understood by a people having fallen victim to Godwin's self-appointed tasks of liberation:

> I ought to be thy Adam; but I am rather the fallen angel. . . .Everywhere I see bliss, from which I alone am irrevocably excluded. I was benevolent and good; misery made me a friend. Make me happy, and I shall again be virtuous.[43]

Notwithstanding the inconsistencies in the logic and values of his theoretical argument, Godwin in his homage to rationalism remains distinct from those anarchist thinkers who emerged in the next one hundred and thirty-odd years. Intellectually, Godwin's anarchism streamed out of the Christian fundamentalism of English Dissent as characterized by Gerald Winstanley and Sandeman. There were, too, those residues of Calvinist training in the rigid admixture and articulations of values, visions and belief. And the French Enlightenment, represented by the influences of Rousseau, mediated and subtly metamorphosed these influences.

Godwin's religiosity had been transmuted into ideational presuppositions which resembled more the social ethic of the "classical liberalists"[44] than the individualism of some later anarchists. His perceptions of history and education as progressive forces and instruments do seem more manifestations of collectivist paradigms than the commemoration of the uniqueness and singularity implied in the concept of autonomous man. For perhaps some of these very same reasons, the influence and penetration of Godwin's philosophy (and those of his utopian adherents) on anarchist thought were interdicted by the emergence and development of very different anarchist traditions. The convergence between Godwin's work and schools of anarchist thought was, as such, suspended for ninety years.

The Individualists and the Anarcho-Socialists

It is in the 19th century that anarchism became "schooled," that is, the traditions and movement crystallized into at least two observable streams. Though the boundaries of each one of these streams within the body of anarchy are somewhat arbitrarily imposed, clear relationships do appear to exist between, on the one hand, Max Stirner, Sergei Nechayev[45] and Friedrich Nietzsche, and, on the other, Pierre-Joseph Proudhon, Michael Bakunin, Karl Marx, Petr Kropotkin, Leo Tolstoy, and the major French (Joseph Dejacque, Faure, Camus), Spanish (Durruti, Montseny), Italian (Malatesta) and "American" anarchists (Most, Berkman, Goldman). Using crude and therefore dramatic analytical categorizations, the former collection of writers and activists might be distinguished by their outraged refusal to accept an identity or proximate relationship between social freedom and individual liberation. The latter group is, of course, marked by their analytical and ideological commitment to social revolt. For this second group, the freeing of the individual was consequent and made possible only by the agency of an unquestionably inevitable revolution of society, but not its destruction. Proudhon, in a way representative of them all, put his argument this way:

> A revolution is a force against which no power, divine or human, can prevail, and whose nature it is to grow by the very resistance it encounters. . . . The more you repress it, the more you increase its rebound and render its action irresistible, so that it is precisely the same

177

for the triumph of an idea whether it is persecuted, harassed, beaten down from the start, or whether it grows and develops unobstructed. Like the Nemesis of the ancients, whom neither prayers nor threats could move, the revolution advances, with sombre and predestined tread, over the flowers strewn by its friends, through the blood of its defenders, over the bodies of its enemies.[46]

Yet, Proudhon had a clear notion of the purpose of such a force and could thus indict the French Revolution for its failure: "The Republic should have established Society; it thought only of establishing Government. . . ."[47]

To the contrary, the solipsistic and narcissistic strains in the nihilism and existentialism of Stirner, Nechayev and Nietzsche seemed to reflect a savage psychic aloneness quite distinct from the disciplined solitude of Proudhon and the others—a solitude which was always predicated on and immersed in the optimism of a vision of an ultimate and final reconciliation. As Stirner in the moment of a more particular indictment might declare for all the social revolutionists, they were finally humanists, humanity was their authority. However for himself:

> My business is neither the divine nor the human, it is not what is True, Good, Right, Free, etc., but only what is *mine*, and it is not something general but is individual as I am individual. For me nothing is higher than myself.[48]

We have uncovered again the contrast between absolute individual freedom and absolute social freedom. We have thus returned to an earlier presumption made here that anarchy, as a vision, is critically dependent on one's construction of the social reality of order.

If one means by order familiarity mediated through institutions, then one must insist on the inevitability of some form of institutional authority. There is no theory inside socially prescribed and defined sanity which can begin elsewhere. It follows then that only the insane can lead us to some different place, crossing the epistemological boundaries of the inevitably tautological nature of understanding.[49] We have seen that the 'world was too much with' Godwin in his attempts to transgress against political authority resulting in a disappointingly trite philosophy, part contradiction and part confusion.

The same is true for Proudhon, Bakunin, Marx, Kropotkin and Tolstoy. All stood at the margin of a transcendent, intellectual triumph only to betray the anarchist movement by the tradition they constructed and represented. Only Marx escaped the pedestrian warrant of criticality by the authoritarian use of an intellectual and biographic dialecticism to forge in state communism a force antithetic and alien. A good deal of the *theoretical* foundation of Marx's thought can be identified by appending a knowledge of political economy to the personal alienations, denunciations, scholarship and treatment of European political and social history reflected and found in his "On the Jewish Question."

The theories of Proudhon and Kropotkin replaced political authority with an authority which had at its base economic calculi masquerading as systems and instincts. Proudhon's prescriptions resulted from projections out of his experience with peasant society in eastern France. Kropotkin's conceptualizations were consequent to his geographical, ethnological and anthropological observations in Siberia, China, Mongolia and elsewhere. Their "observations" were, of course, idealizations of peasant culture, idealizations which had no room for the authoritarian excesses of elementary kinship structures or the occasional horrors of cannibalism of the 19th and 20th centuries' French and Russian peasantries.

The point is that each theorist was inspired by his own "empirical" reality, that is an experience mediated by and sensitive to a specific reality. It is not strange then that those systems are at root the family writ large and as evidenced in the agrarian extended family forms characteristic of peasants and/or tribes, as well as in the packs and herds characteristic of other animal species.[50] The force of biographic development continues undiminished in their theories in which they insist that because a being emerges from institutions as a discrete organism in evolutionary and historical series, that individual is bound to such institutions for survival. The circularity of the insight is manifest, the analytical vision remains sane.

If we were to pursue the insight that grand social theory were somehow directly related to the projection of familial experience, we would discover among the egoists and their nihilism an explicit repulsion from the imagery associated with revolutionist theory of the family as a cooperative and integrative phenomenon. In its stead, they extracted a very different reality. Their experience seemed more a reaction to a competitive, isolating and starkly authoritarian model of the family. In its social projection, they sought to remove the authoritarian aspect or perhaps suspend it as a given in the form of Nature, human nature, history, etc. By positing authority in the sub-matrix of human experience, in the infrastructure as perhaps Claude Levi-Strauss might see it, it could be at once indulged and ignored. On it could rest the final security, self-righteousness, and, since it was unalterable, the permanence of continuity without the requirement of close or conscious attention.

Stirner, for example, shouted of authority residing within himself and thus relieved himself of human (social) responsibility or sensibility except as a theorist. It was his own survival, according to him, which authorized his life:

> In crime the egoist has hitherto asserted himself and mocked at the sacred; the break with the sacred, or rather of the sacred, may become general. A revolution never returns, but a mighty, reckless, shameless, conscienceless, proud *crime* does it not rumble in distant thunders, and do you not see how the sky grows presciently silent and gloomy?[51]

Coming to a kind of ontological closure with his contemporaries in German Romantic literature who would lay the foundation for the ascetic tyrannies of subjective idealism, surrealism, expressionism and symbolism, he seemed to be bounding back over the Christian philosophies of Augustine and Pelagius in order to proceed toward a more ancient perfectibility quite alone. Society indeed was family as fantasy, a fearful, brutal blunder and criminal assault against the individual. One could not with the diseased social instruments of society—economics, religion or politics—repair the injury but simply dress the festering wound with filthy, tattered rags. And these were rags which would have to be discarded:

> Revolution and rebellion must not be looked upon as synonymous. The former consists in a overturning of conditions, of the established condition or *status*, the state or society, and is accordingly a *political* or *social* act. The latter has indeed for its unavoidable consequence a transformation of circumstances, yet does not start from that but from

men's discontent with themselves; it is not an armed rising, but a rising of individuals, a getting up, without regard for the consequences that spring from it. The Revolution aims at new arrangements; rebellion leads us no longer to let ourselves be arranged, but to arrange ourselves, and sets no glittering hopes on "institutions."[52]

Each man-race—for every individual was that unique to Stirner—would have to diagnose his marks in his own way, but realize ultimately that escape from the human colony was unobtainable except through crime and force, the instruments of a morally and socially unfettered ego.

Stirner and the Romantics in Germany of the 19th century represented opposite forces from the same nucleus in the social arena, one pure aggression, the other pure passivity. Social authority was destroyed (Stirner) or suspended alone and beyond (Schiller, Goethe, Wieland) and the tension between individual and collective perfectibilities was resolved by choosing the former and turning inwards toward the tasks of self-assertion or self-indulgence. The German Romantics eschewed socially explicit independence and non-conformity. Their preoccupations were with the private perfectibility of the individual who remained unreconciled with the society around him. Those works of theirs (e.g. Goethe's *Wilhelm Meisters Wanderjahre*) in which the individual became reconciled to his society asserted this resolution to be quite an unsatisfactory one, leading ultimately to conformity and capitulation of creativity. Social consciousness was thus better suspended or perhaps never developed because of its irrelevance to the central process of acquiring individual spiritual integration. For the Romantics, according to Nietzsche:

. . .their general effort was directed toward gaining a place of honor for more ancient, primitive feelings, and especially Christianity, the folk soul, folk sagas, folk language, medievalism, Oriental aesthetics, Indianism.

The whole great tendency of the Germans ran counter to the Enlightenment, and to the revolution of society. . .piety toward everything that had ever existed, only to make heart and spirit full once again and to leave no room for future goals and innovations. The cult of feeling was erected in place of the cult of reason.[53]

Stirner sought to destroy the society around him, while the romanticists sought to ignore it by conforming to its social "superficialities."

Though Stirner as his alter-ego Johann Casper Schmidt failed to act out any of his asocial dictums, the Russian, Sergei Nechayev, several decades later, was the egoist incarnate. There was little compromise in Nechayev's campaign against organized society and the race in general.[54] In conspiracy, murder, betrayal, extortion, and lies, Nechayev proceeded against his world infecting many of those with whom he came into contact with the pure hatred evidenced in his nihilism. Woodcock argues:

> Nechayev was no anarchist. . . .[He] carried nihilism to that repulsive extreme where the end justifies every means, where the individual is negated along with everything else in society, and where the authoritarian will of the terrorist becomes the only justification for his actions. This, moreover, was no mere theoretical position; Nechayev actually used his theories to justify the murder, theft and black-mail which he himself practiced.[55]

It is believed that Nechayev entered Russian literature as Bazarov in Turgenev's *Fathers and Sons*, and most dramatically as Verkhovensky in Dostoevsky's *The Possessed*.

Stirner, Nechayev and the mid-19th century French anarchist, Joseph Dejacque, anticipated, and perhaps gave some impetus to, the violence in assassinations and bombings which would characterize the anarchist movement of the late 19th and early 20th centuries in Russia, Germany, France, Spain, Italy and the United States. They were not, however, in any way solely responsible for such commitments any more than they were themselves freaks of society. The social forces which induced their own experiential, psychological and intellectual development—the maturation of nation states, the oppression and repression of lower and higher orders of men and women by political, economic and dogmatic institutions, the terror and social disintegration induced by industrial and para-industrial changes, murderous wars, scientism, omniscient authorities—were present too for those generations of anarchists which succeeded them. For many, peasants, bourgeoisie and aristocrats alike, the simplest predicate of order had been rent. The authority and authorizations of

Weltanschauugen had been consciously, hurtfully penetrated and compromised by intolerable "fact" and the shamanistic integrations of intellectualism were hard put to find and declare new "orders of permanence" upon which to rest.

The egoists had understood, or better, intuited the fundamental paradox upon which the anarchists as social revolutionists had posited their intentions. The egoists understood that the autonomy for which Godwin, Proudhon, Bakunin, Marx, and Kropotkin theorized could not be consummated by structural revolution. They understood that the social revolutionists could proceed no further toward the total liberation of the individual from society because they could neither judge, consider nor conceptualize such a phenomenon: the individual unfettered by any social predeterminants.

Most of the social revolutionists had begun their philosophies with a tense, abortive fiction—the solitary Nature beast—which was only understandable to them in contrasts and contradistinctions. They had celebrated a negation, a non-thing which existed only while its antithesis survived. They had not understood that the processes and experiences called society could never result in the freeing of the individual but rather in his alienation, and alienation is the estrangement from a "rightful," "proper" station (with all the profound, contextural senses such a word should conjure). What they recognized as alienation was not the beginning of freedom or the search for freedom, as they would have it, but an index to the extent to which men and women had become beings whose lives were characterized by the surrender of all but the most illusory pretensions of freedom. Alienation developed out of the frustration of this passion for submission, not from the submission itself. It was reflex. In the absence of a collector of submissions—authority—all collectors were cursed for their exposed impotence rather than the pervasiveness of their power. Institutions were corrupting, history was contradiction, the political state was an instrument of a specific class, religion was illusion. The ambiance of authority had been dissipated so that no structure was unequivocal.

In the philosophies of the social revolutionists, the autonomous individual was an anthropological fiction—a beginning point fit for those self-same, unrealizable flights of the imagination which had first given it life. The measure of the goodness in each being was the lack of mischievousness in and against a proto-society which was the proximate company of other beings. The individual's goodness was a testament, too, that all beings had not closed upon each other in the cowed association of society—so close together as to require for each of them to survive that one tear away his or her life from the grasp of another's hand. Mankind was by nature and in Nature untutored in the arts of abuse and exploitation, the artifact of greed was without its necessary precondition: abundance, and fear was formed into gods, beasts, and the mysteries.

Proudhon, whom Woodcock called a "social individualist," exemplified this consciousness in both his *Confessions of a Revolutionary:*

> In my father's house we breakfasted on maize porridge; at mid-day we ate potatoes; in the evening bacon soup, and that every day of the week. And despite the economists who praise the English diet, we, with that vegetarian feeding, were fat and strong. Do you know why? Because we breathed the air of our fields and lived from the produce of our own cultivation.[56]

and his *What Is Property?*:

> If I were asked to answer the question: "What is slavery?" and I should answer in one word, "Murder!," my meaning would be understood at once. No further argument would be needed to show that the power to take from a man his thought, his will, his personality, is a power of life and death, and that to enslave a man is to kill him. Why, then, to this other question: "What is property?" may I not likewise answer, "Theft"?[57]

Such was the humanism which though so closely resembling Rousseau's thought was left a parallel uncharacteristically but understandably not remarked upon.

But the egoists failed as well not because they loved the individual too well, but too little. The egoists were consumed by their failure to distinguish the presence of their fellow creatures from the tyranny which only *might* result from that presence. In the hatred and contempt the egoists felt for the masses—submissive fungus suffocating them—they became convinced of the need to destroy the institutions called society to insure their own frightful solitude. They read promise deliberately betrayed, closeness abandoned, continuity broken where, in truth, commitment had only been a fortuitous, adventitious phenomenon. Nietzsche aphorized fittingly the measure by which to understand them when he declared this analytical methodology: from "the deed to the doer, from the ideal to the man who *needs* it, from every way of thinking to the commanding *need* behind it."

The egoists, brutal men from brutal experience who, in turn, brutalized all life they contacted, scorched the air and the page with their cries of "brutality!" They fought back against their experience, projected constructions of reality with those very same instruments of authority, the hatred and contempt they understood to be descending from all around upon them. They were indeed betrayed by all those events in life to which most men and women come to owe allegiance and call by the name of intimacy. Their personal biographies are without exception marked by excessive abandonment, death, insanity and morose love affairs. Yet, out of their work and their lives there did reverberate the echo of an astounding, invaluable insight which had been lost to Europeans in the cacophony of radical thought: the human individual could construct the experience of autonomy proceeding deliberately from conception to inception. They discovered once again that ideas were those night creatures of the dreams and myths of mankind which possessed the power to subvert, transform and transmutate the very substance of the earth between the twilight and dawn of consciousness. Reality and human nature were like the sculptor's stone to these steeled instruments. With ideas, themselves the products of cultures, histories and experiences, members of the species had always been able to chisel and engrave some new expressive constellation from the countenance and form of their kind. If the social revolutionists in suggesting the transformation of society through institution-rearrangement posited an instrument markedly perverse and primitive, the egoists in recalling the sheer force of commitment to ideas bequeathed a perverse mark onto idealism, an instrument presumably characterized by an exquisite, extraordinary sophistication.

It is of interest to note here that the historians of anarchist thought and action, in assessing the "death" of the anarchist movement or its supercession by other radical ideologies, have most frequently argued from the reference and character of closed analytical systems. Most, like Irving Horowitz, Eric Hobsbawn and George Woodcock, have attributed its demise to the fact that it was not particularized, concretized—a radical system which would have offered to its proponents the "strategic" perspectives [or] quick tactical reaction on a national scale"[58] which were characteristic of some of its contemporary systems (e.g. Marxism or Fascism). Anarchism thus failed, they continue, to confront human beings where they are.

What these critics seem to be really arguing is that what the 19th and 20th centuries required to engage the mass, industrialized mind of European workers were closed systems with beginnings, ends, and bounded, rewarded, tangible dimensions—ideological playpens whose form would have supplied the authority for social action, reconstruction and survival. There is much of the Dostoevskyian Grand Inquisitor here. Anarchist philosophy we are told, like the Christ of the Inquisitor, had demanded too much of men by presuming them capable of autonomous choice. Anarchist theory was historically and psychologically premature in not being characterized by the presupposition of the worker as a neotenic creature. To the contrary, through it was sought the instruments by which individuals could celebrate the meaning-filled endings and achievement of existence rather than just another formula for avoidance and the forfeiture of personal responsibility. Yet, to assert that the failure to present a program was the critical weakness in the anarchist philosophy is to avoid the fundamental tragedy that perhaps it represented the groping search for human beings, where they *could not* be found.

To suggest that anarchist theoreticians did not develop explicit formulations is, of course, somewhat absurd. Godwin, Proudhon, Fourier, Kropotkin and the others developed systems which possessed extravagant detail, conceptualizations of society which were rationalized to the most extreme degree. There were always particularized visions available for whomever might enjoy and require them, but there was too, at the same time, the doctrine that each individual or community in anarchy would have and would have to have the responsibility for defining, articulating and consummating his, her, or its own vision. It is obvious too, that the critics in interning anarchy as a movement were engaged in a premature burial. It is not so clear, as some analysts now have acknowledged, that anarchy has been "by-passed by history" and once done so, as Woodcock would have it, could never reassert itself in even the questioned "moderate success it enjoyed in the present and past centuries." Paris of 1968 has brought into question such funereal presumptions.[59] It is precisely a peculiarity of anarchism that by its very nature it confounds the attempts by some of its students to maintain a differentiation between thought and action. What other conclusions could one draw, presumably, from Woodcock's argument that the anarchistic "ideal" had survived? As an intellectual force it is bound to precipitate to some degree the resurrection of behavioral complements. The tragic element for us as in Icarus' fatal quest for recognition through flight, is not that the individual by nature cannot fly (for he or she obviously can by spreading intellect rather than arms) but that the individual must fly in his or her own way.

Yet, anarchy is in many ways—to continue the metaphor—like a sparrow which once wounded never flies again. Its injuries are attended to, its feathers grown out and put in order, but the critical psychological, instinctual trauma is never healed.

The anarchists were reflex to an evil history which penetrated their own remarkable and macabre achievements. In their efforts, the state was countered by the dissolution of the state, centralization by decentralization, elitist intellectualism by pedestrian peasantism, force by reason, obedience by disobedience, familiar entropy by ordered familiarity. They had failed to free themselves, to disengage meaningfully from the existential boundaries and force of their own experience. They were (and are) forever in the state clawing out to a thing perceived through the eyes of naive, desperate infancy.

Anarchism was a theory of society conscious of and in opposition to political society. Though anarchist theorists attempted to reconstruct social order mainly on the basis of economic authority, their conceptualizations of social order had identical epistemological and metaphysical foundations to that which they sought to oppose. Anarchism became a political force against the state, a political force in opposition to political authority. Such a contradiction anticipated the degeneration of anarchism into tragic idealisms and conspiracies of terror and assassination. The root of that contradiction lies in a consciousness dominated by political authority.

The historical example of the anarchists might suggest to some a finalizing adjunct to their theories: that political freedom is only *prior* to political organization and experience, never following out of it.

The "Stateless" Society

There are, however, other experiences of political autonomy which possess some healthier fortune for our concern here. These experiences, or at least, some impression of them, are to be found, for one, in the anthropological literature of the present century and have been most systematically engaged and uncovered in the studies specifically of African peoples.

In the "stateless societies" (or "tribes without rulers") of the Tonga, Amba, Lugbara, Tiv, Konkomba, Tallensi, Dinka and Mandari, evidence emerges of the capacity of human beings to hold together their social structures without the authority of rulers or the presence of political leaders.[60] As such, in an immediate sense these societies represent a contrast to and potential alternative to Western societies.

However, these societies can only fulfill these roles when certain preconditions have been satisfactorily met. It seems to me that there are three such preconditions. First, these societies must be understandable. If the rules and meanings of their social organization resist the categories of Western thought and consciousness, then these societies cannot be used to contrast the rules and meanings of Western social organization and history or to contradict or affirm the universality of Western social structures.

Secondly, these societies must be evaluated through some criterion of success (continuity) if they are to be accepted as relevant models of social organization. Depending upon what we can arrive at as a meaningful criterion of success, stateless societies must either persist, expand, or progress in some arena or constellation of arenas of human activity in order to be classified as successful.

188

Thirdly, the critical aspects of these societies, that is their conceptualizations and experiences of social order, must be in some way
transferable to Western experience. Again, depending on what we can
agree to as the fundamental identity of interculture transfer, these
aspects must either be capable of exchange for, adaptation and
integration, or displacement of the meanings of Western social
experience which confirm the authority of society looked at in a
political way. These critical aspects must in some way "transfer" to
the contexts of urbanized, industrialized, rationalized and politicized
humanity.

This is not the order in which these preconditions can or must be
addressed. To the contrary, the first and the third questions require,
as response, experience presumably not yet available to the reader, but
the second demands only logic; so we will deal with it first, suspending
the exploration of the others until later.

I have suggested above that the question of the "success" of a
society relates somehow to its continuity. Continuity will be taken to
mean through time as manifested in human society by its inheritance
through subsequent generations (I was tempted to say "successive
generations"). According to this definition, an institution is deemed
"successful" if it passes on and beyond its present adherents with
formal and functional sameness. This longitudinal, mechanistic
meaning is the only interpretation of "success" which can be
appropriated to the evaluation of "stateless societies" without major
reservations for reasons peculiar to such societies which will be treated
below. As I warned, it is a question requiring the tools of elementary
logic while eschewing for the major part the more familiar elements of
normative analysis. (There are, of course, some Platonic suggestions
of the good in anything of human origin which survives since its
survival is presumed—understood—as the resultant of some
correspondence between it and the fundamental nature of things.)

If we retain in our immediate grasp the points of discrepancy between continuity and permanence—that is by analogy, a thing which
crosses between points in space and that space itself—then it can be
said that these "stateless" human organizations have been as
"successful" as any other given variant and most definitely of longer
duration. Peasant or farming peoples, including the society from

which we will draw detailed materials, have frequently survived wars, raids, famines, epedemic diseases, translocation, etc., with their social and epistemological structures intact. That is, often, this survival has been accomplished without their resorting to the instruments which would destroy or disturb their constructions of reality.

With a seeming precociousness the matter of "success" must rest here at this rather unsatisfactory point. To pursue it further even in this patently narrow fashion would perforce require that we recognize and confront the fact that we had already penetrated a quite different metaphysics of time and space which passively denies the very fundament of "success:" the notion of change. It is this element in the ethnography of peoples like the Tonga, Amba, etc., who have dealt in "statelessness" which makes of "success" a term particularly alien and quite peculiarly esoteric to their would-be recorders. As for the other questions, we must first come to grips with the "language" or "languages" of our mediators, the political anthropologists, before continuing.

For the relevant social anthropologists, the problem of constructing an identity as political anthropologists through interests-convergence, conceptualizations and analyses came to a head with the introduction written by E.E. Evans-Pritchard and M. Fortes to a work they edited and published in the early 1940s entitled *African Political Systems*. Their essay, in seeking to differentiate the structures of political systems, of course, had precedents in those writings of L. H. Morgan[61], H. S. Maine[62], Max Weber,[63], and Robert Lowie[64] (to name a few of their most frequently cited and immediate predecessors in the fields of political anthropology and sociology) but as the latter had succeeded in mastering "isolated" elements of the empirical theory of politics and constructing binary systems from them, the former in their work merged inclusively their mentors' thoughts into a system of classification and analysis.

The work of Evans-Pritchard and Fortes proceeded quite directly from the presumption of the earlier social evolutionists that "primitive" and "civilized" societies could be distinguished in their political organization by their respective dependencies on the personal relations of kinship and territorial contiguities. This presumption had been developed by the American anthropologist, Morgan, as a theory of social history tracing the species' development from Savagery through Barbarism, ending in Civilization. In this latter aspect of his thought, Morgan was probably influenced by Maine with whom he corresponded. Maine, more than a dozen years previous to the appearance of Morgan's work, had argued that primitive society was characterized by kinship and communal property, while civilized society was organized by contract between individuals with property being held privately. Through the 19th and mid-20th centuries, as indicated above, the legacy of this classificatory scheme was a rich one. It included the *Communist Manifesto* of Marx and Engels, the *Gemeinschaft und Gessellschaft* of Ferdinand Tonnies, and Durkheim's *The Division of Labor*. Weber, of course, who read "primitive" as domestic authority, i.e. concerned with struggle against nature, and "civilized" as state and/or political authority relating to relations between men, is also to be included. The "final" variant of this opposition between primitive and civilized societies was Lowie's argument that the "modern" state was founded on the integration of the kinship and territorial principles through the agency of non-kin "association."

This was the tradition from which Evans-Pritchard and Fortes constructed a triple classification of political systems in Africa. What follows is a concise summary of their morphological scheme as presented in the work of John Middleton and David Tait[65]; a summary not only convenient but which also bears the stamp of authenticity having been reviewed and prefaced by Evans-Pritchard:

> In the Introduction to *African Political Systems* three types of political system in Africa are distinguished. The first is examplified by the Bushman where the largest political units embrace people all of whom are interrelated by kinship so that 'political relations are coterminous with kinship relations and the political structure and kinship organization are completely fused' (Fortes and Evans-Pritchard 1940: 6-7). The second type includes those with specialized political authority that is institutionalized and vested in roles attached to a state administration. They are unitary states, with a king or paramount chief at the centre who holds authority to wield supreme political power as part of his status. He may delegate it to others but their authority is subordinate and can originate only on his. Here there are typically specialized political roles and structures. Relations between component

groups of the society are internal administrative relations, and political roles are hierarchically arranged in a series of superordinate and subordinate statuses. The third type includes societies in which political authority is uncentralized. In them there is no holder of political power at the centre, and specialized roles with clearly defined political authority are less easy to find. Local groups are recruited by unilineal descent or by fiction of such descent and relations between them are characterized by their being in a state of segmentary opposition. . . they are called 'segmentary lineage systems'.[66]

Although the Evans-Pritchard and Fortes essay sought to distinguish the two latter models of political organization in rather too simple terms, it did have interesting consequences for the intensity, quantitatively and qualitatively, with which the two categorizations were treated in subsequent ethnographic work. The writings of Tait, Middleton, Nadel[67], Radcliffe-Brown[68], Gluckman[69], Southall[70], Fortes[71], and Leach[72] were an immediate response compelling Evans-Pritchard finally to defensively comment in 1957:

. . .the tentative typology Professor Fortes and I put forward, and which was intended to be no more than a convenient start towards a more detailed classification of types of African society, in which the absence or presence of forms of descent groups and of state institutions were two criteria, has been expanded and refined.[73]

What the revisionists (in their own estimations) or addendists (in Evans-Pritchard's view) seemed in general to be saying was that: 1) the second type of political system, the state, was not necessarily related (as its formulators suggested) to the processes of internal diversification or of external conquest but could also be explained, for example, by coalescence between groups with certain "complementarities" (Southall) and proximity of long duration; 2) that the second and third types of political system, state and stateless, were not mutually exclusive and might merge into what Southall had termed "the segmentary state;" and 3) that "stateless societies" or those with uncentralized political authority were not necessarily characterized by or based upon segmentary lineage systems. Yet whatever the merits of the initial contributions to a social theory of politics, the ensuing dialogue resulted in the emergence of a post-structural-functional empirical theory of politics suspicious of not only European "empiricisms" (i.e., those which grew out of the study of European political history) but European political philosophy as well.[74]

In the African setting at least—but as well among some of the peoples indigenous to southeastern Asia, Australia and South America—the notions of kinship (clan) and ranked kinship and descent (lineage) were discovered in some societies to possess what are generally recognized in Western society as political and para-political utility. Rather than power and stratifications of power, the metaphysics of order (as familiar experience) and continuity were founded on what European scholars believed to be truly remarkable perceptions of intimacy, distance and their functions as they related to familial origins. The discovery of these principles of social organization, however, did not so much displace the more familiar ones of class, sovereignty, state, nationalism and competitions for power, but expanded that area of thought and theory concerned with social cohesion and stability. Authority as a singularly political pheno-menon was supplemented in anthropological analysis and observation by kinship even though the bulk of ethnographic data tended to confirm the generality and spatial diffuseness of political forms. (It is evident in even those "stateless societies" with which we are presently treating, village chiefs, elders, age-grade status holders, councils and associations were a frequent and clearly "political" phenomenon to these analysts.[75])

Notwithstanding, the presence of distinct variance from the political organization of society was an indication that the postulary dialogue had been prematurely closed. It would thus perhaps be useful at this point in our pursuit of understandability and the assessment of transferability to review in some detail the substance of one such discovery of the kinship-based system of socio-political organization.

The Ila-Tonga and the Social Authority of Kinship

The Ila-Tonga are a Bantu-speaking people living largely in the Mazambuka District of Zambia which was formerly known as Northern Rhodesia—a colonial appellation. The Tonga[76] were and are an agrarian people living in small, scattered villages whose economic technology centered around a system of shifting cultivation. Within the "boundaries" of Tongaland, the soil is, on the whole, poor with pockets of fertility around which the migration of Tonga has pivoted for as long as anyone can recall. It is estimated that eighty years ago, when the Tonga were first conscious of the colonial presence of the British, their number exceeded 60,000. Yet this estimate could have contained a possible error in the order of several thousands due perhaps to the fact that the Tonga had not developed the political and demographic patterns which are the usual predeterminants for such an accounting.

The Tonga are a people by kinship and descent (understood factually as well as fictionally), but by culture, language and residence, they are somewhat indistinguishable at their peripheries from other proximate peoples who do not consider themselves Tonga. Because they did not develop a centralized political organization and because they are in the "midst" of other peoples possessing an array of "tribal" and political apparatus, the Tonga are without networks of social and political machineries which would have made their demarcation convenient to those primarily familiar with European political history. The "known" boundaries of Tongaland thus showed some marked variance.

The Tonga, as has been mentioned, are a relatively mobile people but these migrations were of a greater complexity than the simple economic determinisms of earlier ethnographies[77], since causes could be as varied as poor soil, depleted soil, sanitation (the flight from insects or rotting huts), the maturation of young people and subsequent marriage, quarrels, or new friendships.

Mobility, thus, is manifested among the Tonga on several different levels: the village, household clusters, sibling fragments and/or individuals. Yet some patterns of movement have been more dominant than others. For example, as the Tonga are virilocal, women are more mobile than men—a survey[78] published in the early 1950s told of 36 percent of the men and 20 percent of the women living in their natal villages. The virilocal pattern however was itself made complex by the matrilineality of the Tonga in reckoning descent and its subsequent influences over the succession of social position and property inheritance. So the same investigator postulates that 37 percent of husbands have moved subsequently to their wives' villages. Thus any particular adult male might migrate with his family out of his native village to establish a new one; move to his wife's village; or move on his own. And any female might accompany her village, her father's household, or husband's household in such movements while, regardless of this, being expected to join her husband in establishing her own immediate household and family. It is this same pattern of theme and countertheme, yielding a multitude of competing, conflictual, demanding allegiances, loyalties and mores as consequence through Tonga metaphysics, economics and kinship, which forms the matrix of Tonga social stability. The social integration of the Tonga rests on the dynamic composition of their epistemological, metaphysical and identity systems. The establishment of a new household is of interest in the pursuit of this pattern.

There is a word among the Tonga, *mukowa*, which has been taken to signify a group of matrilineally-related kin or, more inclusively, a clan of matrilineal descent. There are thousands of the first class of *mukowa* but only fourteen of the second. When speaking of $mukowa_1$, all its members must be of the same $mukowa_2$, but not all members of $mukowa_2$ are in the same $mukowa_1$. Though Max Gluckman in his treatment[79] of the Tonga suggests that a means of distinguishing these *mukowas* is that the first "functions as a unit while the members of a clan never meet together,"[80] his clarification seems more in the order of gross simplification and distortion than illuminating reflection. He is asserting that the functionality of the "clan" must be judged by that element peculiarly characteristic of the smaller group: coming together, i.e. a face-to-face relationship. Once accepted, such an absurd proposition would be analogous to tearing away from each of us the ground of past and future, abandoning us all to the narrow precipice of what is NOW! Gluckman fails to record the significance that Tonga consciousness has for any interpretation of their social structure. He might have referred to Elizabeth Colson's "Ancestral Spirits and Social Structure Among the Plateau Tonga"[81] which appeared in a collection for which he wrote the foreword. Or he might have consulted either J. Jahn's *Muntu* (1961) or W. Abraham's *The Mind of Africa* (1963). Perhaps we have him at a disadvantage having had available John Mbiti's *African Religions and Philosophy*

(1969), but it appears extraordinarily ethnocentric for Gluckman not to have taken into account that generally the African, and certainly specifically the Tonga, presume the ubiquitous presence of visible, transparent and invisible kin (the dead are represented by the term for personal and "ancestral" spirits, *mizimu*). The following excerpts from Colson's essay indicate Gluckman's misunderstanding in asserting that "the members of a clan never meet together," a legacy perhaps of his legalistic training.

> The belief in the unity of the matrilineal group is reflected in the belief that they are all one before their *mizimu*. In defining membership within the group, the Tonga are apt to say: 'We name with the same names. Therefore we are one matrilineal group.' (p. 37)
>
> Since ancestors are not remembered, what then are the *mizimu*? Apart from the belief in their ritual powers, they are a set of names, which refer either to known members of the group who have died so recently that they are still remembered or they refer to a few people of a generation or so earlier who were sufficiently striking in some way so that tales about them are still current in the community. And lastly, of course, they are the names current among known members of the matrilineal group. . . .(p. 39)
>
> Although the Tonga see the matrilineal group as a unit held together by a mystical relationship involving a common set of *mizimu*, the *mizimu* are seldom invoked to enforce the obligations of kinship. (p. 40)
>
> [*mizimu*] are conceived to act rather like important men among the living, who attempt to attract followers from amongst their kinsmen without regard to their degree of relationship and in return give them some measure of support. (p. 41)[82]

Yet, one can sympathize with Gluckman's "instincts" for he is declaring that one can not call different things by the same name without inviting confusion, further, awkwardness, and insoluble difficulties. In the Tonga instance, one may presume that either this semantic axiom is not true, or that is is not accepted in its entirety without exception, or that *mukowa* like the fundaments of any epistemology is arbitrarily the same but different in its meaning(s). With some slight shove from Levi-Strauss converging with the validation of Karl Polanyi, I choose the latter.

Regardless, we have once again come across a phenomenon whose origins and development are alien to its equivalents in our own experience so we thrust at it with "parallels," or better said, distortions. Though Gluckman and others treat the phenomenon as distinct phenomena (spatiotemporal discreteness is opposed to spatiotemporal diffuseness), there exists nothing in these studies to suggest that the Tonga would agree with them. In point of fact, as Gluckman would read—in sociological terms—the most significance in his first "sense" of *mukowa*, the Tonga themselves argue that the larger, more incorporative "sense" is the most important conceptualization they possess. Gluckman repeats on their behalf that "they cannot conceive of a society without clans."[83] Yet he goes on to demur that "We may well ask why they so regard it when it never assembles as a group, and has not property and no ritual."[84] The response which seems to satisfy him is in actuality a tautology which takes the form that clan-*mukowa* are of permanent significance because they are the most persistent and enduring elements of Tonga society. The Tonga thus appear to have continued their metaphysical stroll quite comfortably beyond the borders of our never-never land. On one level, then, this characteristic of *mukowa* is suggestive in a slight fashion of the Tonga capacity for constructing complements of conflict and solidarity.

On the second level, that of behavioral mores and patterns, *mukowa* presents a much more concretized example of this skill. At this level, Gluckman's necessarily lengthy description will suffice:

> . . .a man must be married to be ritually independent in the sense of having a shrine at which he can approach the spirits that control his destiny: if his wife dies, or they are divorced, he loses this privilege. An unmarried man is in religious belief incomplete, while a woman can make offerings from the beer she brews.
>
> The family household is a group of great importance, since in it children are born and reared, and its members co-operate in productive activities and consume the produce together. But in it there is a meeting of the interests of a whole series of groups: 1. the husband and his *mukowa* own the hut, and his *mukowa* fellows will inherit its goods when he dies. They should visit the household's members when they are ill, should come to mourn at deaths, should help with the marriage-payments of its members and with paying the husband's fines and damages, should purify his wife if he dies and find another man to inherit his position—and only marriage, be it noted, enables him to

197

establish an inheritable position. In the past, his *mukowa* also helped him to enforce his claims and avenged wrongs done to him. 2. The wife's *mukowa* performed the same duties for her, and for her children who belonged to them, not to their husband's *mukowa*. 3. The *mukowa* of the husband's father's mother and also of the wife's father's mother, to neither of which they belonged, also had important duties. This extension of duties might proceed to the husband's father's father's mother's *mukowa* and the wife's father's father's mother's *mukowa*. . . . Intermarriage between the *mukowa,* which has to be spread widely by the rules prohibiting marriage, thus compels a wide spread of links of this kind; and so long as people believe that their fortunes and misfortunes, and those of their children, depend on the spirits of various groups, they are forced into relationships of dependence with a whole series of these groups.[85]

And additionally because the Tonga, though aware of them, have no formalized ranking of descent and kinship in their *mukowas* and believe it to be "bad manners" to formulate such rankings, the guardians of the gates of kin and relatedness are without consistency in their vigilance:

In result, any individual who can establish a claim of any kind to a member of the *mukowa*, can be absorbed and treated as if he or she were a close relative, through uterine links, of all other members. A man establishes this claim by practical activity, such as helping at funerals, contributing to the marriage-payments made by men of the *mukowa*, helping pay fines and damages—and in the end he will be helped in turn and share in the *mukowa*'s marriage-payments coming in from the mating of its women and in inheritances of the property of members which are distributed at their deaths.[86]

The Principle of Incompleteness

To the discriminating eye, important threads of the tapestry of a society can already be discerned. By ingenuous design, accident, experience and whatever other processees and machinations are decisive to the evolution of a social mesh, the Tonga have come into possession of an understanding of human organization which gives little prominance to the familiars of public-private, autonomy-subject, secret-shared, interest-exclusion oppositions. Each element of Tonga consciousness embraces another to secure its "own" vitality—a game of life of running, jumping, spinning for a thousand-headed, millipede beast whose members would each, if severed, be unfit to survive. But before proceeding with the Tonga in ethnographic terms, let us for a moment consider a significance of words and meanings we might attach to Tonga thought and belief. For a moment, let us stand back for that Nietzsche who stood for the savage, monstrous monument of individualism whose strength was in its serene aloneness.

If, in some spiteful play, one were compelled by some demon or god to choose a transgression against Nietzsche so profound and fundamental to his temperament and intention as to break apart the ground upon which his philosophy stood, one could do no better than this: a society which has woven into its matrix for the purpose of suspending and neutralizing those forces antithetic to individual autonomy, the constructed reality that *all are equally incomplete.* A logic is being jousted here. Is it not so that the emergence of power as the instrument of certainty in human organization is seen by many[87] to be the *consequence of* and *response to* the circumstances of inequality and sensed social entropy? Is it not so that individual autonomy, rare enough in the first condition and imperiled by the second, is in the final construction made foreign? And does not, logically, even autonomy require for its nurturance a hothouse of certitude similar to that required for the evolution of power—autonomy being to a degree a variant of power?

Then the principle of incompleteness—the absence of discrete organistic integrity, if it were to occupy in a metaphysics the place of inequality in political philosophy, would bring to human society a paradigm subversive to political authority as the arche-typical resolution, as the prescription for order.

The recognition of a consciousness which contains a metaphysics of the relatedness of things has occurred from time to time in Western thought. This recognition has been embodied in concepts which inevitably have been thought to have either a transitional function for the political or an antagonistic relationship to it. Among the more recent examples to be found in Western literature are the "libidinal" ties Freud believed existed between the individual, the leader and other members of the group—the groups in question being the Church, the

Army and the crowd (*Group Psychology and the Analysis of the Ego*); the absolute authoritarianism of the revolutionary mass in the act of destroying the State which Marx, Engels, and Lenin recognized and accepted (*The Alliance of Socialist Democracy and the Working Men's Association; The State and Revolution*); the charismatic relationship between followers, and followers and the charismatic figure that Weber postulated (*The Theory of Social and Economic Organization*); the instinct of mutual aid developing into a stage of ethical morality foreseen by Kropotkin (*Ethics: Origin and Development*); and the collective will, the Jacobinism of Gramsci's *condottiere* (*The Modern Prince*).

In each of these formulations, there was a kind of spontaneity, an explosive moment of combination, which culminated an historical and social process. Each of these constructions was thus associated with a situation of crisis or social fragmentation. Additionally, to the degree to which they could be described as occurring within a political society, they were either apolitical in the sense of taking place outside of political relationships (Freud, Kropotkin), or antipolitical—a transitional phase or transformational process between political orders (Weber and the Marxists). As such, they were either fundamentally antithetical to political order or fundamentally subversive of political order. They were its negation.

These examples present instances in which one can begin to recognize the impact which an authority like that of the Tonga might have on political authority. At the immediate level of recognition, it would dismantle that authority, replacing it, perhaps, with an authority which identified order and responsibility in terms of the indivisibility of things. In these terms, there might be discovered a more powerful image of the species-being than was posited in Hegel's philosophy of history or Marx's historical materialism. The problem of alienation, to which to some degree both of the latter systems were addressed, must be understood to be an epistemological question. That is to say that separation can only be understood in its own terms—given the duality of subject-object. Consequently, it is immaterial what system is employed to reconcile it, it persists by way of consciousness. J.G.A. Pocock came to this conclusion in his discussion of what he called "romantic politics:" ". . .this posture is not merely transient or recurrent but integrally and existentially part of the human condition. . .alienation and revolution as human norms.''[88]

However, a testament to the corrosiveness of this metaphysics of complementarity has also been witnessed in the penetration of Western social thought by psychoanalytic metaphor and the concepts of development theory in ego psychology. As political science, sociology and economics (and their progeny in schools of history) have evolved into scientism—the progression of empiricism, analyticism, and quantitativism from approach to ideology—their probings into the nature of human organization have become situation-specific to a particular case of that organization: Western industrialized society, and have settled down into a tangential, self-indulging universe of queries and data indices. And as they have done so they have sought the measure and dimensions of reality by positing for every particle in their systems an existence exorcised from the presence of any other thing: reification. So it followed that when Freud wrote *das Es* (Id) and suggested—if not to himself then to so many others—that he meant *all* of it (phylogenetic history), when the psychoanalysts said "identity" and suggested a dynamic complementarity, they became, ironically, "reductionists." Eric Erikson is one of the few in the field of "American" ego-psychology who remembers the ontological character of one of the founding myths of psychoanalysis:

> But who or what is the counterplayer of the ego? First, of course, the id and the superego, and then, so theory says, the "environment." The first two are awkward terms in English, which does not cultivate the academic-mythical grandeur of German, where *"das Es"* or *"das Ueber-Ich"* are never thinglike entities, but demonic and primal givens.[89]

(It is, of course, a paradox for the behavioral sciences that atomistic theories of physics—the penultimate of reductionists in the physical sciences—have also declared that, at the base, all material and form-variants are interchangeable and characterizable only by their absence of something.[90]

Notwithstanding its vulnerability, we have glimpsed an authority of organization which is dissimilar to political authority, and with a different consciousness we can reflect on certain questions of political theory which we have looked at earlier (see specifically chapters 1-3). Is power a rational-like adjustment, i.e. an adjustment informed by the mythology of the political, to inherent disadvantages in the organization of human beings, or is it fundamentally irrational, the consequence of what men believe to be so? Is power a variant of the political process, which is itself a complement to the "infant" nature of mankind, or is it the insurer of that infancy proceeding out of historical moments of crises and collective weakness? Or is it now, for whatever its origins might be, quite irrelevant to human development as survival?

As we turn to another aspect of Tonga solidarity and integration, the suggestion of a trunk of responses to these questions emerges. At the same time, the conceptual and methodological paradigms of Western social science seem to recede further from relevance. Their staple of universal laws resemble more and more a coincident or the correspondence of the study and projection of one epic phenomenon: the history and development of Western institutions. Western social thought is not merely ethnocentric, but epistemocentric as well.

The Instruction of the Tonga Jokester

Among the Tonga, in keeping with their awareness of and sensitivity to the principle of incompleteness, shame rather than guilt is the fence through which a community expresses its disapproval of acts counter to mores and transgressing morality.[91] The specific instrument for precipitating shame is what anthropologists have termed the "joke"—a formalized and deliberate verbal antagonism whose conscious construction is bared to the "joker's" antagonist in order to emphasize the absurdity of the antagonism while ministering, on another level, to a real conflict which is frightful and unacceptable to either party.

Among most peoples, but to somewhat varying degrees, the joker and his "victim" are possessors of social roles which contain elements of ambivalence (as for example between wife and mother-in-law in the nuclear family of contemporary Anglo-Saxon society). The joker and his partner if not for this pecking dyad might otherwise be understood to be inevitable rivals since one survives on what he or she has managed to sequester from the other "rightful" claimant. The joking relationship in being highly formalized, in prescribing the identity of joking pairs as well as the proper interchange code, protect the exchange from becoming violent while relieving it of the underlying tension.

Yet in some societies the relationship has even further functions. Among the Tonga (and as well the Cheyenne, Crow, Tsonga and Tallensi[92]), it is the estrangement itself which is the vehicle for maintaining the continuity of mores and moral integrity among members of the clan-*mukowa*:

> Tonga stress the importance of the whole web of joking relationships between the clans, for in practice each clan is linked with a number of other clans. Each clan can call on its clan-joking partners in a number of specific situations. . .If we survey these duties, we see that the clan-jokers are concerned with morality, with care for property, with food, with maintaining the rules of exogamy that spin the network of kinship ties, with symbolizing all kinship, with preserving life, with burial of the ill-omened dead, and with urging life despite death. . . .The social interest in life, in property, in morality, in kinship, and in intermarriage of 'enemies', is thus attached to the only enduring groups of Tonga society.[93]

As Gluckman goes on to review the role of the court jester in Tudor England, 19th-century Zululand and other South African Bantu-speakers, I am also reminded of Erikson's portrait of Mahatma Gandhi as sly jokester to his English colonials. What stands out in these instances is an element which Gluckman captures succinctly:

> Beyond a certain point, for each clan, there comes an end to the range of friends, and here there are clans who are friends of one's friends but also friends of one's enemies. These are 'clan-jokers'. . .who are almost your enemies—some of them are the people who can exercise the strongest 'moral coercion' (Fortes) over you. . .the person who emphasizes these values is a stranger, someone from outside of the normal run of activity in which a man engages. I use 'stranger' here to cover persons who are outside the particular type of relationships involved in a specific situation. Here again we are dealing with a very common occurrence frequently institutionalized: the manner in which 'strangers' are called in, or enter, to solve internal crises in the life of a group.[94]

Thus the functions of the stranger in Tonga social philosophy contrast sharply with that emerging out of Western social and political theory where the stranger *as a threat* induces as response new forces of social solidarity and cohesion and renewal of ties in the threatened community. In the Tonga case, at least one case among politically uncentralized peoples if not typical, the "stranger," the "enemy" is responsible for, and has the obligation to demand that the member reintegrate into the community.

Conjunction and disjunction merely characterized by *mukowa* and the pattern of joking relationships are elements of Tonga society which demonstrate the principle upon which that society proceeded. To be sure, that principle's significance is much more extensive institutionally than presented here, it is thematic:

> I have had to analyse Tonga social organization in detail, though still over-simplifying, to show how societies, the smaller social groups, derive their integration from the divided allegiances of their members. Out of the interweaving of relationships, all established by custom and validated by mystical beliefs, emerges what social cohesion there is around the *mukowa,* the clans with their joking partners, and the ephemeral rain-shrines which give fixed points of reference.[95]

Distinct from the legacy of anarchy and those elements it shares with the presumptions of Western political thought, this is the receipt of a social philosophy which does not proceed from the basis of a political system or State as fundamental authority. It is a perspective which is compelling as an authentic alternative, conceptually and methodologically.

The principle of inequality concludes in the vision of society as a bounded, discrete system. Inequality logically proceeds to the presumption of just (skills) and unjust (tradition in anachronistic dysfunction) hierarchies or stratifications which maintain themselves by the set articulation of roles which is a dynamic order or system. The roles are equilibrated to each other, suggesting the possibility of missed articulation, or breakdown, or disequilibrium. Entropy is a description of a state of randomness or lack of order which suggests, for perhaps no stronger reason than an intellectual relief, its counter and referent phenomenon: order; or as one would describe it among dynamic elements, system (again). Whether one's basic conceptual model of development is mechanistic or organistic, the elements peculiar to this table of organization—inequality, equilibrium, system, boundaries, entropy—exists in a single analytical plane. And that plane is ultimately shored by its own sense of that which is rational—substantively expressed mathematically as that which "adds up"—so dominant that even the irrational is rationalized.[96]

On the other hand the anthropological materials with which we have been concerned contain an opposite truth. Here we find—in the progress of our own perceptions—an exchange of metaphysical functional emphasis for analytical structural-functionalism. The principle of incompleteness yields a word picture of complementarity which resists a philosophy of numbers which presupposes those numbers to be precise expressions of reality. Political authority is evaded by a psychological authority based in kinship. The establishment of power is circumvented by intentionality—the will and the need to remain one with all. This is much more than the "mutual aid" of Kropotkin whose theoretical work came closest to it among those committed to economic authority. It goes much beyond his rational or historical progression from mutual aid as an instinct proceeding to an ethic of justice and finally to morality, for it does not even entertain, epistemologically, the presumption of the individual or the possible antagonism of interests between individual and community. This was an antagonism which Kropotkin consciously had to resolve by posing evolutionary dynamics and contradictions in instincts to aggrandizement and instincts to reciprocity. What I am arguing is that the Tonga positivity is an anthropological critique of social order as political order as rational order. The Tonga are not an alternative but a negation (one could say a negation by parrallax). They are a negation in the mind of the analyst, a *perceptual* and *conceptual* negation, not a *historical* one. In developing an epistemology based on a metaphysics of kinship, the Tonga, for one, have preserved a mythology which is transferable and translatable into a variety of social and historical milieu. It is a mythology whose primeval presumptions are constantly referred to in the "brotherhoods" and "sisterhoods" which characterizes the movements of oppressed peoples from the most highly industrialized to the most primitive of contexts.

But one must be careful with the notion of transferability. Transferability is a formal proposition. Social movement, that is praxis, does not beg the question of transferability but it is based on a presumption which precludes the conceptualization of change as exchange: the dialectical development of society. Transference is a concept tied to the appearance of things. It is not possible to equate the experiences of reality of different cultures. Consciousness of reality is formed in the dialectic between existential reality and epistemological systems.

The singular significance of the mythology, one which is yet to fully be understood, is that it is, at one and the same time, a revolutionary instrument and a post-revolutionary vision. It is capable not merely of cohering a political challenge to political authority as an epistemology and as a system of social order, but more importantly, projects an alternative epistemology and a postrevolutionary system of integration.

Our immediate questions appear now to have been responded to for we have found another people's way intelligible, successful and tentatively acceptable to the degree that what has been done has at its base conceptions, presumptions and beliefs. In short, we have recognized a social ideology.

CHAPTER VI

Conclusion

In these few pages, what I have attempted is deceptively simple. It was simple because at one level it had more to do with demonstration than conceptualization. As demonstration it was the identification of something (order) which had to be seen for what it is not, to be believed. It pointed to a paradigm of society both obscured and reinforced by Western epistemology. What was recognized was a paradigm of order complemented by an epistemology which had order as a base to its metaphysics. This is the reason the demonstration on another level was deceptive: it substituted concept for empirical proposition. In the context of thinking about this paradigm and its relationship to order, one might usefully apply Pocock's statement on the paradigmatic content of language:

> It follows, not only that there is always more implicit in the language we use than we realize—we know what we say, but know not what we may be saying—but that in using a socio-political language at all, we commit ourselves to a tissue of political implications, to a variety of political functionings, and to the recommendation of a variety of authoritative structures, greater than we can critically distinguish at any one moment. . . . To speak of a thing at all *is* to imply the possibility of its acceptance.[1]

I tried to demonstrate that within Western social and conceptual history, a variety of ontological identities existed. There have been brought into realization complexes of understandings concerned with the natures of the relationship between things. This demonstration

207

was meant to expose the possibility and actuality that orthodox Western thought was neither universal nor coherent. I meant to demonstrate that all social and political theories possess this mixed character, specifically all social theories which are themselves expressions of the presumption of the political as the basis of order and authority. At that point the task became conceptual.

In the West there have been, as there presumably still are, people who have conceptualized the ontological foundations of their society and experiences in ways fundamentally alien to the ways which have become orthodox. They do not see, feel or believe what they "should." But these conceptualizations are not truly alien for the following reasons.

Some forms of Western consciousness are the persistence of pre-scientific, dualistic metaphysics. They are most frequently identified by the terms mysticism and mythology. Their epistemologies and metaphysics are root elements in Western thought. When we are occupied with concepts, analytical methods, logics, etc., sometimes we discover these "archaic" forms are still conscious and vital in the mainstream of thought, e.g. dialectics. But sometimes this is not the case. More frequently, it appears, myth, mysticism and metaphysics are unconscious but vital.

Yet consciousness is not merely generated by the persistent force of concepts. Historical and objective factors play parts in the development of consciousness. New and unexpected events are added to the constellation of things to be known. These new events do not merely create space in epistemologies where words had formerly never gone. They are not merely additions, but assume a dialectical relationship to that which preceded them.

The results of these processes can be very different. A society might be best understood as a mix of peoples, each possessing distinct consciousness. That is to say that human history may be thought of as the "history" of tribes and peoples.

On the other hand, what is recognized as a universal and consistent consciousness in the society may be a fragile mix of themes and integrations. These social legends, instructions, etc., have been extracted from the constituent groups of that society and have contributed to the establishment of a widely-received ideology. It consists of systems which are generated from social and historical particularities and which bear, borrowing from Wittgenstein, family resemblances to each other. In social, that is synthetic terms, ideological sets co-mingle through sympathy and sentiment: the sociological manifestations of family resemblances. But as such an ideology is often contradictory, there is for some few more certainty and coherence in older understandings.

Societies, then, can consist of and contain quite different epistemologies. These epistemologies appear subject to history, structure and institutions.

Presuming this, I have tried to demonstrate further that the true or, alternatively, *significant* character of social organization is still problematic. It is problematic, that is, if one systematically peruses the nature of the constructs with which or through which are arranged one's insights into social theory. Such an investigation reveals contradictions.

Specific to Western social thought, we have come to perceive *things* extracted from the context of their social and historical processes, or in their object-fixity.[2] Through this mode of recognition, the apparent loci of our lives is best defended and/or conserved. A similar defense might be found in the determined way that the bulk of 17th- and 18th-centuries European intelligentsia protected "scripture" from the contradictions and heresies of the modernists posing as anatomists, astronomers, geologists and naturalists.[3] For these defenders, too, the world had an immutable, definable character.

One consequence of this doubly useful conservatism is that the dislocations and horrors of human society continue to be mistakenly approached. As the dynamics of these problems are mis-identified, their resolutions are mis-informed.

We recognize as immutable object-phonomena those dynamics whose process is no longer accessible because of the presumptions we have accumulated about the nature of things. Such a practice is that which the historicist in Hegel described as "monochrome formalism", "monotonous and abstract universality."[4] For Marx, this same practice was similarly "this process of objectification which appears in fact as a process of alienation. . . ."[5]

Thus, in general, the social sciences as taught and applied in

Western experience, prepare the intelligence for formal, structural ontology, eschewing metaphysics and transformation as well as their implications for social and/or historical understanding.

Yet, this culture of knowledge and its sociology of knowledge, are not without contradiction, not without challenge and negation. Systems of conceptualization alternative to the familiar, or as it is presented, the rational, continually do arise. Responses to such systems, of course, are according to their recognizability in the terms of the resident paradigms or epistemologies. They are, therefore, on occasion ignored and/or dismissed, and on other occasions, may reap more active forms of rejection: anger, ridicule, suppression, etc. Nevertheless, the culture of knowledge, in contradiction to appearance, is fundamentally unstable, having not as yet in any text formed a constellation of world knowledge which may be the basis for general human development.

As a consequence, this instability consisting of penetrations; degenerations and generations; revitalizations of idea-systems, is continuous. It results in at least disjunctive epistemological systems, and at worst, the ideological systems Kuhn described as "normal science." The former process, sometimes in the form of mixed paradigms, is tantamount to change as adaptation; the latter to change as crisis. Each occur within the same system or culture, at some times synchronously but not coterminously.

The distinction between adaptation and crisis is in the relationship—the possibilities of relationships—that constructs of reality have for "discovered" reality. Consequent to this conjunction, adaptation and crisis have to do with the *degree* of reformulation which follows. Mixing paradigms, the first degree, is a description of a response in which no fundamental penetration of the structure of knowledge has occurred. Normal science, the critical degree, is a description of precisely that penetration.

In an historical situation, the theocratic feudal order of 16th- and 17th-centuries Europe may be described as having adapted to it an economic system characterized by redistribution and reciprocity, but was subsequently transformed by a mercantilism motivated in a crisis for the feudal structure, mobilizing the proto-bureaucratic state to respond to the disturbance of its patterns of symmetry and its principles of social reciprocity and redistribution. The result was the "market society."

> Instead of economy being embedded in social relations, social relations are embedded in the economic system. The vital importance of the economic factor to the existence of society precludes any other result. For once the economic system is organized in separate institutions, based on specific motives and conferring a special status, society must be shaped in such a manner as to allow that system to function according to its own laws. This is the meaning of the familiar assertion that a market economy can function only in a market society.[6]

At other times, the process is in sequence, e.g. adaptation leading to crisis to subsequent new forms of adaptation. Still at other times, the process has leap-frogged from one sphere to others causing turbulences whose intensities are determined by the cumulative states of the second- or third-order spheres. These processes of trans-formations were contained in the notion of the dialectical in Hegel's science of logic: the negation of the negation. Steady-state systems of knowledge are, as such, convenient illusions.

In language and subsets of language, however, we possess ontological preservatives—that is, structures which serve to conserve aspects of reality in the forms of epistemologies and ideologies. We presume that through language, we feel out and identify the object-ness of that order to which we are a part, whether it be of material or essential quality. But clearly, language and languages are paradigms, and as such they are text which bring subject and object into "conditions of possibility": realization. By employing language to identify what is outside our selves, we indicate as well the nature of alienation peculiar to our text.

Predictably, the relationships between such understanding and social institutions are tautological rather than dialectical. In our social experience, we demonstrate to ourselves, over and over again, in the most rigorously "objective" ways, what we have been saying, what we have been thinking. Thus the appearance of authenticity in the way we understand is attributable to the language by which we identify reality, the activity in which we engage in this empirical reality and the "reactivity" we experience as response-confirmation.

The attentive care through which we become tolerable social beings is transformed into other forms of strain, that is "domesticated" forms of strain: aesthetic fetish, e.g. the symmetry of the world, its "pairness" or its duality; rationalistic fetish, e.g. latent-manifest or patterned variables; philosophic fetish, e.g. existentialism, positivism, and the like. Counterforms lose their capacities to generate anxiety as they recede from consciousness, from the range of accessibility.

Thus language as grammar, syntax, vocabulary, myth and metaphor, impresses meanings which bind the appearance of things, the ordering of things as well as the metaphysical grounding of things.

It is for these reasons, we must begin to understand the severe gravity of Levi-Strauss' attempt to subvert language, his attempt to force language back onto itself, his attempt to force language to say, and thus reveal, what it was never possible for it to say. Levi-Strauss has attempted to deform language by imposing on it the "grammar" of music, a grammar which he is convinced transcends, that is fails to be restricted by the "topological constants" of mind-structure. This subversion of language is Levi-Strauss' considered response to Kant's antimonies. It is, as well, Levi-Strauss' critique of the German Critical Philosophy's idealistic and materialistic dialectics.

It would be as if he were saying that if the structures of the human mind unavoidably create in language paradoxical constructions of reality then the logical mind must be circumvented through the subversion of its reflexive and authoritative instrument. Language must be confronted by a construction of reality or the *suggestion* of a construction of reality whose base is metaphysically illogical.

It is not "language" which Levi-Strauss is treating with a vengeance but the historicity of a civil society[7] which is founded on the twisted social meanderings of an alienated sub-order, a sub-order alienated from itself and its universe: the self-subsisting positivity. This language option is the expressive form of a human consciousness which was made to set and certify human society apart from all other systems.

It becomes possible then through theory to set "cultures" truly against themselves, apart from the contained contradiction of derived negations. By juxtaposing noncommensurable sets of symbols, crises of metaphysics are accomplished, characterized by consciousness of the "deep structures" (Chomsky) or "single ideas" (Boaz) which are the base of cognitive and emotive systems. Just as Habermas would suggest,[8] in treating deformity of language as the most profound reaction of the human psyche in crises, public language, that is coherence and paradigm, is thus dissolved as the nexus for social organization. It is not organization itself which is challenged, for it is legitimated by anthropomorphic requirements, but it is the authorization of that organization.

I have briefly argued elsewhere[9] that being historically and conceptually contexturalized by liberal thought, Western anarchist theory could not accomplish this juxtaposition as it was a contained contradiction (some Marxists would say, opposition). It bore a family resemblance to the tradition it was designed to subvert. This form of anarchism: anti-state, liberal anarchism,[10] was bounded by presumptions and values which were shared with the sentiment authorizing its contemporary forms of civil and political society. But by compelling that idea of anarchism generated by that same authority beyond its tolerance, that is beyond the historical and anthropolitical integument of that authority, such a juxtaposition of non-commensurables might be accomplished.

The purpose of the Tonga materials was to turn the language back onto itself by taking a statement of that language, anarchism, a contained opposition, and forcing it into the attempt at realizing a social order phenomenologically alien to it.

. . .the general problem of all ethnology is in fact that of the relations (of continuity or discontinuity) between nature and culture. But in this mode of questioning, the problem of history is found to have been reversed: for it then becomes a matter of determining, according to the symbolic systems employed, according to the prescribed rules, according to the functional norms chosen and laid down, what sort of historical development each culture is susceptible of; it is seeking to re-apprehend, in its very roots, the mode of historicity that may occur within that culture, and the reasons why its history must inevitably be cumulative or circular, progressive or subjected to regulating fluctuations, capable of spontaneous adjustments or subject to crises. . .

Ethnology, like psychoanalysis, questions not man himself, as he appears in the human sciences, but the region that makes possible knowledge about man in general. . . .[11]

The anarchism of the mutualist, the collectivist, the individualist, the syndicalist, bears only a formal resemblance to the anarchism of the Tonga (and contra-doxically, to the apolitical organization of the 19th-century Jura craft workers, and Siberian and French peasantries). One is *not* the expression of the other in a technologically different context. They are each manifestations of different orderings of things, distinctly different epistemologies or paradigms—that is, languages. They bear a superficial *familiarity,* but at the phenomeno-logical level, no *familiality.*

Thus, we can come to recognize that Western anarchism was a political expression generated against the political, a contradiction in the literal and logical meanings of the term. As such, this contra-diction was a condition of possibility for militant Marxism, that is for the ideology that the state (proletarian) must be used to destroy the state (either as a bourgeois instrument or its reification) and, furthermore, that it is in the very nature of the bourgeois state to anticipate and generate its own destruction. As well, it could be anticipated, or could have been anticipated without the support of retrospection, that such an anarchism because it was a political movement in contradiction to itself would develop forms of terrorism. That is to argue that, over and above those dynamics which have been most conveniently encompassed by clinical, inflation-of-authority and frustration theories, but analytically consistent with them, the gener-ation into acts of terror by elements of European lower and middle classes influenced by the idea of anarchism are manifestations of the inherent contradiction within the idea itself.

It was not that the Western notion of anarchism was naive or utopian, but that—as Marx ironically recognized and argued without referring himself to the roots of his own thought in anarchism—it was an ideology. It was a form of anarchism generated from bourgeois political society.

Marx, presumably, sincerely believed anarchism was a reactionary ideology of a specific class, and as such remained unconscious of its more profound roots in his *civilization.*[12] Once he had made the former identification, lumping Stirner and Proudhon with Bakunin, he could unambiguously polemicize against the dynamic which posed an intellectual, political and organizational threat to his interests and purposes. But in so doing, he was using an analytical procedure which disingenuously distinguished him from the heroic dialectician resurrected by Lukacs and Marcuse.

The idea of anarchism which evolved in Western experience by the 19th century was meaningless without authority being understood as power. The general language or dominant paradigm of Western civil society (that is dominating the intercourse whose purpose was to develop a social theory) was enmeshed with that particular form of social authority which was recognized in political order. The expression of anarchism which was a revolt against the authority of the secular order was forged in the armory of that authority's ideological weaponry.

Reason (Godwin), trade association (Proudhon), the ego (Stirner), the self-subsisting village group (Kropotkin), all in one way or another the expression of principles which were the consciousness of the new class order of things, were the "alternatives" of this revolt. It was a revolt against the State, to be sure, but not so much because it was a structure whose social function was alien but because it was redundant. Of these spokesmen, only Kropotkin was certain that it was indeed alien. The political order for the others as an order of human groups was already present in the form of institutions and structures which had no explicit political character. Political freedom, which Marx had already recognized as a false emancipation,[13] was to be constructed without the apparatus of the State, in contradistinction to it.

As historically dispersed observers of the developing bourgeois state, these men reacted to different manifestations of the fundamental character of that State: to the violence of its inception; to the alienation of man from man and man from nature; to the deception of liberty grounding utilitarian theory; and to the debasement and terror which resulted from the necessary apparatus of violence and coercion. They reacted by rearranging the *ideas* of that bourgeois society: reason, scientism, interests, the self, the group as an economic unity, etc., not by subverting them.

The face of things which was a reflection of the objectivation that Marx, Michel Foucault, Karl Polanyi and Lukacs so incisively identified, dominated, too, as a paradigm the thought of these 19th-

215

century anti-statists. Just as this paradox was part of the terror of Nechayev, Narodnaya Volya, Pallas, Santiago Salvador, Gallo, Vailliant, Ravachol, Czolgosz, Berkman and the thousands of their comrades, it too was part of the international organized terror of *World War I* to which Kropotkin would lend his name.

Thus the anarchisms[14] *as articulated* in the Western tradition of anarchism were not a true opposition but, instead, an analytically-consistent alternative. It was an alternative *of* the social order, not *to* it. It did not contradict the language of civil society but like Marxism, more specifically the vulgar Marxism represented by the economism of the late 19th-century German Social Democrats, was evidence of the search for a more rational expression of the social vision contained in that language. Of Marxism, Foucault has written a characterization of its placement which is quite as applicable to anarchism:

> At the deepest level of Western knowledge, Marxism introduced no real discontinuity; it found its place without difficulty, as a full, quiet, comfortable and, goodness knows, satisfying form for a time (its own), within an epistemological arrangement that welcomed it gladly (since it was this arrangement that was in fact making room for it) and that it, in return, had no intention of disturbing and, above all, no power to modify, even one jot, since it rested entirely upon it. Marxism exists in nineteenth-century thought like a fish in water: that is, it is unable to breathe anywhere else. Though it is in opposition to the 'bourgeois' theories of economics, and though this opposition leads it to use the project of a radical reversal of History as a weapon against them, that conflict and that project nevertheless have as their condition of possibility, not the reworking of all History, but an event that any archaeology can situate with precision, and that prescribed simultaneously, and according to the same mode, both nineteenth-century bourgeois economics and 19th century revolutionary economics.[15]

Yet the impulse of anarchism was a significant one. It made it possible to question the fundamental pattern of knowledge which evolved into those human sciences of which political science is a subset and the order of things of which political order is an historical and conceptual expression. No real matter how weakly, anarchism suggested that political order and its investigation were contingent, historical phenomena unsanctioned by anthropomorphic necessity or inevitability. Political order could thus be understood as the politicization of order; the imposition of a specific, positive and historical character onto a most pervasive metaphor for human existence. Such a character could then become for a period—and precisely that period that Marx identifies as pre-history—a preoccupation, in psychoanalytical terms, a collective neurosis, or construct-specific, a paradigm.

For whatever secret discomforts gave motive to the discussion in this essay, it is these minimal criticisms through which a subversive methodology and articulation were achieved. I have suggested that despite its antiquity (which has too often been a concealment), despite its institutional and structural facades, and its ideologues, the notion of the political order is a mythology. But because of these same aspects, its representations, the fundamental insubstantiation of the political order of things has continued unrecognized in any persistent way to human consciousness. By way of the "subversive methodologies:" psychoanalysis, ethnology, and linguistics,[16] I have attempted to reconstruct the reasons for and the means through which such a circumstance could come into being—in a particular case. More precisely, this essay is an outline for such a reconstruction.

I agree with Weber that political leadership is the key and have as such given it the place of the founding myth in this mythology. Obviously, this "agreement" with Weber is tendentious since it has been argued here that his understanding of the phenomenon, specific to charismatic leadership and its relationship to charismatic authority and in general to the authority of the political, was distorted by his consistency with the mythology in question.

I have attempted to demonstrate that in the pursuit of understanding of the political, there has occurred an unprogressive dialectic or more precisely a dialectic whose movement could be characterized as circular, transversing the itinerary of what Kuhn once described as normal science, i.e. puzzle-solving. This problematic has resulted in work which encompasses increasingly simpler empirical propositions while employing increasingly more complex instrumentations and techniques. Why this has been so is more complex than the usual reading of Marx, Freud, Lukacs, Foucault, Levi-Strauss, Nisbet and Gouldner[17] would suggest. But the reasons are there subject to the sympathetic (that is sympathies both mutual and to the object:consciousness) touch of their structuralisms for revelation.

By identifying the concept of political order *as a mythology*, I do not intend to argue that because it is, it is of no use, for such a presumption would ultimately contradict the fundamental relationship which is human knowledge; that is the relationship between existential consciousness and truth systems. To the contrary, what I mean to say is that as a myth, as the dominating myth of our consciousness of being together, it is contingent and therefore replaceable. As such there are two uses, each in its own way anti-political, to which it must be applied.

The first application is the utilization of the political to defend ourselves from the destructive objectivation of the myth: the apparatuses of repression and control. This is the activity which Pocock identifies with what he terms "romantic man:"

> . . .he characteristically places himself at that moment in time in which the existing institutions of self-creation are seen as no longer creating or even expressing the self. . .and therefore as malignantly hostile to the self's authenticity. . . . Romantic man tends to assume that his identity requires to be asserted or discovered, and that hostile agencies are operating to thrust an identity not his own upon him; his political action is revolutionary, a transformation of the self, a reconstruction of the conditions under which selves are to be created, and an engagement in the presumed self-creations of others.[18]

Pocock does not trust this commitment, but despite that, he puts the case forward succinctly.

The second application, coterminous with the resistence which is the first, is to subvert that way of realizing ourselves.

I believe the success of both ultimately rests on our ability to hold onto the consciousness that the political is an historical, one temporarily convenient, illusion.

Notes

Introduction

1. For the antipolitical tradition, see Wayne A. R. Leys' "Was Plato Non-Political?" and "An Afterthought," and F. E. Sparshott's "Plato as Anti-Political Thinker" in Gregory Vlastos (ed.), *Plato*, Vo. II, Anchor Books, Doubleday and Company, Inc., New York, 1971. Also of interest is Stanley Diamond's "The Rule of Law Versus the Order of Custom" in Robert Paul Wolff (ed.), *The Rule of Law*, Simon and Schuster, New York, 1971; and Leonard Krieger's "Power and Responsibility: The Historical Assumptions" in Leonard Kriegar and Fritz Stern, (eds.), *The Responsibility of Power*, Anchor Books, Doubleday and Company, Inc., New York, 1969.

2. T. H. Green, *Principles of Political Obligation,* Ann Arbor Paperbacks, Ann Arbor, 1967, p. 122.

3. Karl Marx, "On the Jewish Question" in Robert Tucker, (ed.) *The Marx-Engels Reader,* W. W. Norton and Company, Inc., New York, 1972, p. 30.

4. Quote taken from David Mitrany's *Marx Against the Peasant,* University of North Carolina Press, 1951, p. 48. Mitrany also directs our attention to an interesting passage found in Martin Buber's *Paths in Utopia,* (1949), p. 83: "From this we can see with the greatest clarity what it is that connects Marx with 'Utopian' Socialism: the will to supersede the political principle by the social principle, and what divided him from it: his opinion that this supersession can be effected by exclusively political means—hence by way of sheer suicide, so to speak, on the part of the political principle." Ibid., p. 224.

5. Stanley Diamond, "Rule of Law," p. 136.

6. See Stephen Pepper's *World Hypothesis*, University of California Press, Berkeley, 1966.

7. Michel Foucault, *The Order of Things*, Tavistock Publications, London, 1970, p. 379.

Chapter I *The Order of Politicality*

1. Leonard Krieger, "Power and Responsibility: The Historical Assumptions" in Leonard Krieger and Fritz Stern (eds.), *The Responsibility*

of Power, Anchor Books, Doubleday & Company, Inc., New York, 1969, pp. 10-11.

2. E. V. Walter, in his essay, *Terror and Resistance*, Oxford University Press, New York, 1969, is one of the recent analysts to have forcefully challenged the presumption of a dichotomy between force and consent in the analysis of legitimate political authority. He has suggested that force is an inevitable element of any stable political authority as well as a constituent of its foundations: "...our conventions of political thought have shut out the realities of terroristic systems, for our imaginations cannot grasp the paradox of a regime of terror—a government that destroys part of the community in order to control the rest. . . .We think of proper governments, moreover, as instruments to protect the community against violence, and although history is generous with examples to the contrary, we refuse to imagine a durable government, based on consent, that uses continual violence as a regular technique—not a last resort—on its own people. We identify order with consent, but we also equate violence with the absence of order." (p. 29)

3. *The Politics of Aristotle,* edited and translated by Ernest Barker, Oxford University Press, New York, 1962, pp. 6-7. For my use of the term artifact here, let me quote the note appended to this passage by Barker: "Aristotle here concedes, and indeed argues, that in saying that the state is natural he does not mean that it 'grows' naturally, without human volition and action. There is art as well as nature, and art co-operates with nature: the volition and action of human agents 'construct' the state in co-operation with a natural immanent impulse." (p. 7) In this entire essay, it is my intention to use terms like artifact, authenticity, authentic, rationalize and rationalization in ways which are as close to their literal meanings as possible: e.g. artifact = "any object made by human work" whether that work be manual or mental; authenticity (-tic) = genuine, of the thing itself; rationalize (-zation) = to make something reasonable or to make it fit within a system or set of things.

4. Sheldon Wolin, "Political Theory as a Vocation," *The American Political Science Review,* Vol. 63, December, 1969, p. 1063. As a political theorist, Wolin's critique of political science as a discipline whose practitioners have withdrawn from the direct encounter with the political by immersing themselves in journalism and the mechanics of simple social synapses is not unexpected. His obsession with the political as the foundation of ethical concerns has made him impatient with a science deeply implicated in its own dimunition. It also appears that there are legions within the discipline who share his view. A fairly extensive survey of faculty and graduate students in the discipline recorded wide-spread dissatisfaction with the science and a majority who characterized research in the field as "trivial", see Ellen Coughlin, "Many Political Scientists Are Unhappy About Their Jobs. Salaries, Students," *The Chronicle of Higher Education,* September 11, 1978, p. 9. One account of the historical development of American political science is particularly interesting in its characterization of the mood of political

scientists after the second world war: ". . . .there was widespread dissatisfaction with the 'state of the discipline.' This stemmed from several sources: the discovery that the talents and skills of political scientists were not highly valued by governmental personnel officers; the disconcerting realization, by those who did spend some time in the public service, of the profound difference between the 'accepted wisdom' of the profession and the reality of the governmental process; the inability of traditional political science to account for the rise of fascism, national socialism, and communism, or to explain the continuation of these regimes in power; a growing sensitivity to, and unhappiness with, the basically descriptive nature of the discipline; and a knowledge of apparent advances in other social sciences and mounting fear that political science was lagging behind its sister professions." Albert Somit and Joseph Tanenhaus, *The Development of American Political Science*, Allyn and Bacon, Boston, 1967, p. 184. The response to this malaise was to adapt behavioral science as the model for political science (Ibid., pp. 183ff.); a resolution which only compounded the misdirection of the discipline.

5. For Kuhn, see *The Structure of Scientific Revolutions,* Chicago University Press, 1970; "Logic of Discovery or Psychology of Research" and "Reflections on My Critics" in Imre Lakatos and Alan Musgrave (eds.), *Criticism and the Growth of Knowledge,* Cambridge University Press, 1970; also "Second Thoughts on Paradigms" in Frederick Suppe (ed.), *The Structure of Scientific Theory,* University of Illinois Press, Urbana, 1973. For Popper, see *The Logic of Scientific Discovery*, Basic Books, New York, 1959; *Conjectures and Refutations,* Basic Books, New York, 1962; and "Normal Science and Its Dangers" in Lakatos and Musgrave, *Criticism.*

6. The question of convergence between Kuhn and Popper can for some (e.g. Kuhn and Imre Lakatos), and on some occasions for others, be resolved by accepting Lakatos' declaration that there are different Kuhns and Poppers (see Lakatos' essay, "Methodology of Scientific Research Programmes" in Lakatos and Musgrave (eds.) *Criticism*). This tactic appears in reality to be an attempt to systematize and phase inconsistencies in the writings of the two men. However, there are passages in Popper which seem unmistakably a Kuhnian sense of the thing, and vice versa. To the degree that Popper is authentically presented as the "sophisticated methodological falsificationist" in the following paragraph written by Lakatos, he is conforming to Kuhn's and Polanyi's understanding of the criteria for change encompassed by their respective notions of the paradigmatic vision and "personal knowledge": "If a theory is falsified, it is proven false; and if it is 'falsified', it may still be true. If we follow up this sort of 'falsification' by the actual 'elimination' of a theory, we may well end up by eliminating a true, and accepting a false, theory. . .*The methodological falsificationist separates rejection and disproof,* which the dogmatic falsificationist had conflated. He is a fallibilist but his fallibilism does not weaken his critical stance; he turns fallible

propositions into a 'basis' for a hard-line policy." (ibid., pp. 108-109, author's emphasis). This is certainly the process described by Kuhn and Polanyi. (For Polanyi, see *The Tacit Dimension,* Doubleday & Co., N.Y., 1966, p. 26) Popper and Kuhn do agree as to the existence of "normal" and "extraordinary" sciences (see text below), yet they weight them quite differently. One (Popper) from what he calls an "absolutist" (his) perspective and the other from the logical contradistinction of "historical relativism." Popper, too, makes the error of confusing Kuhn's position as one of sympathizing with the "normal" scientist which is clearly not the case (see Paul Feyerabend's essay "Consolations for the Specialist" and Kuhn's response in Lakatos and Musgrave, *Criticism*). And it does so appear that Popper has somewhat mistaken his own position (contrast the above "reconstruction" of Popper by Lakatos with the quotation cited in Note 7).

7. Popper, *Conjectures*, p. 192.

8. Popper, "Normal Science," p. 56. See also, Margaret Masterman, "The Nature of a Paradigm," in Lakatos and Musgrave, *Criticism*. In the early 20th century, Luigi Pirandello made this same point in the substance and structure of most of his plays. (See especially *Six Characters in Search of an Author*). Ironically perhaps, in the Marxian historical dialectic there is contained a parallel process of subversion: but here in the area of social change. Following Marx, Lukacs, in his discussion of the revolutionary consciousness of the proletariat emerging from "the objective reality of social existence. . .in its immediacy" shared by the proletariat and the bourgeoisie, argues, "The category of totality begins to have an effect long before the whole multiplicity of objects can be illuminated by it. It operates by ensuring that actions which seem to confine themselves to particular objects, in both content and consciousness, yet preserve an aspiration towards the totality, that is to say: action is directed objectively towards a transformation of totality." And further: "The great advance over Hegel made by the scientific standpoint of the proletariat as embodied in Marxism lay in its refusal to see in the categories of reflection a 'permanent' stage of human knowledge and in its insistence that they were the necessary mould both of thought and of life in bourgeois society, in the reification of thought and life. . .The proletariat 'has no ideal to realize'. When its consciousness is put into practice it can only breathe life into the things which the dialectics of history have forced to crisis; it can never 'in practice' ignore the course of history, forcing on it what are no more than its own desires or knowledge. For it is itself nothing but the contradictions of history that have become conscious. On the other hand, however, a dialectical necessity is far from being the same thing as a mechanical, causal necessity." (Georg Lukacs, *History and Class Consciousness,* The MIT Press, Cambridge, Massachusetts, 1971, p. 175 and 177-178.)

9. See note 6 for Lakatos' reconstruction of the Popperian character of self-consistency.

10. Here, I follow the analysis of Margaret Masterman, "The Nature of a Paradigm." It should also be noted that though Kuhn recognized the

importance of "social pressures" in the development of scientific thought (see Kuhn, *The Structure of Scientific Revolutions,* p. 69), he did not give to such forces the character or centrality that Marx and later Marxists have. For instance, B. Hessen, a Soviet historian of science, wrote in 1931: "The brilliant successes of natural science during the sixteenth and seventeenth centuries were conditioned by the disintegration of the feudal economy, the development of merchant capital, of international maritime relationships and of heavy (mining) industry;" and further, "Science flourished step by step with the development and flourishing of the bourgeoisie. In order to develop its industry the bourgeoisie needed science, which would investigate the qualities of material bodies and the forms or manifestation of the forces of nature." B. Hessen, "The Social and Economic Roots of Newton's 'Principia,' " in *Science at the Crossroads: Papers Presented to the International Congress of the History of Science and Technology held in London, June 25th-July 3rd, 1931 by Scholars from the U. S. S. R.,* Kniga, London, 1931, pp. 5 and 20 respectively. Indeed, science was so closely identified with the bourgeoisie which triumphed during the interregnum in England that the Restoration witnessed a renewal of hostility towards science which would dominate until the mid-18th century (See Leonard Marsak, "Bernard de Fontenelle: In Defense of Science," in Leonard Marsak, ed., *The Rise of Science in Relation to Society,* MacMillan, New York, 1964, p. 4) For Marx's explanation for the development of modern science see his *Capital,* Vol. 1, International Publishers, New York, 1977, pp. 348 and 361.

11. A. R. Louch, *Explanation in Human Action,* University of California Press Berkeley and Los Angeles, 1969.

12. Kuhn, "Reflections," p. 262.

13. To Popper's 'charge of relativism,' Kuhn rejoined that he is to the contrary an "evolutionist" in one sense and perceives scientific development "like biological evolution, unidirectional and irreversible." (Kuhn, "Reflections," p. 264) Yet he goes on to assert that he does not believe in scientific "truth" or make the presumption that theories are "representations of nature. . .statements about 'what is really out there'." (ibid., p. 265) Nor does he believe that fundamentally different (paradigmatically) theories possess a neutral, inter-theoretical language but indeed are often incommensurable. It appears here that Kuhn has mistaken in the first instance non-specific sequence for evolution, has rejected as well evolution and revolution as dialectic and has assumed that scientific development proceeds through instrumental (artifactual) sameness but succeeds to metaphysical disparateness. Each new paradigm, then, consists of an epistemology distinct from its competitors. Kuhn, as such becomes in his interpretations a paradox himself, demonstrating a sensitive, critical ignorance of the semantic vagaries which brighten his analyses but obfuscate their defense.

14. It is a temptation to cite for authorization of this statement the entire literature of political science on the State, or to simply give the reader license to read any particular document. Either approach though sufficient would be unsatisfactory to a reader (though I do indeed prefer them). Instead, I refer you to the example made of Dahl in the text which follows this note and for more

general reference, Harold Laski's *The State in Theory and Practice,* Viking Press, New York, 1947, pp. 8-10, and Georges Balandier's *Political Anthropology,* Pantheon Books, New York, 1970, pp. 23-25.

15. Robert Dahl, *Pluralist Democracy in the United States,* Rand McNally & Co., New York, 1967, p. 4.

16. Ibid.

17. Ibid., p. 23.

18. Ibid., p. 24.

19. Ibid., p. 12.

20. Indeed, the contrary is still strongly representative. See Robert Dahl's *Who Governs,* Samuel Huntington's *Political Order in Changing Societies,* and the critical essay of Peter Bachrach, *The Theory of Democratic Elitism.* The following statement by Harold Lasswell is quite typical in its forthright identification of democracy and social science: ". . .science will be directed toward providing the knowledge needed to improve the practice of democracy in which the ultimate goal is the realization of human dignity in theory and practice." ("The Policy Orientation" in D. Lerner and H. D. Lasswell (eds.) *The Policy Sciences, Recent Developments in Scope and Method,* Stanford University Press, Stanford, 1951.

21. It is here, at what should be the very beginning when we decide what our sounds are to signify, that the artifact of controversy is established. I have taken *kratein* to mean "to rule," a supposition which leaves unremarked the instrument of that rule. I do not presuppose, then, politics as it is most familiar to us and has consumed our imaginations, government, i.e. institutions possessing *power* to coerce or persuade or determine for their *subjects* through prescriptive and proscriptive behavioral codifications called *law.* It seems to me thus presumptuous and somewhat tragic to find *kratein* so often translated "government" when the latter term has so precisely matured into a tyranny over vision. The discussion must remain open, even if it were never meant to be, simply because it possesses other suggestions and there is a lingering doubt about the efficacy of the alternative so far explored.

22. There is, of course, little tension between the contemporary sentiment attached to this term and that of its Latin root *vulgas,* translated "the common people." This is, at least, one phoneme which has survived, intact, the augeries of democratic and Christian philosophies and moralities from the stratified society of its origin.

23. According to Ernest Barker, Aristotle classified constitutions "into the two *genera* of right and wrong, or normal and perverted. . ." (Barker, *Aristotle,* p. 113). And these two types of constitutions were further subdivided into three subgroups: Kingship, Aristocracy and Polity, based on the rule of "One, or Few, or Many." Aristotle argued that Democracy, the rule of the Many, though a perversion of Polity, might be defended by the argument that with the Many, ". . .when they all come together it is possible that they may

surpass—collectively and as a body, although not individually—the quality of the few best." (ibid., p. 123) In any case, he warned, ". . .there is serious risk in not letting them have *some* share in the enjoyment of power; for a state with a body of disfranchised citizens who are numerous and poor must necessarily be a state which is full of enemies." (ibid., pp. 124-5)

24. Richard Lichtman, in tracing the development of liberal democratic theory from Locke and Mill to Schumpeter, Dahl, Berelson and others, has made use of the following writings to indicate the nature of what he terms "the contemporary inversion" of that theory. These materials indicate the replacement of the ideal of democracy with techniques of description, efficiency and stability, and the functional interpretation of apathy and formal procedure: "Political theory written with reference to practice has the advantage that its categories are the categories in which political life really occurs" (Berelson, 1954); "Probably this strange hybrid, the normal American political system, is not for export to others. But so long as the social prerequisites of democracy are substantially intact in this country, it appears to be a relatively efficient system for reinforcing agreement, encouraging moderation, and maintaining social peace in a restless immoderate people operating a gigantic, powerful, diversified, and incredibly complex society." (Dahl, 1956); "Like every other political system, of course, the political system of New Haven falls far short of the usual conceptions of an ideal democracy. . .But to the extent that the term is ever fairly applied to existing realities, the political system of New Haven is an example of a democratic system, warts and all. For the past century it seems to have been a highly stable system." (Dahl, 1961); "We need some people who are active in a certain respect, others in the middle, and others passive." (Berelson, 1954); "Viewed in this light, the apathy and caprice for which political democracy have been blamed is seen to be rather to its credit than otherwise. It means at any rate that people are free to interest themselves or to disinterest themselves as they please in political affairs." (Hogan, 1945); "It is no exaggeration to say that in less than two decades this series of studies [surveys of voting behavior] has significantly altered and greatly deepened our understanding of what in some ways is the most distinctive action for a citizen of democracy—deciding how to vote, or indeed whether to vote at all, in a competitive national election." (Dahl, 1961). All cited in Lichtman's "The Facade of Equality in Liberal Democratic Theory" in *Socialist Revolution*, Vol. 1, No. 1, January 1970, pp. 113-114. For a concise discussion of the theory of representation, see Hanna Fenichel Pitkin's *Representation,* Atherton Press, New York, 1969, especially her introductory essay (pp. 1-23). It is of interest for our later discussion of mixed paradigms that Pitkin argues that the modern sense of representation (i.e. in place of something) stems from ecclesiastical doctrine when the higher clerics, in an attempt to establish their authority, began to present themselves as representatives of God and to thus change and temper the revolutionary

individualism of the earlier Christian movement which recognized only divine authority. See also Sheldon Wolin's *Politics and Vision*, Little, Brown & Co., 1960, Ch. IV.

25. Lichtman, "Facade of Equality," p. 106.

26. Support for this interpretation of Locke can be found in Lichtman, "Facade of Equality," and Wolin, *Politics*, Ch. IX. In addition, the reader is referred to C. B. Macpherson's "Locke on Capitalist Appropriation," in *The Western Political Quarterly*, Vol. IV, 1951, pp. 550-66; see especially, pp. 556-59.

27. From John Stuart Mill, *Principles of Political Economy,* Longmans, Green & Co., 1909, p. 139. Cited by Lichtman, "Facade of Equality."

28. Mill, *Political Economy*, p. 143.

29. For a short history of the development of the behavioral approach see Robert Dahl's "The Behavioral Approach in Political Science: Epitaph for a Monument to a Successful Protest," in *The American Political Science Review*, December 1961, pp. 763-772. For the implications of the electoral studies, see Gerald Pomper's "From Confusion to Clarity: Issues and American Voters, 1959-1968," in the same review, June 1972, pp. 415-28.

30. See note 24, especially the quotes from Berelson and Hogan.

31. In addition to Bachrach, *Democratic Elitism*, see Jack Walker's "A Critique of the Elitist Theory of Democracy" in *The American Political Science Review,* Vol. LX, No. 2, June 1966, pp. 285-95.

32. Though there are some similarities, Sheldon Wolin's use of Kuhn's theory of scientific development is different from the one this writer employs. At one point—though he has earlier conceptualized the behavioral movement as a paradigm—Wolin goes beyond political theory in order to locate the significant paradigm informing the work of political scientists. Political society becomes Wolin's paradigm. This choice is dictated by the logic of his argument wherein he perceives political theory as extraordinary science precipitated by historical crises (Wolin's anomalies): "My proposal is that we conceive of political society itself as a paradigm of an operative kind. From this viewpoint society would be envisaged as a coherent whole in the sense of its customary political practices, institutions, laws, structure of authority and citizenship, and operative beliefs being organized and interrelated. . .This *ensemble* of practices and beliefs may be said to form a paradigm in the sense that the society tries to carry on its political life in accordance with them. . .To the degree that a society succeeds in adapting, its efforts might even be likened to a form of puzzle-solving. . .Society's indifference towards theory is matched by the indifference of theorists. Throughout the history of Western political theory we find that most of the major theories have been produced during times of crises, rarely during periods of normalcy. . .This indifference is not the expression of a choice between having a theory or living without one. A society which is operating fairly normally has its theory in the form of the dominant paradigm, but that theory is taken for granted because it represents

the consensus of the society." Wolin, "Paradigms and Political Theories" in Preston King and B. C. Parekh (eds.), *Politics and Experience*, Cambridge University Press, 1969, pp. 149 and 151, respectively. By extending Kuhn's analysis to political society, Wolin has attempted to tie conceptual transformation to historical change. Though this is consistent with Wolin's earlier essay, (*Politics and Vision*, p. 8), it transcends Kuhn's sense of the phenomenon which tended towards idealism and ahistoricism. Nevertheless, the present writer believes that Wolin would have been more successful in his use of Kuhn if he had employed a concept like democracy rather than one such as political society. This would have allowed his analysis a more significant historicity than one dependent upon the ambiguous periodicity inherent in the term political society.

33. Feyerabend, "Consolations," p. 202. Feyerabend makes the point that Kuhn's commitment to normal science is ambiguously deceptive because Kuhn intends to hide the revolutionary consequences of a "monomanaic concern with only one single point of view." (Ibid., p. 201) I believe that Feyerabend here is taking advantage of his special relationship to Kuhn and is excessively dramatizing Kuhn's intentions. One suggestion of this is an article in the same collection authored by Stephen Toulmin. Toulmin reminds us that one year before the appearance of *The Structure of Scientific Revolutions* in print, Kuhn had made this dimension of his work fairly explicit by entitling a paper presented at Worcester College, Oxford, 'The Function of Dogma in Scientific Research.' In support of Feyerabend's point, however, Toulmin also describes Kuhn's retreat from his "original exposed position" for unexplained reasons: "Kuhn, in moving on from his Oxford paper to the 1962 book, withdrew his insistence on the term 'dogma', but attempted to retain a central distinction between 'normal science' and 'scientific revolutions.' " ("Does the Distinction between Normal and Revolutionary Science Hold Water?," Lakatos and Musgrave, *Criticism*, pp. 39-41)

34. Feyerabend, "Consolations," p. 214.

35. Huntington, *Political Order in Changing Societies*, Yale University Press, New Haven, 1968.

36. Ibid., p. 3.

37. To quote A.F.K. Organski, "The reader will find in this volume many new insights, hypotheses and typologies. The best in this volume are chapters 1 and 3 where Mr. Huntington develops the theoretical framework for the study of development and order and explores the difficulties in getting to self sustaining political growth in traditional polities. . .One must certainly acknowledge Mr. Huntington's contribution. His concepts of political decay at the least began to close a gap in the literature of development. Both concepts have been widely used. This pioneering volume, examining as it does the relation between development and stability, is an interesting and exciting addition to the literature." Book review in *The American Political Science Review*, Vol. LXIII, No. 3, September 1969, p. 922; for a later and more

circumspect view of Huntington and theory development in comparative politics, see James Bill and Robert Hardgrave, Jr., *Comparative Politics*, Charles Merrill, Columbus, 1973, pp. 229-38.

38. Stanley Diamond, "The Rule of Law Versus the Order of Custom," in Robert Paul Wolff's (ed.) *The Rule of Law,* Simon and Schuster, New York, 1971, p. 117.

39. Ibid., p. 126.

40. It is to be understood that these remarks concerning "spaces" are not other ways of introducing or identifying the several "determinisms" which have been the stuff of controversy in political science since perhaps Montesquieu. These determinisms miss the mark in several ways. For example, they are used to "explain" the political as a consequence of non-political phenomena thereby substituting one authority for the other, while I am here seeking to explore an insight into groups without politics, securing authority as the definition of the relationship between the individual and his universe. As well, determinism suggests theories of limits relating to social fact and artifact whose generality and inevitability are unsubstantiated. Thus questions of identity and bias intrude, many of which are centrally concerned in that which this essay eschews.

41. See David Pears' *Wittgenstein,* Fontana, London, 1971.

42. See for example Irving L. Horowitz, *The Anarchists*, Dell Publishing Co., New York, 1964, p. 27; and E. J. Hobsbawn, *Primitive Rebels*, W. W. Norton & Co., New York, 1959, pp. 80-82.

43. It appears possible that in the fifteenth century and earlier, the BaKongo of present-day Zaire used political processes only between kingships. That is, political processes were used between the death of one king and the investiture of his successor, during that period that their Western ethnographers have termed anarchic. In interregnum periods, battles were fought between opposing factions of the royal class over succession. But once established, the king dissolved or allowed to dissolve the political instruments used to sanction the legitimacy of his ascendance. He and his former opposition became bound by the traditional cosmology (kinship) and its authority. He became the vessel of the BaNkita: heroic ancestors who had founded the nation. He became the one responsible for the integrity of the forces which made up the BaKongo society, that is, those on the surface of the earth, those below the earth (BaKulu: clan ancestors), those not yet born. As the BaKongo believed that nothing ever dies and conceived of time as circular, they had no ongoing sense of what is called history in Western society. As such a precondition for political order was absent. Their epistemology subverted the historical and the contingent (e.g. the "death" of a king), using pseudo-events (the anarchic interregnum) to affirm its authority by repeatedly re-establishing things as they were. Thus political phenomena, being transitory both in the sense of being temporary and in the sense of being between the establishment of its true order of things, reaffirmed the basic apolitical order.

The history of the BaKongo from the fifteenth century onwards, however, is a record of the politicization of BaKongo life-experience. The BaKongo state emerged from among them, caught as they were between the threat of the Yagga from the east and the penetration of Europeans, Christianity, the Atlantic slave trade, etc. from the west. See Georges Balandier's *Daily Life in the Kingdom of the Kongo,* Meridian Books, World Publishing Company, 1966, and his *Sociology in Black Africa,* Praeger Publishers, New York, 1970; Jan Vansina, *Kingdoms of the Savanna*, University of Wisconsin's Press, Madison, 1966; Leonard Krieger, "Power and Responsibility," especially pages 17-19; Wyatt MacGaffey's "The Religious Commissions of the Bakongo" in *Man,* 1970, pp. 26-38; and Jasques Depelchin's "Incipient Ideologies of the Lower Congo," unpublished paper, Stanford University, 1970.

44. The relationship between the terms "the political" and "politics" must be kept constantly in mind here. I have defined the political as an ordering principle arranging the relationship of things and of people within society. Following Plato, Wolin (for one) argues that the political is a concern with "general interests," "common quality," and "common involvement." (*Politics and Vision,* p. 10) But "politics" for Wolin, though it is "political activity" is concerned with conflict and competition. (ibid.) Thus there is an inherent contradiction or tension between the political and politics (ibid., p. 11). I find this unsatisfactory in its idealistic logic. In its stead, I am suggesting that the conflict of politics as political activity presupposes the element of conflict and opposition in the political. The destruction or avoidance of politics eliminates the political—a social order purged of politics or without politics is not a political order. Wayne A. R. Leys has stated: "In deciding which problems should be called "political," I follow the tradition of Machiavelli and Hobbs, which culminates in the writings of Carl Schmitt. Schmitt contended that the distinction between friend and foe is the essential political distinction. Thus, a person who has political sense is the one who thinks about the opposition and also about the support, actual and potential, that may be connected with any idea, activity, or institution." ("Was Plato Non-Political?" in Gregory Vlastos' (ed.) *Plato*, Vol. II, Anchor Books, Doubleday and Company, New York, 1971, p. 168) Once this is said, however, disclaimers are necessary. One of Leys' disclaimers is appropriate here: "To define 'the political' as 'that which pertains to divisions, disagreements and conflicts' is not the same thing as asserting that political institutions, as a matter of fact, have no other function than that of dealing with conflicts. . .but a definition of 'political' merely defines a characteristic that is especially prominent in government." (ibid., p. 169)

45. Diamond, "The Rule of Law," p. 136.

46. Hannah Arendt, *Between Past and Future*, Faber and Faber, London, 1961, p. 96.

47. Ibid., p. 123.

48. Ibid., p. 113.

49. Ibid., p. 116. Arendt also reminds us that in Greek mythology the gods had not created the world which was to the contrary "ever present." The terms "order of things" and "natural" thus represented in Greek thought immutability, immortality and permanence. Ibid., p. 42.

50. Krieger, "Power and Responsibility," pp. 17-18. Arendt herself states: "If authority is to be defined at all, then, it must be in contradistinction to both coercion by force and persuasion through arguments. . .This point is of historical importance; one aspect of our concept of authority is Platonic in origin, and when Plato began to consider the introduction of authority into the handling of public affairs in the polis, he knew he was seeking an alternative to the common Greek way of handling domestic affairs, which was persuasion. . .as well as to the common way of handling foreign affairs, which was force and violence. . . ." (*Between Past and Future*, p. 93).

51. Arendt, *Between Past and Future*, pp. 122-3.

52. Ibid., p. 121. Pitkin and Arendt thus agree that in separating out authority from rule, the early Christian hierarchy constructed the more primitive category of our contemporary political authority: "The separation of church and state, on the other hand, far from signifying unequivocally a secularization of the political realm and, hence, its rise to the dignity of the classical period, actually implied that the political had now, for the first time since the Romans, lost its authority and with it that element which, at least in Western history, had endowed political structures with durability, continuity and permanence." Ibid., p. 127. In such ways, too, does history become political history and thus the record of disobedience or challenges to political authority. We, also, join those others who have congratulated Marx on the perspicacity of his innocent vision which sought to identify this process of politicization in the destruction of feudalism by capitalism. See Marx's "On the Jewish Question" in Robert Tucker (ed.) *The Marx-Engels Reader,* W. W. Norton & Company, Inc., New York, 1972, pp. 24-51.

53. Stanley Diamond, "The Rule of Law," p. 135.

54. I am to a degree made uncomfortable by the clearness and obviousness of a conceptual error of such simple dimensions being found in Arendt's work. And so I suggest that more properly it must be understood not as error but as a myth consequent to the strategy of this particular work. (*Between Past and Future*) which seeks to indict the modern intellectual with, in Benda's words, his "betrayal" of his age and his community. What the modern intellectual as apologist has failed to do was to oppose and counterpose the contemporary emblems of fear and despair. This intellectual has failed to challenge the political propaganda which contains in it the support of the enpowerment of and deference to this age's political thugs and bandits and their inevitable retinue of court jesters and magicians. Instead, of course, he has rationalized them and, as well, given them some of the instruments for their obscene reigns. In several of her works (notably *The Origins of Totalitarianism*), Arendt has

demonstrated not only a lack of passion for the mass politics of the twentieth century but also a precise understanding of the systemic vagaries of human thought, faith and vision (*Eichmann in Jerusalem*). In *Between Past and Future*, she again seems to be intent upon the making of a record of successive betrayals and succumbings of the magnificent and heroic to the banal and so the sense of authority which she employs will always be an historical sense. What I am employing, to the contrary, as the relevant sense of authority immediate to any discussion of order, is a psychological interpretation, that is a conceptual framework to which Arendt has elsewhere demonstrated a great deal of sensitivity. Her "myopia" in this instance is, then, consequent to the choice of stratagems and nothing more. But others have found very different base from which to suspect Arendt and her colleagues in their submission to liberal political philosophy and theory: "The line of this philosophical approach ["withdrawal" and "contemplative" idleness] goes from Schopenhauer and Kierkegaard, through Unamuno, Ortega y Gasset, Huizinga, Berkyaev, Gabriel Marcel and others down to their present-day epigoni like Hannah Arendt. The last named characteristically closes her book, *The Human Condition* (!), with these words: "how right Cato was when he said:. . .'Never is he more active than when he does nothing, never is he less alone than when he is by himself.' The idealization of individual autonomy, carried to its extreme, leads inevitably not only to the acceptance of inactivity but also to conferring on it the highest moral praise." Istvan Meszaros, *Marx's Theory of Alienation*, Harper Torchbooks, New York, 1970, pp. 261-2.

55. Herbert Rosinski, *Power and Human Destiny*, Richard Stebbins (ed.), Pall Mall Press, London, 1965, pp. 13f.

56. Polanyi, *Tacit Dimension*, p. 38.

57. Ibid., p. 40.

58. The models for 'understanding' the perceptual skills of nerve cells, nerve fibers, axons, dendrites, nerve-end synapses, cortex, cerebellum lobes, current-impulse, circuits, transducers, etc., which describe in most primitive ways the structures and mechanics of what is known as the human brain, largely derive, we are told, from communication, computer and electronic theory and engineering: "We must however be careful not to assume *detailed* similarities between biological and engineering systems, even when they seem to be performing the same functions. *General* engineering concepts will apply to both, but this does not mean that identical or even similar circuits and components will be found." this is how Richard Gregory, a professor of "perception bionics" sees it in his "Perception" in David Paterson's (ed.) *The Brain*, British Broadcasting Corporation, 1969, pp. 21-22. Later Gregory summarizes the work of two American physiologists, Hubel and Wiesel: ". . .the patterns of electrical activity on the surface of the back of the brain—the so-called 'projection area' from the eyes—is 'described' in terms of circuits which respond to specific shapes, and movement in certain directions. In other words, the brain responds only to certain selected visual features. . .Deeper in the brain, cells respond

to more and more abstract features; until finally, perhaps a few cells indicate the identity of the external objects, their sizes, distances and so on. . .What is important about objects are features which are not represented directly to the eye. Optical images—the eye's pictures—are not hard or soft, hot or cold, eatable or poisonous. The pictures in the eyes are only biologically useful when they can be used by the brain to 'read' *non-optical* qualities from these patches of light. . .The patterns in the eye are not biologically important in themselves, but only when their significance is read by the brain." (Ibid., pp. 23-24) These image-styles to which the brain is inherently responsive become objects when associated with "stored information" or "models of reality," internal models whose origin is partly in the images of all sensory experiences and partly unknown: "A curve of nose, an eyebrow—it is a face. The rest is unnecessary, because objects are redundant. They are redundant in space and in time. The brain uses the redundancy of the world of objects to make perception possible; in real time, with a finite brain computer." (Ibid., p. 29)

59. Wolin, *Politics*, p. 33. Charles Drekmeier objects to Wolin having attributed to Plato the historical role of being ". . .first to view political society in the round. . ." Instead, Drekmeier asserts that the Indian caste society presents to us a conceptualization which predates the Greek Enlightenment. (Personal communication.) Drekmeier's objection raises another issue. At what historical point does Western civilization begin? In anthropological terms (tribal-kinship base, transhumanance) the peculiar admixture of Western European locatization, specific language-groups, social structures, mythic and ideological compositions, and seigneural (manorial) agriculture which is described as "the Western tradition" is no older than the 4th century B.C. In intellectual and ideological terms, through elements of Egypto-Greek thought were borrowed by the ideologues of the early medieval period for their own purposes, it would be centuries before Egypto-Greek thought would be appropriated into Western thought as its intellectual origins. (William Carroll Bark, *Origins of the Medieval World,* Stanford University Press, Stanford, 1974, pp. 69-73.

60. Edmund Leach, "Anthropological Aspects of Language: Animal Categories and Verbal Abuse," in Pierre Maranda's (ed.), *Mythology*, Penguin Books, Middlesex, England, 1972, p. 47. See also C. K. Ogden and I. A. Richards, *The Meaning of Meaning,* Harcourt, Brace & World, New York, 1968 (first published in 1928): "Symbols direct and organize, record and communicate. . .It is Thought (or, as we shall usually say, *reference*) which is directed and organized, and it is also Thought which is recorded and communicated." (p. 9)

61. Charles Drekmeier, "Knowledge as Virtue, Knowledge as Power," in Nevitt Sanford and Craig Comstock (eds.), *Sanctions for Evil*, Wright Institute, Beacon Press, Boston, 1971, p. 209.

62. Ernest Gellner, *Thought and Change*, Weidenfield and Nicolson, London, 1964.

63. G. G. Simpson, *Principles of Animal Taxonomy,* New York, 1961, p. 5, as cited in Claude Levi-Strauss' *The Savage Mind,* University of Chicago Press, Chicago, 1970, pp. 9f.

64. Claude Levi-Strauss, *Savage Mind,* p. 3 and p. 10.

Chapter II   *The Parameters of Leadership*

1. Susan Buck-Morss, "The Dialectic of T. W. Adorno" in *Telos,* No. 14, Winter 1972, p. 135.

2. Murray Edelman, *The Symbolic Uses of Politics,* University of Illinois Press, Urbana, 1967.

3. Ibid., pp. 20-21.

4. Ibid., p. 73.

5. Ibid., p. 94.

6. "Adorno: Love and Cognition," review in *The Times Literary Supplement,* Number 3705, March 9, 1973, p. 253.

7. Edelman, *Symbolic Uses,* p. 75.

8. Ibid., pp. 74-75.

9. Ibid., pp. 142-5.

10. See page 16 of this essay for metaphysical, sociological and artifactual paradigms.

11. Peter Berger and Thomas Luckmann, *The Social Construction of Reality,* Anchor Books, Doubleday & Company, Inc., Garden City, 1966.

12. In Chapter IV, a close analysis of the structure and origins of that myth will be attempted.

13. Barrington Moore, Jr., *Social Origins of Dictatorship and Democracy,* Beacon Press, Boston, 1966.

14. Jeremiah F. Wolpert, "Toward a Sociology of Authority," in Alvin Gouldner (ed.), *Studies in Leadership,* Harper, New York, 1950, p. 681.

15. Gabriel Almond and G. Bingham Powell, Jr., *Comparative Politics,* Little, Brown and Company, Boston, 1966.

16. Gouldner's introduction, *Studies in Leadership,* pp. 12-13.

17. See Gouldner's *The Coming Crisis of Western Sociology,* Avon Books, New York, 1970, pp. 29-40.

18. Gouldner, *Studies in Leadership,* p. 11.

19. Dankwart Rustow, "Introduction to the Issue 'Philosophers and Kings' " *Daedalus,* Summer 1968, Vol. 97, No. 3, pp. 683-4.

20. See Chapter IV.

21. Albert Hirschman, "Underdevelopment Obstacles to the Perception of Change and Leadership," *Daedalus,* Summer 1968, Vol. 97, No. 3, pp. 935-6.

22. Fred Fiedler, *A Theory of Leadership Effectiveness,* McGraw-Hill, New York, 1967, p. 261.

23. Gouldner's introduction in *Studies in Leadership*, p. 15.

24. Ibid., p. 19.

25. An instance of this is John MacGregor Burns' biography of Franklin Roosevelt. Reconstructing Roosevelt's relationship to the development of the labor movement of the mid-1930s, Burns writes: "On the labor front. . .the New Deal unleashed surging and dynamic forces. Probably Roosevelt never fully understood those new forces or the new leaders they lifted to power. Certainly he had little conscious role in bringing about social and legislative changes that were to recast radically the structure of political power in the 1930's. . . Quite unwittingly the new President acted as midwife in the rebirth of labor action." *Roosevelt: The Lion and the Fox*, Harcourt, Brace & World, New York, 1956, p. 215. This was hardly the view of most workers caught up in a unionization movement which included the CIO banner PRESIDENT ROOSEVELT WANTS YOU TO JOIN THE UNION (Ibid., p. 216)

26. Sidney Hook, "The Hero as Event and Problem," in William McPherson, ed., *Ideology and Change: Radicalism and Fundamentalism in America*, National Press Books, Palo Alto, 1973, p. 56.

27. William Foote Whyte, "Informal Leadership and Group Structure," Ibid., p. 115.

28. Gouldner, *Studies in Leadership*, Ibid., p. 20.

29. Ibid.

30. The suggestion of this analogue to the role of leader as envisioned by Gouldner can be made clearer by another reference using the same model. Engels in his "On Authority" expressed the presumptions of this paradigm quite forcefully: "On examining the economic, industrial and agricultural conditions which form the basis of present-day bourgeois society, we find that they tend more and more to replace isolated action by combined action of individuals. Modern industry with its big factory and mills. . .has superseded the small workshops of the separate producers. . . . Everywhere combined action, the complication of processes dependent upon each other, displaces independent action by individuals. . .a certain authority, no matter how delegated, and, on the other hand, a certain subordination, are things which, independently of all social organization, are imposed upon us together with the material conditions under which we produce and make products circulate." (in Robert C. Tucker, ed., *The Marx-Engels Reader,* W. W. Norton & Company, Inc., New York, 972, PP. 662-4) The more enveloping analogue would of course be mathematical integration—with some special attention being paid to the resemblance between social and symbolic "integrations". However, I have chosen economic organization—and more precisely industrial organization— because Gouldner, in a momentary lack of consciousness or in the absence of candor with his reader, reconstructed the functions and styles of that role in political terms. In part this may be explained as the consequence of the kinds of restrictions he reads into his particular interpretation of the democratic (which has its roots in classical liberalism and one of its emanations: Parsonianism) but it

seems also another confirmation of Kuhn's understanding of the penetration of the metaphysical paradigms by artifactual paradigms (that is the influence of industrial organizational history and experience on social thought): the sociology of knowledge. Gouldner has, of course, grown markedly in intellectual terms in the intervening years, see his *The Coming Crisis*. But his personal growth is not the issue here since he is being referred to as a representative of a tradition in Western social thought which persists. For an interesting confirmation, see the review on Gouldner's *The Coming Crisis of Western Sociology* by Leo Kaplan, *Trans-action*, September 1971. For a view of the role of Marxist thought as a corrective to liberal thought alternative to that projected by Gouldner, see Michel Foucault's *The Order of Things*, Tavistock Publications, London, 1970, pp. 261-2, and Marshal Sahlin's *Stone Age Economics,* Aldine-Atherton & Company, Inc., Chicago, 1972.

31. Anthony Piepe, *Knowledge and Social Theory*, Heineman, London, 1971, p. 76.

32. Immanuel Wallerstein, *The Modern World-System*, Academic Press, New York, 1974, pp. 151-56. See also Wallerstein's reference (Ibid., p. 153), to Christopher Hill's *Reformation to the Industrial Revolution, 1530-1780,* Vol. II of the Pelican Economic History of Britain, Penguin Books, London, 1967. In his review of Quentin Skinner's *The Foundations of Modern Political Thought,* (Cambridge University Press, Cambridge, 1978), Keith Thomas summarizes Skinner's treatment of the historical development of the modern concept of the state: "For most of the period, 'state' meant the condition in which the ruler found himself; his 'state' was something he had to maintain. But by the mid-sixteenth century the world had begun to acquire its modern meaning of an entity independent of both ruler and ruled. Professor Skinner lists the intellectual changes which had encouraged the evolution of the new concept: the challenge of fourteenth-century jurists to the Emperor's sovereignty over subordinate principalities; the denial by theologians of both the papal plenitude of power and the Church's right to secular jurisdiction; and the emerging view that rulers should devote their energies to purely secular functions. The whole process, he observes had been under way since the reception of Aristotle's *Politics* in the mid-thirteenth century." "Politics Recaptured," *New York Review of Books,* Vol. XXVI, No. 8, May 17, 1979, p. 29. Another instance of the consanguine complementarity of Church and State is found in the political character of early Protestantism (Lutheranism) which we discover "at first helped to strengthen the claims of the secular state by demanding the absolute obedience of its subjects." (Ibid., p. 27)

33. Karl Polanyi, *The Great Transformation*, Beacon Press, Boston, 1967, pp. 163-5; Karl Marx, *Capital*, Vol. I, Chapters X and XV; See also Anthony Wallace's amplification of Neil Smelser's treatment of this process (*Social Change in the Industrial Revolution*) in the Appendix to *Rockdale*, Alfred Knopf, New York, 1978, p. 494.

34. Charles Moraze, *The Triumph of the Middle Classes,* Anchor Books,

Garden City, 1968, pp. 105-38; and Karl Mannheim, *Ideology and Utopia*, Harcourt, Brace & World, New York, 1936, ". . .bourgeois intellectualism expressly demanded a scientific politics, and actually proceeded to found such a discipline. . .just as parliament is a formal organization, a formal rationalization of the political conflict but not a solution of it, so bourgeois theory attains merely an apparent, formal intellectualization of the inherently irrational elements." (p. 122)

35. Jurgen Habermas, *Knowledge and Human Interests*, Beacon Press, Boston, 1968, p. 28.

36. Trent Schroyer, "The Critical Theory of Late Capitalism," in George Fischer (ed.), *The Revival of American Socialism*, Oxford University Press, 1971, New York, p. 305.

37. I am suggesting here that the irrational has often been demonstrated to possess logical systems—e.g., the schizophrenic patient whose presumptions are different from the rational while also possessing asystemic, illogical elements related to no order of things.

38. See Karl Marx's *Das Kapital*, especially "Chapter X: The Working Day" reproduced in Tucker, *Marx-Engels*, pp. 249-264.

39. For Fritz Redl, see Gouldner, *Studies in Leadership*, pp. 41-4.

40. Hook, "The Hero," p. 54.

41. The literature of the rebellions and revolutions of slaves, serfs, peasants and other plebians is extensive. For some examples, see C. L. R. James, *The Black Jacobins,* Vintage Books, New York, 1963; Roland Mousnier, *Peasant Uprisings in 17th Century France, Russia, and China,* Harper Torchbooks, New York, 1972; Karl Polanyi, *The Great Transformation, op. cit.*; and Frantz Fanon, *The Wretched of the Earth,* Grove Press, New York, 1963.

42. For example, Lewis Edinger remarks: "The study of political leadership is as old as the study of politics for the one is inseparable from the other. Since time immemorial men have asked, debated, and sought to establish who governs or should govern, what are or ought to be the bases of political authority in a community, and why and how some individuals obtain and exercise exceptional influence over the making of public rules and policies when others do not." "Editor's Introduction," in *Political Leadership in Industrialized Societies,* John Wiley and Sons, New York, 1967, p. 3. Sidney Hook makes the same point: "The basic fact that provides the material for interest in heroes is the indispensability of *leadership* in all social life, and in every major form of social organization." "The Hero", p. 49. It might be useful to maintain a perceptual tension by insisting that leadership is a style *within* organization. Thus we retain in the forefront of our analysis the suggestion that organization and leadership are not inevitable concomitants.

43. See, for example, E. Victor Wolfenstein, "Some Psychological Aspects of Crisis Leaders," in Edinger, *Political Leadership*, pp. 155-181.

44. Anthony Wallace, "Revitalization Movements," *American Anthropologist*, Vol. 58, 1956.

45. Alex Comfort, *Authority and Delinquency*, Sphere, London, 1970, p. 34.

46. Consider, for example, Abraham Kaplan's use of Kenneth Arrow's logico-analytical legitimation of the leader. Arrow suggests that the need for leadership is evidenced by the paradox of three individuals (A,B,C,) with three alternatives (X,Y,Z). Basically, the "proof" is as follows:

Group Members' Preferences

A	B	C
X	Y	Z
Y	Z	X
Z	X	Y

"Now, what would happen in our group if we were to use majority rule? A prefers X to Y, and C prefers X to Y, so a majority of the group prefers X to Y. A prefers Y to Z, and B prefers Y to Z, so a majority of the group prefers Y to Z. But, unfortunately, B prefers Z to X, and C prefers Z to X, so a majority of the group also has this preference. Thus a majority of the group prefers X to Y, Y to Z and Z to X! And now your rule of majority has just tossed you around in a circle, and no choice has emerged at all." Abraham Kaplan, "Power in Perspective," in Robert Kahn and Elise Boulding (eds.), *Power and Conflict in Organizations,* Tavistock, London, 1964, pp. 26-7. According to Kaplan, then, leadership is justified by the need to resolve intra-group conflict. But if a leader does make a choice for one preference over the others, do the others disappear? The implication of this example is that other dynamics than expedience are active but they remain unidentified. The implication is that the leader represents resolution outside the logic of choices.

47. A. J. Ayer, *Language, Truth and Logic*, Dover Publications, New York, 1952, p. 95.

95. John O'Shaughnessy, *Inquiry and Decision*, George Allen & Unwin, ltd., London, 1972, pp. 15-17.

49. Richard Snyder, H. W. Bruck, Burton Sapin, *Decision-Making as an Approach to the Study of International Politics*, Princeton: Foreign Policy Analysis Project, Princeton University Press, 1954.

50. David Braybrooke and Charles Lindblom, *A Strategy of Decision*, Free Press, New York, 1963.

51. Norman Campbell, *What is Science?*, Dover Publications, New York, 1952, p. 79.

52. James Rosenau, "Premises and Promises of Decision-Making Analysis" in James Charlesworth (ed.), *Contemporary Political Analysis*, Free Press, New York, 1967, p. 201.

53. Braybrooke and Lindblom, *Strategy of Decision*; see also Lindblom's "The Science of 'Muddling Through'" in *Public Administration Review*, Vol.

29, Spring 1959, pp. 79-88.

54. Rosenau, "Premises and Promises", p. 199.

55. Lindblom, *The Intelligence of Democracy*, Free Press, New York, 1965, p. 178.

56. Ibid., p. 148.

57. Comfort, *Authority and Delinquency*, pp. 42-3.

58. Systems analysis and crisis management are two forms of incremental decision-making utilized in public-and foreign-policy spheres. One of the fall-outs of U.S. involvement in the Vietnam war was the re-analysis of the performance of American strategists. Of crisis management, Colin Gray had this to say: "The stress laid by theorists upon the need for clear and limited objectives, the value of resolve, the virtue of a gradual increase in the pressure applied, and the absolute necessity for rapid inter-adversary communication, all contributed to miscalculation in the less apocalyptic circumstance of Vietnam." "What RAND Hath Wrought," *Foreign Policy*, No. 4, Fall, 1972, p. 118. In his response to Gray, Bernard Brodie admitted: "Classical systems analysis. . .had had just about zero relevance to everything concerned with Vietnam. Our failures there have been at least 90 percent due to our incomprehension and inability to cope with the political dimensions of the problem, not forgetting that part which is internal to the United States." "Why were we so (Strategically) Wrong?," *Foreign Policy,* No. 5, Winter 1972, p. 157.

59. One instance of the indulgence in this symbolic signification of the leader is the collection of policy essays organized by the Brookings Institution on the event of President Nixon taking office in 1969. Kermit Gordon, President of Brookings at the time, had this to say in his introduction to those essays: "At the opening of a new administration—even in times more benign than the present—the public seems to turn away from the memories of the struggles, per-plexities, and frustrations which clouded the record of the outgoing regime, and to nourish the hope that the new leaders, making as fresh and confident start, will find the therapies for the nation's ills which eluded their predecessors. The voters expect new diagnoses, new strategies, and new initiatives, and most are inclined to suspend their doubts while the new administration has a fair chance to show its skills. It is a time when measure of faith is rekindled." Kermit Gordon, ed., *Agenda for the Nation*, Doubleday and Co., Garden City, 1968, p. 3.

60. See Erik Erikson's *Insight and Responsibility*, W. W. Norton & Company, New York, 1964, pp. 90-4.

61. Comfort, *Authority and Delinquency*, pp. 42-3.

62. Petr Kropotkin, *Mutual Aid, A Factor of Evolution,* McClure Philips & Company, New York, 1902, p. 111.

63. Ibid.

64. See Chapter IV.

65. Wilhelm Reich, *Mass Psychology of Fascism,* Farrar, Strauss & Giroux, New York, 1970, p. 53; and Max Horkheimer in his *Critical Theory*, Herder &

Herder, New York, 1972, especially the section called "Authority and the Family."

66. See Ian Clegg's *Worker Self-Management in Algeria*, and/or Seymour Melman's "Industrial Efficiency Under Managerial vs. Cooperative Decision-Making: A Comparative Study of Manufacturing Enterprises in Israel," in *The Review of Radical Political Economics*, Vol. II, No. 1, Spring 1970; there is also Stephen Jones and Victor Vroom, "Division of Labor and Performance Under Cooperative and Competitive Conditions," *Journal of Abnormal and Social Psychology*, No. 68, March 1964, pp. 313-20; and James L. Price, *Organizational Effectiveness;* as well as Andrew Gorz, *Strategy for Labor: A Radical Proposal,* Beacon Press, Boston, 1967.

67. For Arendt, see Chapter 1; for Kropotkin, see *Mutual Aid,* pp. 76-114; for others see the essays in John Middleton and David Tait (eds.), *Tribes Without Rulers,* Humanities Press, New York, 1958.

68. See Erik Erikson, "The Concept of Identity in Race Relations," *Daedalus,* Winter 1966, Vol. 95, No. 1, pp. 163-70.

69. Comfort, *Authority and Delinquency*, p. 8. Hegel also advanced this explanation of some developments in history involving his "world-historical figures," see Robert Tucker, *Philosophy and Myth in Karl Marx,* Cambridge University Press, Cambridge, 1971, pp. 64-68; and the same historical "force" was used by Marx but described as the capitalist class, see Tucker, pp. 136-49.

Chapter III *The Question of Rationality*

1. *See* A. R. Louch, *Explanation and Human Action,* University of California Press, Berkeley, 1969, p. 3. He distinguishes here rationalization from explanation.

2. Ludwig Wittgenstein, *Tractatus logico-philosophicus,* Routledge and Paul Kegan, London, 1922, p. 151.

3. I. M. Lewis, *Ecstatic Religion,* Penguin, England, 1971, p. 29.

4. See the section entitled "Irrationality and Theory-Choice" in Kuhn's essay "Reflections On My Critics" in Imre Lakatos and Alan Musgrave (eds.), *Criticism and the Growth of Knowledge,* Cambridge University Press, Cambridge, 1970, pp. 231-78.

5. Feyerabend comes close to this position in the construction which follows from his critique of Kuhn: ". . .the transition from pre-science to science does not replace the uninhibited proliferation and the universal criticism of the former by the puzzle-solving tradition of a normal science. It *supplements* it by this activity or, to express it even better, mature science unites two very different traditions which are often separate, the tradition of a pluralistic philosophical criticism and a more practical. . .tradition which explores the potentialities of a given material. . .without being deterred by the

difficulties that might arise and without regard to alternative ways of thinking (and acting)." Feyerabend, p. 212.

6. The presumption that all societies, communities, associations, etc., persisting through time have a similar if not identical social structure or social construction (that is, social, economic, political and religious spheres) is seldom critically discussed. It is not enough to declare that the forms of these spheres may change, if by that one is simply still insisting that the functions are omniscient (and by inference the needs they meet). Finally, one must break away; question the existence of the presumed parallelism; question the significance of "alien" historical developments not merely values and paradigms (if one can justify somehow indeed such things as paradigms and values being brought to the alien event); find the root (again if we can justify its existence within the total that is the physical and metaphysical existence and consciousness of the alien people); e.g. it may be so true that all peoples but regularize their process or actions engaged with their existence, but does that make these relationships with their environment economic (i.e. presuming a specific, linear, geometric rationality exists)? Is it not possible that what is presumed economic by us is to the creators-participants, heirs of that 'system', a fundamentally differently understood phenomenon? Could not its rationality rest on epistemology of appearances and invisibilities, on symbols and significances drawn from those totally minimized senses of representation found among ourselves? It is also instructive that the means of discovering an equally different understanding of the world among members of our own societies is effectively precluded by such analytical constructs as subculture (flinging up images of organizational charts with their lines and boxes, for example). But do we then recall the imprecision, even the mysticism of that term's prefix: sub? Sub: below, earthly, dark, fetid, beneath human attention, etc.

7. Recall that both true and valid are terms which describe the relationship of the phenomenon to the epistemological system of the subject. These terms thus suggest an *a priori* alienation of subject from object and a bridge by which a convenience between the two may be effected by exchanging the nature of the phenomenon for one system-specific to the subject.

8. Arnold Levison, *Knowledge and Society,* Pegasus: Bobbs-Merrill Company, Inc., New York, 1974, p. 87.

9. Anthony Wallace, "Revitalization Movements," *American Anthropologist,* Vol 58 No. 2, April 1956, pp. 264-81. Some readers may be more accustomed to the term millennial or the derived term millenarian. Sylvia Thrupp's comments may clarify their relationship with the notion of salvationism: "It was necessary for our purpose only to draw some line of demarcation between millennial movements on the one hand and utopian movements and revolutionary socialism on the other. Norman Cohn's opening paper draws this line primarily in terms of the element of salvationism in the former. [Cohn states that " 'millenarism' becomes simply a convenient label for a par-

ticular type of salvationism.''] The movements that his definition allows us to class together as millennial (or, to use the 17th century term that some of our contributors prefer, as millenarian), have frequently a political as well as a religious character. But their political character derives its strength largely, if not wholly from millennial inspiration, and some idea of preparation for salvation is always present if not central.'' "Millennial Dreams in Action: A Report on the Conference Discussion." in Sylvia Thrupp, ed., *Millennial Dreams in Action,* Schocken, New York, 1970, p. 11.

10. Roland Robertson comments: ". . .a major interest of such social scientists was in arriving at 'theories' of the origin of religion—among the most prominent of which were so-called *animist* and *naturist* theories. Very broadly, animist accounts emphasized the imputation by primitive societies of spirit-like qualities to animals; while naturist theories stressed the attribution of spiritual qualities to natural phenomena. The former kinds of theory relied a great deal on the theses advanced by Tylor and Spencer; that originally spirit beliefs emanated from such practices as ancestor worship and from dream experience. . .Naturism, on the other hand, rested on the claim that belief in spiritual phenomena arose out of the feelings of awe aroused by such natural entities as mountains and the sun or such natural occurrences as storms and volcanic eruptions. . .what was common to most nineteenth century evolutionists was the conviction that primitive religion (and magic) arose out of ignorance of the 'true' nature of and relationships between social, psychological and natural phenomena." *The Sociological Interpretation of Religion,* Schocken, New York, 1972, p. 13.

11. The irrational will be treated here as a framework which elicits incoherence since its constituents lack fit having emerged from fundamentally different metaphysical systems. The "irrationalists" described here are those analysts who attempted to treat with physical, empirical, social phenomena while grounding their explanations on the presupposition of the existence of phenomena which have no tangible, manifest or physical character—explanations grounded on the artifacts of faith, belief, speculation or imaginings.

12. See Alvin Gouldner's *The Coming Crisis of Western Sociology,* Avon Books, New York, 1970, Chapter II.

13. See Paul Kecskemeti's introduction to Karl Mannheim's *Essays on Sociology and Social Psychology,* Oxford University Press, New York, 1953, pp. 1-11.

14. Rudolph Sohm, *Outlines of Church History,* MacMillan & Company, Ltd., London, 1904 (original 1892) p. 32.

15. G.W.F. Hegel, *Early Theological Writings,* University of Chicago Press, Chicago, 1948, the essay entitled "The Positivity of the Christian Religion."

16. Sohm, *Church History,* pp. 34-35.

17. Freud, Fromm, Reich and Comfort will have the relevant pieces of their works cited elsewhere in this essay if they have not already been identified;

for Ernst Cassirer, see *The Myth of the State;* and for Theodore Adorno, of course, see *The Authoritarian Personality.*

18. Sohm, *Church History,* pp. 40-41. For Weber's use of Sohm's work see Reinhard Bendix, *Max Weber: An Intellectual Portrait,* Doubleday, New York, 1962, pp. 325 and 386.

19. M. A. Smith, *From Christ to Constantine,* Inter-Varsity Press, London, 1971, pp. 47-60.

20. See Chapter I, note 52 and accompanying text.

21. Sohm as well identifies the significance of the Jews in early Christian history but opposes the stress on the struggle between two ideologies to the fact of later development of the Church as *the* Christian institution: "The enemy of the Church from its very birth was Pharisaic Judaism. . .The mass of the Jewish people was Pharisaically inclined. In Pharisaism it found its own innate zeal for the law. . .proud self-consciousness of Jewish nationality. . . hatred against the heathen conqueror. . .the kingdom of Judah. . .And now in sharpest contrast to this slavish zeal for the law, appeared the Christian doctrine of the freedom of God's children from the law; in contrast to the image of a Jewish Messiah coming in earthly glory, the form of the Crucified who called heathens and Jews without distinction into His heavenly kingdom. Pharisaism meant the completion, Christianity the abolition of national Judaism." Sohm, *Church History,* p. 7.

22. Ibid., pp. 42-43.

23. Max Weber, *Economy and Society,* Bedminster Press, Inc., New York, 1968, p. 1116.

24. Ibid., pp. 1115-17. William Barrett in his discussion of "irrational man," found another, perhaps more instructive way of identifying the dynamic between these metaphysical traditions and its history in Western experience. Following the cues of Matthew Arnold's distinction between Hebraism and Hellenism—the experience of faith as opposed to the idea of reason—Barrett deepened Arnold's insight by contrasting the cries of Job and the Psalmist to the etiological record of the imprint on Western thought of the Greek concepts *theatai, legein,* and *kalokagatnia:* to see; to speak, and the beautiful and the good. The conflict between the two traditions as Barrett saw it was between the man of faith, the poet and the committed and the man of reason, the spectator, the detached: "Biblical man too had his *knowledge,* though it is not the intellectual knowledge of the Greek. It is not the kind of knowledge that man can have through reason alone, or perhaps not through reason at all; he has it rather through body and blood, bones and bowels, through trust and anger and confusion and fear, through his passionate adhesion in faith to the Being whom he can never intellectually know. This kind of knowledge a man has only through living, not reasoning, and perhaps in the end he cannot even say what it is he knows; yet it is knowledge all the same, and Hebraism at its source has this knowledge." (Barrett, *Irrational Man,* Doubleday & Company, New York, 1962, p. 70). "The conception of human

finitude places in question the supremacy that reason has traditionally been given over all other human functions in the history of Western philosophy. Theoretical knowledge may indeed be pursued as a personal passion, or its findings may have practical application; but its value above that of all other human enterprises (such as art or religion) cannot be enhanced by its claim that it will reach the Absolute." (Ibid., p. 80) Yet Barrett is characterized by a rationalism rather than the poise of a "knight of infinite resignation." (to use Kierkegaard's phrase)

25. Weber, *Economy and Society,* p. 1116.

26. Ibid., p. 1120.

27. Margaret Murray, *The God of the Witches,* Oxford University Press, London, 1970 (originally published in 1931). For a similar treatment of satanism, see Jules Michelet's *Satanism and Witchcraft,* Citadel Press, New York, 1971 (originally published in 1939).

28. William James, *The Varieties of Religious Experience,* Modern Library, New York, 1929 (originally published in 1902) p. 29.

29. Ibid., p. 36. For some of the most perplexing problems of the application of psychological methods to religious experience, see Pierce Butler, "Church History and Psychology of Religion," *American Journal of Psychology,* Vol. XXVII, No. 4, Oct. 1921, pp. 543-551.

30. Sohm, *Church History,* p. 234.

31. Ibid., p. 232.

32. Ibid., pp. 236-7.

33. Ibid., p. 218.

34. Quoted in Cushing Strout, "William James and the Twice-born Sick Soul" in Dankwart Rustow (ed.), *Philosophers and Kings, Daedalus,* Summer 1968, p. 1075.

35. James, *Religious Experience,* pp. 490-1.

36. Ibid., pp. 352-3.

37. Ibid., p. 29.

38. The mechanisms for the transmission of this "racial memory" were and are somewhat ambiguous in Freudian and psychoanalytic theory. Some of Freud's writings (as do those of Jung and Erikson) suggested a Lamarckian inheritance while at other points the implication was that the "memory" was a cultural phenomenon (totem, taboo) and the mechanism learning. A not too curious consequence of scientific revolutions of the late 19th and early 20th centuries in those various empirical treatments of the mind and the brain is that the question is left entirely unresolved. Genetic code, neurology and social theory continue to successfully compete for paradigmatic authority over this phenomenon whether Freudian or some other system or element is intended by memory. Freud did use the notion of "collective unconscious" in the last of his major works, *Moses and Monotheism,* Vintage, New York, 1939, pp. 167-70.

39. See Cushing Strout, "William James" and Gay Wilson Allen's *William*

James, Viking Press, New York, 1967. Allen especially integrates his biography with the several writings of James.

40. See David Bakan's *Sigmund Freud and the Jewish Mystical Tradition,* Schocken, New York, 1969. For an interesting treatment of Freud's ambiguity toward being a Jew, see Immanuel Velikovsky, "The Dreams that Freud Dreamed," *Psychoanalytic Review,* Vol. XXVIII, October 1941, pp. 487-511.

41. Sigmund Freud, "Group Psychology and the Analysis of the Ego," in *The Complete Psychological Works of Sigmund Freud,* Vol. XVIII, (1920-22), Hogarth Press and Institute of Psychoanalysis, London, 1957.

42. Ibid., p. 78.

43. Ibid., p. 127.

44. Ibid., p. 116.

45. Ibid., p. 103.

46. Ibid., p. 140.

47. Ibid., p. 142.

48. Ibid.

49. Ibid., p. 143.

50. In the midst of the surge of 'suggestive' strengths Freud's explanatory theories were often characterized by, it is perhaps less than fully just to ignore conveniently Freud's own ambivalences concerning his analytical constructs. He did somewhere declare that they were to be used for the moment, instead of empirically manifest phenomena—an assertion that the sciences of the mind had not yet achieved an expected capability. If this were in time to occur it would not alter the fact that Freud proceeded in the founding of theory clothed in metaphysics, intuition, speculation and a private genius for 'imagining' relatedness. He would remain an irrationalist despite such apologia as put forth by followers like Fromm (see Harry K. Wells' *The Failure of Psychoanalysis,* International Publishers, New York, 1963, p. 120).

51. Wilhelm Reich, *The Mass Psychology of Fascism,* Farrar, Strauss & Giroux, New York, 1970, p. 53.

52. According to one of Freud's accounts of the origins of his interests in sexuality, it was owed to the almost cavlier asides made to him by Rudolf Ckrobak, J. M. Charcot and Josef Breuer which did indeed treat with orgasmic sexuality rather than the mere undifferentiated, liebe-libido, polymorphic perverse sexuality of the child, See Freud's *A History of Psychoanalysis* in the collected papers of Sigmund Freud, Vol. 1, p. 294; and Norman O. Brown's *Life Against Death,* Wesleyan Press, Middleton, Conn., 1959.

53. This is, of course, the title of two of Reich's works, one, the first, differentiated from the second by the retention of its title in German rather than in the English. See Constantin Sinelnikov, "Early 'Marxist' Critiques of Reich," *Telos,* No. 13, Fall 1972, p. 131.

54. This is a reference to Reich's "sex-pol" movement begun in the

mid-1930s. For Reich's meaning of this term, see his *Mass,* pp. 170-204, and "What is Class Consciousness" in *Liberation,* Vol. 16, No. 5, October 1971, pp. 15-49; also see Norman O. Brown, *Life Against Death,* pp. 27f, for polymorphic perversity. Reich had the distinction of being censored from both the German Communist Party and the International Psychoanalytical Association. Each was on the basis of his involvement with the other. See Paul Robinson, *The Freudian Left,* Harper, New York, 1969, pp. 37 and 56; and Howard Press, "The Marxism and Anti-Marxism of Wilhelm Reich," *Telos,* No. 9, Fall, 1971, pp. 65-82.

55. Freud, *Civilization and Its Discontents,* W. W. Norton & Company, New York, 1962, p. 80.

56. Ibid., pp. 91-2.

57. Reich, *Mass Psychology,* p. xii.

58. Ibid., p. xv.

59. Ibid., pp. xii-xiii.

60. Erich Fromm, *Escape From Freedom,* Avon Books, New York, 1966, pp. 317-318.

61. Ibid., p. 161.

62. Ibid., pp. 240-1.

63. Ibid., p. 242.

64. Ibid., p. 245.

65. Wells, *Failure of Psychoanalysis,* p. 130.

66. Ibid., p. 132.

67. Modern, presumably with its suggestion of spontaneity and only quite tenuous links with the past.

68. Norman Cohn, *The Pursuit of the Millennium,* Oxford University Press, New York, 1970, p. 284.

69. For the influence of Marx on Cohn, see Cohn, *Pursuit of the Millennium,* pp. 26-32.

70. Ibid., p. 176.

71. Ibid., pp. 281-2.

72. I have in mind, specifically, Max Weber, but as well Engels and other analysts of the advent of bourgeois society.

73. Zevedei Barbu's work, *Problems of Historical Psychology* (Grove Press, New York, 1960), is of interest here because in it he attempts to confront the presumption of a racial continuity suggested in the historians' use of categories like "the French," "the English," etc. Granted that the flow of institutions, language, culture, etc., do mean something when one is concerned with continuity, yet Barbu is struck by the evidence of critical psychological discontinuities between "the French" over historical periods (that is periods whose boundaries are marked by societal events presumed traumatic in their consequence and impact). Cohn and Barbu are thus complementary, suggesting the prominences and depressions on the side of a coin, as the first is concerned with unremarked continuities and the latter with change.

74. Cohn, *Pursuit of the Millennium,* p. 309.

75. Ibid., p. 283.

76. Ibid., p. 286.

77. See Eric Wolf's conclusion in his *Peasant Wars of the Twentieth Century,* Harper & Row, New York, 1969; and his two essays in Roderick Aya and Norman Miller (eds.), *National Liberation,* Free Press, New York, 1971.

78. E. V. Walter in his *Terror and Resistance* (Oxford University Press, New York, 1969), if you recall, has suggested that totalitarian regimes are not unique if they are to be characterized as reigns through terror. Walter argues that rule and some form of terror are concomitants. It is then another way of saying that order may be accomplished through terror. Theoretically, this should not be so since epistemological terror and order are anti-material to each other, that is dialectically contradictory but not conflictual as historical or dialectical materialisms would demand. It is not terror, the experience of being without an order, which is used as an instrument of control, but fear: the experience of terror organized into meaning. It is the second-order phenomenon: fear of something, fear of something to be done, fear of something to be lost, which has been and is a social device. Terror is existential while fear—within the confines of social and political mechanisms is the consequence of the engineering of choice—the manipulation of rationality—so that the options are unmanageable for the victim. Historically, the "terrors" of rules have been survived, lived with, accomodated to, because offering an order to which the individual might or might not adjust, they were not really terror but terrible. No individual, no madman or woman can produce terror, for he or she operates within a system or a set of systems, whether alone or augmented by legions.

79 .J. G. A. Pocock, *Politics, Language and Time,* Atheneum, New York, 1971, pp. 277-8.

80. Cited in F. S. C. Northrop's introduction to Heisenberg's *Physics and Philosophy,* Harper and Row, New York, 1962. For a corroborating item, see the articles by Walter Sullivan in *The New York Times* on the progress of the publication of Einstein's private papers, manuscripts, etc., March 28, 29 and 30, 1972.

Chapter IV   *The Messiah and the Metaphor*

1. An interesting and much earlier example of pre-scientific explanation of political development (?) is found in Plato's concept of *eros.* It is interesting because it is dialectical and evidences, in part, the antiquity of the belief in the tendency toward perfectability caused by the tension between things and Forms, a tension manifested and resolved by *eros:* "The *Republic,* finally, teaches that *Eros* [casual energy; the bond between opposing objects] and *Eidos* [Forms] are effective only within the *Polis,* just as the *Polis,* in turn,

is founded on *Eros* and *Eidos*. For it is founded around the *Agathon*, and *Eros* is the union of its rulers in their striving toward this center. "Man and *Polis* are Part of the cosmic order. Without *Eros,* the heaven and earth would break asunder. Thus the function of *Eros* is fulfilled only within the widest possible context. . .Aristophanes, finally, expresses the hope that *Eros,* in the future, will lead the divided fragments of men, that is, will restore us to the state of original perfection resembling that of our creators." Paul Friedlander, *Plato,* Bollingen Series LIX, Pantheon Books, New York, 1958, p. 55.

2. Sigmund Freud, *Moses and Monotheism,* Vintage, New York, 1939, p. 81.

3. See for an example of the conceptual confusion surrounding the advent of the charismatic leader and his role in reconstructing or creating a political society and system, David Apter's *Ghana in Transition* and his subsequent "rethinking" in his essay 'Nkrumah, Charisma and the Coup," in *Daedalus,* Summer, 1968, pp. 757-92. Ann Ruth Willner has as well contributed to this revision of charismatic theory by her use of the phrase "quasi-revolutionary leaders" in an unpublished paper ("Quasi-Revolutionary Charismatic Political Leaders and Periods of Crisis," presented at the Sixty-Fifth Annual Meeting of the American Political Science Association, New York, September 2-6, 1969), comparing Nkrumah, Nasser and Sukarno. The revision may be most simply summarized as the recognition that the charismatic leader in the role of facilitator for "modernization" (the institutionalization of Western technology, organizational patterns, instrumental mores, etc.) and adaptation to crises and change in nonindustrialized societies is an incomplete social mechanism when institutional (e.g., indigenous bureaucrats) social (e.g., traditional elites, voluntary associations, mass political parties) and cultural supports are not mobilized.

4. G. van der Leeuw, "Primordial Time and Final Time," Joseph Campbell (ed.), *Man and Time,* Bollingen Series XXX, Pantheon Books, Inc., New ork, N.Y., 1957, p. 326.

5. Ibid., p. 337.

6. "The Middle Ages had lived on a vision which was itself inherited from the most ancient times. This vision consists in distinguishing in space two regions which form as it were two worlds apart, different not only in format but in nature: the *terrestrial region* and the *celestial region.* The heavens are the seat of those necessary and perfect movements of which we have a direct intuition in the case of circular motion, and in comparison with which the changes which we observe on earth seem corruptions and degradations. The passing from the celestial plane to the terrestrial plane was accomplished in time, or more precisely at the beginning of time, by an intervention from above which is at once mysterious and explanatory, and which the religious traditions of the various peoples all aim at revealing." Leon Brunschvicg, "History and Philosophy," in Raymond Klibansky and H. J. Paton, eds.,

Philosophy and History, Harper, New York, 1963, p. 28.

7. Helmuth Plessner, "On the Relation of time to Death," *Man and Time,* p. 240-1.

8. Just as Weber had argued that in constructing ideal-types his intent was the establishment of pure concepts rather than descriptions of reality, it is assumed here that one of his "accentuations" or "emphasized viewpoints" was an idealized Time. Few, if any conceptual systems have as foundation an unmixed awareness of Time, i.e., Time is only linear, only cyclical, etc., but most do have present in them a dominating sense of Time.

9. H. H. Gerth and C. Wright Mills (eds.), *From Max Weber: Essays in Sociology,* Oxford University Press, Inc., New York, 1946, p. 229.

10. Leszek Kolakowski, *The Alienation of Reason,* Doubleday and Company, New York, 1968, p. 61.

11. van der Leeuw, "Primordial Time," p. 336.

12. Talcott Parsons, ed., *Max Weber: The Theory of Social and Economic Organization,* Free Press, New York, 1-64, p. 342.

13. At other times, Weber meant by the irrational in political systems, that which was abritrary in style and personal in nature. See Otto B. Van Der Sprenkel, "Max Weber on China" in George Nadel (ed.), *Studies in the Philosophy of History,* Harper Torchbooks, New York, 1965, p. 204.

14. Ibid.

15. R. G. Collingwood, *The Idea of History,* Oxford University Press, London, 1956, pp. 43-44.

16. Rudolf Bultmann, *History and Eschatology,* Harper Torchbooks, New York, 1957, pp. 25-26.

17. See Collingwood, *Idea of History,* pp. 32-41.

18. G. W. F. Hegel, *The Phenomenology of Mind,* Harper and Row, New York and Evanston, 1967, p. 252.

19. Ibid., p. 253.

20. Hegel, *The Philosophy of History,* Dover Publications, Inc., New York, 1956, p. 29. See also J. N. Findlay, *Hegel: A Re-Examination,* George Allen and Unwin Ltd., London, 1964, pp. 330-31.

21. Bultmann, *History,* pp. 26-27. See also Hugh Schonfield, *The Passover Plot,* Bernard Geis, New York, 1965.

22. Bultman, *History,* p. 28.

23. Peter Berger is critical of Weber's sociohistorical account in *Ancient Judaism* of the rise of eschatalogical teachings. Citing more recent studies of pre-Exilic Israelite prophecy, studies which have had at their disposal data not available to European Old Testament scholars in the late 19th century, Berger joins the argument that the prophets arose from within the cultic or institutional offices of the established priesthood, not from without. Rather than the "socially detached individuals" interested in ethics and not cults, the "prophets of doom" emerged from the traditional and established priesthood, warning the Jews of the consequences of having broken the cove-

nant with their God. Yet, Berger concludes: "They do not invalidate the ideal-typical construction of charismatic authority as against traditional and legal-rational authority. More importantly, these modifications in no way weaken Weber's sociologically crucial elaboration of the process of the routinization of charisma. . .In other words, the new interpretation of prophecy, as located socially not on some solitary margin but within the religious institutions of ancient Israel, does *not* weaken the Weberian notion of the innovating power of charisma. . .charisma may also be a trait of individuals located at the center of the institutional fabric in question, a power of 'radicalization' from within rathar than of challenge from without." Peter L. Berger, "Charisma and Religious Innovation: The Social Location of Israelite Prophecy," *American Sociological Review,* December 1963, Vol. 28, No. 6, pp. 949-50.

24. Bultmann, *History,* p. 29. See also Max Weber's *Ancient Judaism,* Free Press, New York, 1967.

25. According to Walter Kaufmann, it was George Bernard Shaw who "popularized the ironic word 'superman' which has since become associated with Nietzsche. . ." *The Portable Nietzsche,* edited by Walter Kaufmann, Viking Press, New York, 1968, p. 115.

26. See Bultmann, *History,* Chapter III.

27. See Jean Cohen's "Max Weber and the Dynamics of Domination," in *Telos,* Winter, 1972, pp. 63-86, for an interpretation of Weber's understanding of the irrationality of bureaucratic society.

28. Max Weber, *Theory of Social and Economic Organization,* MacMillan Co., New York, 1947, pp. 386-7. Both Reinhard Bendix (in his *Max Weber, An Intellectual Portrait,* Anchor Doubleday, New York, 1962, pp. 30-31, and his "Max Weber and Jacob Burckhardt," in *The American Sociological Review,* April, 1965, pp. 176-84) and Carlo Antoni (in *From History to Sociology,* Wayne State University Press, Detroit, 1959) remind us that Weber was committed to the principles of power and Germany's national struggle. And thus his concern with the leader:

" 'Great men are necessary for our life, so that the world-historical movement frees itself periodically and abruptly from forms of life that are dead and from ruminating idle talk.' " (Burckhardt)

"Weber, like Burckhardt, emphasizes the inherent cultural significance of this phenomenon, its absolute transcendence of routine and its independence from ordinary moral standards, as well as the basic distinction between greatness and mere power." (Bendix, "Max Weber and Jacob Burckhardt," p. 182)

and Antoni:

"One might even argue that Weber was closer to the ideas of Machiavelli than were Droysen and Treitschke, for they still lived in the Bismarckian atmosphere, whereas Weber laboured under the privation of a genuine political direction of the nation. Just as in Machiavelli the humiliation of political impotence gave impulse to the formulation of the doctrine of the prince, so in Weber it gave birth to the idea of the leader or Fuhrer. *History to Sociology,* p. 137. See also Max Schapiro, "A Note on Max Weber's Politics," in *Politics,* February 1945, p. 44.

29. This discussion follows closely those found in Collingwood, *Idea of History,* and Ernst Cassirer, *The Myth of the State,* Yale, 1946.

30. Joseph Campbell, *The Hero with a Thousand Faces,* Meridian, New York, 1956, pp. 37-8.

31. A sense of this can be found among what I consider some of the most extraordinary lines written by Gabriel Almond. Among the three most influential experiences of his life he includes: ". . .my early apprenticeship to my father around Old Testament themes. . ." (*Political Development,* Little, Brown and Co., Boston, 1970, p. 5). He goes on to state: "The experience began with an acute sense of injustice and deprivation, with mixed feelings of boredom, defiance and fascination with the bloody, complicated and often inscrutable, often beautiful material to which I was exposed. Repeating this experience year after year I recapitulated in my own theological development the centuries-long history of Israel's search for deity and for national identity." (Ibid.) "Thus from boyhood on I was set on course in a search for this elusive form of redemption, separated from ritual and liturgy on one hand, and mysticism on the other. And on the question of means and approach to problem-solving, I have had no other real choice than continuity and adaptation together. Though it surely was never spoken in these terms, I believe my father, pious man though he was, intended it this way." (p. 7)

32. Robert Georges, *Studies on Mythology,* Dorsey Press, Homewood, Illinois, 1968.

33. Harry Levin, "Some Meanings of Myth," in Henry Murray (ed.), *Myth and Mythmaking,* Beacon Press, Boston, 1969.

34. Ibid., p. 354.

35. Ibid., p. 355.

36. Eric Hobsbawm, *Primitive Rebels,* W. W. Norton and Company, New York, 1965, pp. 60-1.

37. Clifford Geertz, "Ideology as a Cultural System," in David Apter (ed.), *Ideology and Discontent,* Free Press, New York, 1964, p. 64. The term phatic is borrowed apparently from Bronislaw Malinowski's phrase "phatic communion:" "An act of serving the direct aim of binding hearer to speaker by a tie of some social sentiment or other. Once more language appears to us in this function not as an instrument of reflection but as a mode of action." From Malinowski's "The Problem of Meaning in Primitive Languages" in C. K. Ogden and I. A. Richards (eds.), *The Meaning of Meaning: A Study of the Influence of Language upon Thought and of the Science of Symbolism,* Harcourt, Brace Press, New York, 1945, p. 316.

38. Erik Erikson, *Identity, Youth and Crisis,* W. W. Norton and Company, New York, 1968, p. 134.

39. Geertz, "Ideology," p. 49.

40. See Reinhard Bendix's historicization of the appearance of ideology in the "modern" period in his "The Age of Ideology: Persistent and Changing," in David Apter (ed.); *Ideology and Discontent.* In it, Bendix argues that ideology developed once culture had set aside the belief and presumption that human history was subject to the will and purpose of God. Once humans freed themselves from a fate subject to, and temporalized their vista, the preconditions for ideology came into existence.

41. See Hannah Arendt's *The Origins of Totalitarianism,* World Publishing, Cleveland, 1966, esp. Chapter 10; and Karl Popper's *The Open Society and Its Enemies,* Vol. I, Routledge, London, 1969, Chapter 10.

42. For Gouldner see *The Coming Crisis of Western Sociology;* for Leites, *Operational Code of the Politboro,* and for Kuhn, *The Structure of Scientific Revolutions.*

43. See Claude Levi-Strauss, *The Raw and the Cooked,* and Michel Foucault's *The Order of Things.*

44. Levi-Strauss, *The Raw and the Cooked,* Harper Torchbooks, New York, 1969, pp. 15-16.

45. Ibid., p. 12. At the time of this writing, two of the four works which make up *Les Mythologiques* have not been translated from the original French, so I am dependent on English reviews of those works: *The Origin of Table Manners,* and *The Naked Man,* (my version of their French titles), accompany *The Raw and the Cooked* and *From Honey to Ashes.*

46. Claude Levi-Strauss, *The Savage Mind,* University of Chicago Press, Chicago, 1966, p. 246.

47. Levi-Strauss, *Raw and the Cooked,* p. 341.

48. Levi-Strauss, "The Story of Asdiwal," in Edmund Leach (ed.) *The Structural Study of Myth and Totemism,* Tavistock, London, 1969, pp. 27-28.

49. Ibid., p. 29.

50. Ibid., p. 30.

51. Levi-Strauss, *Raw and the Cooked,* pp. 10, 11 and 12.

52. Ibid., p. 240.

53. See Foucault's introduction to *The Order of Things* (Random House, New York, 1970). "In France, certain half-witted 'commentators' persist in labelling me a 'structuralist'. I have been unable to get it into their tiny minds that I have used none of the methods, concepts, or key terms that characterize structural analysis." (p. xiv)

54. Kuhn's "Reflections on my Critics," in Imre Lakatos and Alan Musgrave (eds.), *Criticism and the Growth of Knowledge,* Cambridge University Press, Cambridge, 1970, pp. 266-68.

55. Foucault, *Order of Things,* p. xi.

56. Ibid., p. xx.

57. Levi-Strauss, *Raw and the Cooked,* p. 12.

58. Foucault, *Order of Things,* p. 209. One recent interpretation, that of Hayden White, attempts to explain the vagueness in Foucault of the relation-

ship between *epistemes:* ". . .these *epistemes*. . .do not succeed one another dialectically nor do they aggregate. They simply appear alongside one another—catastrophically, as it were, withot rhyme or reason. Thus, the appearance of a new 'human science' does not represent a 'revolution' in thought or consiousness. A new science of life, wealth, or language does not rise up against its predecessors; it simply crystallizes alongside of it, filling up the 'space' left by the 'discourse' of earlier sciences. . .of expression which consiousness takes in its effort to comprehend its essential mystery. As thus envisaged, the human sciences are little more than products of different wagers made by men on the possibility of grasping the secret of human life in language." See White's "Foucault Decoded: Notes from Underground" in *History and Theory,* Vol. XII, No. 1, 1973, p. 27. The text of note 55 would appear to substantively refute this interpretation. Each *episteme* determined the "space" possible for its successor.

59. Ibid., p. 310.

60. Ibid., p. 314-15.

61. Without entering into any of the latest debates surrounding Marx's philosophy and science (that is, as Louis Althusser in *Lenin and Philosophy,* distinguishes them): historical materialism and dialectical materialism, respectively, let me state that Hegel (*Philosophy of History*) and, subsequently Marx, had peculiar, at least "racist," senses of history. Marx began *Das Kapital* denying the significance of history except as HISTORY. The absence of "soul" which Hegel understood to preclude the possibility of history, became the absence of a developed capitalism and classes in Marx, and for both the crucial factors *mutatis mutandis* for denying a history to particular peoples. Within the eschatological tradition, Marx attempted to destroy history, substantiating Hegel's phenomenology through an economic theory which presumed universal parallels and ended with the precondition of history removed: class struggle. Dialectical materialism was, as Lukacs proudly delcared, a theory of capitalist society. And thus dialectical materialism was unequipped to produce an historical anthroplogy: "Thus historical materialism is, in the first instance, a theory of bourgeois society and its economic structure. . .Marx frequently emphasizes the distinction between capitalist and pre-capitalist societies as being the difference between a capitalism which is only just emerging and is therefore locked in a struggle for the control of society and a capitalism which is already dominant." Georg Lukacs, *History and Class Consciousness,* MIT Press, Cambridge, Mass., 1971, p. 229. See also Marshall Sahlins, *Stone Age Economics,* and the extraordinary essays by Ernest Mandel (*Marxist Economic Theory,* Vol. I) and Emmanuel Terray (*Marxism and Primitive Societies*) for critique and examples of Marxists at work, respectively.

62. Foucault, *Order of Things,* p. 317.

63. Maurice Godelier, "Myth and History," in *New Left Review,* London, Oct.-Sept., 1971, p. 108.

64. Zevedei Barbu, *Problems of Historical Psychology,* Grove Press, New York, 1960, p. 9.

65. Ibid., p. 13.

66. Two English-language reviewers assert that Foucault's *The Archaeology of Knowledge* is an appendix to the earlier *The Order of Things,* see White, "Foucault Decoded" and Frank Kermode's "Crisis Critic" in *New York Review of Books,* May 17, 1973, p. 37-39.

67. Godelier, "Myth and History," p. 103.

68. "The Archaic Age is usually made to end with the Persian Wars, and for the purposes of political history this is the obvious dividing line. But for the history of thought the true cleavage falls later, with the rise of the Sophistic Movement. And even then the line of demarcation is chronologically ragged. In his thought, though not in his literary technique, Sophocles (save perhaps in his latest plays) still belongs entirely to the older world; so, in most respects, does his friend Herodotus. . .Aeschylus, on the other hand, struggling as he does to interpret and rationalize the legacy of the Archaic Age, is in many ways prophetic of the new time." E. R. Dodds, *The Greeks and the Irrational,* University of California Press, Berkeley, 1971, p. 50.

69. Ibid., p. 180.

70. Ibid., p. 195.

71. Ibid., p. 189.

72. Ibid., p. 184.

73. Bruno Snell, *The Discovery of the Mind,* Harper Torchbooks, New York, 1960, p. 185.

74. Sheldon Wolin, *Politics and Vision,* Little, Brown & Co., Boston, 1960, Chapter II, see particularly pp. 29-30.

75. This citation is taken from Godelier, "Myth and History" p. 109, and which he attributes to J.P. Vernant, *Les Origines de la Pensee Grecque,* Paris, 1962, p. 117. See also Popper, *Open Society,* pp. 248-53 to which to the text closely clings.

76. Isaiah Berlin, "Machiavelli," in the *New York Review of Books,* November 4, 1971. The recognition of several processes and/or phenomena is critical to this assertion concerning the significance of mathematical and geometrical systems to Greek political philosophy: The breach between the beliefs of the people and the beliefs of the intellectuals (Dodds, p. 180), demonstrated in the dialogues between Socrates and Crito and Socrates and Meno (see Arthur Adkins' *Merit and Responsibility,* Oxford University Press, 1960, pp. 226-32) was one such process. In the area of politics, this manifest itself as a conflict between politics seen as State administration, helping friends, and harming enemies, etc., and politics as justice and perfectability ("And indeed, Plato hints that historical decay might have been avoided, had the rulers of the first or natural state been trained philosophers. But they were not. They were not trained (as he demands that the rulers of his heavenly city should be) in mathematics and dialectics; and in order to avoid degeneration,

they would have needed to be initiated into the higher mysteries of eugenics, of the science of 'keeping pure the race of the guardians', and of avoiding the mixture of the noble metals in their veins with the base metals of the workers.'' Popper, (pp. 81-2) Aristotle opposed the metaphysics of forms and numbers associated with Plato and the Academy (see Aristotle's *Metaphysics,* Book Alpha, and his *Politics,* Book V, Chapter XII for specific critiques of Plato's political philosophy). However, mathematics retained its position in the Academy (see T. A. Sinclair's *A History of Greek Political Thought,* Routledge & Kegan Paul Ltd., London, 1951, chapter XII and especially p. 247); Plato's influence on Greek political philosophy more than matched that of Aristotle during the period in question, Plato's Academy outlasting Aristotle's Lyceum by nearly 800 years (William Anderson, *Man's Quest for Political Knowledge,* University of Minnesota, Minneaplos, 1964, p. 263). For another reference to the role of physis in Greek political philosophy, see John Myles, *The Political Ideas of the Greeks,* Greenwood Press, New York, 1968, p. 248. For an entirely different approach, see Bruno Snell's comments on the capacities of the Greek language for conceptualization in his *The Discovery of the Mind,* pp. 244-45; Snell's observations would tend to support the text of this essay.

77. Dodds, *The Greeks,* pp. 182-83.

78. Ibid., p. 44.

79. Ibid., pp. 42-3.

80. Ibid., p. 48.

81. Ibid., Chapter V. By reproducing more of the text from which an earlier quote was taken (note 78), we can see that Dodds anticipates the charge of reductionism: But it was the Archaic Age that recast the tales of Oedipus and Orestes as horror-stories of blood-guilt; that made purification a main concern of its greatest religious institution, the Oracle of Delphi; that magnified the importance of *phthonos* until it became for Herodotus the underlying pattern of all history. This is the sort of fact that we have to explain.

"I may as well confess at once that I have no complete explanation to give. . . No doubt general social conditions account for a good deal. In Mainland Greece. . .the Archaic Age was a time of extreme personal insecurity. The tiny overpopulated states were just beginning to struggle up out of the misery and impoverishment left behind by the Dorian invasions, when fresh trouble arose: whole classes were ruined by the great economic crisis of the seventh century, and this in turn was followed by the great political conflicts of the sixth, which translated the economic crisis into terms of murderous class warfare. It is very possible that the resulting upheaval of social strata, by bringing into prominence submerged elements of the mixed population, encouraged the reappearance of old culture-patterns which the common folk had never wholly forgotten. . .development of a belief in daemons. . .increased resort to magical procedures. . .It is also likely, as I suggested earlier, that in minds of a different type prolonged experience of human injustice might give rise to the compensatory belief that there is justice in Heaven.'' Ibid., pp. 44-45.

82. Ibid., pp. 155-6.

83. Ibid., p. 152.

84. Foucault, *Madness and Civilization,* Mentor, New York, 1967, p. x. The term in Greek is translated "wanton violence."

85. Popper, *Open Society,* p. 253.

86. See Weber's *Ancient Judaism,* Schonfield's *The Passover Plot,* Joseph Campbell's *The Hero with a Thousand Faces,* and his *Myths To Live By,* Bantam Books, New York, 1973, p. 8.

87. Weber, *Ancient Judaism,* pp. 287-88.

88. See Chapter III, this essay.

89. Petr Kropotkin, *Memoirs of a Revolutionist,* Dover Publications, 1971, New York, pp. 288-89.

90. It should be recognized as evident in works like Victorio Lantenari's *Religions of the Oppressed,* Eric Wolf's *Peasant Wars of the 20th Century* and Eric Hobsbawm's *Primitive Rebels,* that not every oppressed people give expression to their anguish in terms of the messianic or charismatic leader-deliverer. The charismatic figure, however, does seem to be of great antiquity and is especially frequent in those cultures and people who were participants in or affected by the cultures of the Mediterranean region. Surprisingly enough, perhaps, there are people who were not in that particular tradition who did generate charismatic-like movements, e.g. see Peter Worsley's *And the Trumpet Shall Sound.*

91. Erikson, *Identity,* p. 210.

92. See Erikson's treatment of Gandhi in *Gandhi's Truth,* W. W. Norton and Company, New York, 1969, esp. pp. 223-24 and pp. 265-67.

93. The following is the context in which Weber introduces the term "war psychosis": ". . .it is quite correct that pre-exilic ethic developed under the pressure of fear, one is almost tempted to say of 'war psychosis' in view of the frightful wars of the great conquering empires. The basic mood of the Deuteronomic circle was the conviction that only a divine miracle, not human power, could bring salvation." *Ancient Judaism,* p. 246.

94. This appears to be the explanation which most satisfactorily treats with the self-destructive impulses of the charismatic figure, e.g. Martin Luther King and Malcolm X, as recent examples. See my "Malcolm Little as a Charismatic Leader," in *Afro-American Studies,* Vol. 3, 1972, pp. 81-96. See also *The Confessions of Nat Turner* and George Shepperson's and Tom Price's *Independent African* for historical examples of such trainings.

95. Schonfield, *Passover Plot.*

96. John Schaar, "Reflections on Authority" in the *New American Review,* #8, New American Library, New York, January, 1970, p. 79. This is one of the most delightful pieces written on the subject of authority. Yet it is especially frustrating as one almost feels Schaar thrashing about inside the paradigm of political authority as salvation, yet not realizing that the logic and momentum of this disenchantment will inevitably hurl him beyond it.

97. I am here, finally, only slyly alluding to the difficulty I have with Marx-

ist analysis, especially that analysis of peasant populations, from Lenin to Eric Wolf (no progression intended). Marxist, socialist revolutionaries and their sympathizers have historically as well as theoretically taken a dim view of the capacities of peasant communities to achieve, autonomously, liberation. Lenin, for example, used pen and state to suppress Russian peasantry, linking them with the reactionary characteristics of Marx's lumpen-proletariat and petit-bourgeoisie (see Lenin's *The State and Revolution*), and so did many of his national (Stalin) and ideological colleagues (Ho Chi Minh and young Mao Tse Tung). Wolf, in his *Peasant Wars,* in some confusion in characterizing the nature of peasant autonomy and capacity, rests, finally, with the assurance that the lower peasant is hopeless without, at the very least, the middle peasant (i.e., Mao, Ho, Zapata, etc.).

98. Cohen, "May Weber," pp. 82-83.

99. Edmund Leach, *Genesis as Myth and Other Essays,* Jonathan Cape Publishers, London, 1969, p. 7.

100. Ibid., p. 9.

Chapter V *On Anachism*

1. It might be useful to remind the reader of the preceding discussion of authority (Chapter I) as it is necessary that political authority be seen as a special case of authority on two levels. The first level is the more obvious, that is that political authority is political rather than non-political: it is political rather than some species of authority which is based on economic, kinship or religious principles. The second level is that as authority it is constituted in actual and contemporary terms by the possession of superior (actual or perceived) force (identified in additive and numerical terms) by some subsocietal unit. As such, political authority relates most authentically and appears most useful to societies rather than to communicate as I have defined and understood these terms.

2. There is of course here some suggestion of the anthropological myths of origins of human society constructed by such social analysts as Freud, Mill, Rousseau, and certainly most of the anarchist theorists of the 19th century. This is a form of what Karl Popper has marked as "historicism." This interpretation of the terms "replaced" and "primitive" as used in the text is understandable if not correct. What is meant here is that political authority is "legitimated" by its reliance upon crude and primal emotive and rational structures as well as skills (modes) contained in the group. Crises precipitating the choice of political authority to restore order represent in terms of individual psycho-social development a regression to choice skills (modes) acquired within the context of early socialization whenthe individual is confronted with an objective reality which consists of his own relative weakness and dependency in contrast to the strength and seeming autonomy of older, larger and more experienced members of his immediate social environment. At

the analytical level of the group, such crises incur a collective response which is the accumulation and emanation of individual biographies. The political response is only literally primitive or "first" in these terms. Moreover, there would appear to be a logical contradiction in liberal or individualistic cultures which rely on actual or potential violence and coercion as means of social organization.

3. It is important to keep in mind here the distinction drawn between history and evolution by Leslie White. In a critique of the anthropologist, A. R. Radcliffe-Brown, White commented: ". . .he confused history (the name of a temporal-particularizing process) with evolution (the name of a temporal-generalizing process)." In a subsequent paragraph, White gave this example of the difference. "The temporal-generalizing process manifested in the evolution of money is not the same as the temporal-particularizing process involved in the diffusion of coinage." *"The Social Organization of Ethnological Theory," Rice University Studies,* Vol. 52, No. 4, 1966, p. 35; see also his "History, Evolutionism and Functionalism," *Southwestern Journal of Anthropology,* 1, 1945, pp. 221-248.

4. In our non-Western example, the people classified as the Ila-Tonga, it is questionable whether traditionally anything was conceived in economic terms. We are told: ". . .in the past land for the Tonga was practically a free good, neither sold, rented nor inherited. . ." (M. A. Jaspan, *The Ila-Tonga Peoples of North-Western Rhodesia,* International African Institute, London, 1953, p. 45); also though cattle were "owned" individually, they ". . .are regarded as links in a system of social inter-relations." (Ibid., p. 46) In other words, cattle were (are) part of the kinship network. It may be that in a traditionally subsistence economy, the absence of wealth served as an inhibitor to the development of economic relations independent of kinship.

5. James Joll, *The Anarchists,* Methuen and Company Ltd., London, 1964, p. 148.

6. To a large degree, that editor's (Edwin Babelon) sense of the influential role played in scholarship by the public usage of terms has been confirmed in the "crowd" studies of Elias Canetti (*Crowds and Power,* Viking Press, New York, 1966) and George Rude (*The Crowd in History,* John Wiley & Sons, New York, 1964). Both authors see the phenomenon of crowds in terms approximating the Durkheimian phrase "anomic violence." Perhaps one of the most powerful refutations of these theses of "anomic" behavior is contained in C.L.R. James' "Colonialism and National Liberation in Africa" in Norman Miller and Roderick Aya (eds.), *National Liberation,* Free Press, New York, 1971.

7. As cited in Ernst Cassirer's *Rousseau, Kant and Goethe,* Harper Torchbooks, New York, 1963, p. 19.

8. Ibid., p. 24.

9. Joll, *Anarchists,* p. 30.

10. Cassirer, *Rousseau,* p. 26.

11. Lester Crocker, *Rousseau's Social Contract,* Case Western Reserve

University, Cleveland, 1968, p. 36. See as well Crocker's *Jean-Jacques Rousseau, The Quest,* MacMillan Company, New York, 1968. For the extraordinary ambiguity of Rousseau's writings see Ernest Barker (ed.), *The Social Contract: Essays by Locke, Hume and Rousseau,* Oxford University Press, New York, 1948, p. xxxi.

12. Sheldon Wolin, *Politics and Vision,* pp. 243-44.

13. Christopher Hill, *The Century of Revolution, 1603-1714,* Thomas Nelson, Edinburgh, 1969, pp. 111-90.

14. Wolin, *Politics and Vision,* p. 273.

15. Thomas Hobbes, *Leviathan,* Collier Books, New York, 1962, p. 163.

16. See Crocker, *Rousseau's Social Contract:* "Rousseau's personality was complex. He was an 'anarchist,' or at least an outsider, in his own society. He was also a revolutionary, a Christ-like Legislator (in his fantasies), an authoritarian (in his thinking). (p. 166) "Rousseau loved mankind, if not men. He looked around him and dreamed of a better life than the one he saw." (p. 184)

17. Joll, *Anarchists,* p. 30.

18. As we shall see below, Godwin identified as the instruments for the rationalization of human existence, education and democracy. Though both concerns have extraordinary ambiguities (and thus potential), as systems they lack characterizable integrity. As processes they must be suspended in environments which contain conflict by segmentation or channel it into other processes and structures. Neither education nor democracy are effectively useful except as subsequent or secondary instruments, since they rest upon presumed communities of value, procedure and perception.

19. Recall here the discussion which posed the two fundamental senses of order. The first, and most common meaning was, succinctly, approximate and proximate integration of institutions which serve to provide a primitive psychological security; the second meaning suggested was the elimination of history or the end of the record and social experience of disobedience to authority by the dissipation of authority. See also note 36, this chapter.

20. George Woodcock, *William Godwin,* Porcupine Press, London, 1946, p. 6.

21. Ibid.

22. As quoted in Woodcock, ibid., p. 10.

23. Ibid., p. 15.

24. Ibid., p. 20.

25. George Woodcock, *Anarchism,* Meridian Books: The World Publishing Company, Cleveland and New York, 1962, pp. 74-5.

26. William Godwin, *Enquiry Concerning Political Justice,* edited by F. E. L. Priestley, Vol. II, University of Toronto, 1946, p. 2.

27. Several analysts have suggested that Godwin anticipated many of the critical analytical concepts attributed to later socialist and anarchist writers. Alexander Gray, for example, in his *The Socialist Tradition* (Longman,

Greene & Co., London, 1946) recognizes the class war in Godwin, and the role of the State as the instrument of a class (p. 119). Godwin was also a classical rather than historical materialist, emphasizing the relationship between the development of justice and the stage of production society had attained.

28. Godwin, *Enquiry,* p. 82.

29. Ibid., p. 25.

30. Ibid.

31. Of course "his" Athens was a historical utopia, but in the following discussion we are concerned with what Godwin had called "the future history of political societies."

32. Godwin, *Enquiry,* p. 67.

33. Ibid., p. 60.

34. Woodcock, *William Godwin,* p. 65.

35. Woodcock, *Anarchism,* p. 60.

36. Ibid., p. 83.

37. Ibid., pp. 83-4.

38. See G. D. H. Cole's introduction to *The Social Contract and Discourses,* E. P. Dutton and Co., Inc., London, 1950, pp. xxxv-1.

39. For some inexplicable reason, Woodcock identifies this phase in Godwin's scenario as "extreme democracy." Apropos to Joll's sensitivity to any particular aspect of anarchist history, he would presumably join in Woodcock's estimation here since Joll identified Godwin as a "cold rationalist" which suggests perhaps the deceptive talent for calling a spade (elitist tutorship) a spade (democracy). In fairness to Godwin, though, it should be recalled in subsequent editions of his work he sought to exorcise any mention of transitional political forms. He came to rely fully on the agency of Reason. This expunging certainly doesn't excuse Woodcock's unfortunate description mentioned above nor clarify the tactical choices made by Godwin. In Godwin's altered text, men would become enlightened enough by Reason to change radically their social institutions toward liberalization. Yet he was also to argue that this enlightened phase would be nurtured and dependent upon liberalized social structures. The critical boundaries to the imagination being described here retain their tyrannical links with their past. The definition of timocracy used here is borrowed from Karl Popper: "First after the perfect state comes 'timarchy' or 'timocracy', the rule of the noble who seek honour and fame. . ." (*The Open Society and Its Enemies,* Vol. I, Routledge, London, 1969, p. 40); "The first form into which the perfect state degenerates, timocracy, the rule of the ambitious noblemen, is said to be in nearly all respects similar to the perfect state itself." (ibid.). See also T. A. Sinclair: "Giving the name aristocracy in the strict sense of 'rule of the best' to his own constitution, in which the most wise rule, he considers next how it may degenerate into something like the Spartan way, something intermediate between aristocracy and an oligarchy of the rich. This he calls Timocracy because in it great importance is attached to Honour. . . .The rulers become a military

caste. . ." (A History of Greek Political Thought, Routledge & Kegan Paul Ltd., London, 1951, pp. 161-62.

40. Godwin did suggest that the contest between "truth and falsehood" was so weighted in the favor of truth as to preclude any need for intervention on the side of truth. There was no "need of support from any political ally." Godwin thus anticipated and perhaps contributed to the disfigurement of the vision of that later theorist, Friedrich Engels, who contained in his thoughts similar *denouement* ("the withering away of the state") through the mediation of rationalized political authority ("the dictatorship of the proletariat"). Marx, though, was much less ambivalent toward the State as an instrument for social change than Godwin.

41. Godwin, *Enquiry,* p. 302. Jeremy Bentham would have agreed with Godwin, for he argued that education was itself "a particular form of government—'government acting by means of the domestic magistrate,' " John Passmore's *The Perfectability of Man,* Duckworth & Company Ltd., London, 1970, p. 175.

42. Woodcock, *Anarchism,* pp. 84-5.

43. Mary Shelley, *Frankenstein,* Everyman's Library, London, 1818, p. 101.

44. The following excerpts from Sheldon Wolin's *Politics and Vision* (Little,Brown & Co., Boston, 1960), are used to identify possible interrelations of 18th-century Liberalism and Radicalism: "In many ways the political thought of the two centuries after Locke constitute one long commentary on the three themes just discussed: the equating of government with physical compulsion, the emergence of society as a self-subsistent entity, and the willingness to accept compulsion from an impersonal source." (p. 312) "Liberals, however, were not the sole beneficiaries of the Lockian heritage. Radicals, such as Tom Paine and William Godwin, showed that a shift in emphasis combined with doctrinaire reasoning could produce a conception of society markedly different from that advocated by Locke but not without strong suggestion of his influence." (p. 313) "To model the political order after society, to re-create the spontaneity, naturalism and peaceful relationships of society in a political setting was but to hanker after a non-political condition. The hostility towards politics gained further momentum in the nineteenth century and again it was the Lockian notion of society as a self-subsistent entity which supplied the inspiration for a wide variety of theories each sharing in this animus." (Ibid.)

45. Nechayev is a somewhat enigmatic figure in anarchist historiography. Most analysts would accord to him only a most peripheral role in this intellectual movement and primarily through his disjunctive relationship with Bakunin. Nechayev was committed to dictatorship (autocracy), a convergence of power and narcissism which would seem to settle the question, yet he merges again with the tradition through the resemblance of his techniques and designations with those of late 19th- and early 20th-centuries anarchist activists. The autocratic nature of his narcissism precluded any moral or social

proscriptions—"any rulers," and as such he articulates historically with such men as the unquestionably anarchistic leader of the Russian anarchist army and movement, Nestor Makhno, and the Mexican agrarianist, Emiliano Zapata. Nechayev like most individuals resists the imposition of analytical categorization. His life taunts paradigmatic assessment. He is described as murderer, fanatic, extortionist, thief, liar, traitor, nihilist and finally as insane. In short, he was "possessed" of a singular freedom of action for one bred in human society. In our own time, the clinicians assuredly will have the final word.

46. P. J. Proudhon, *Oeuvres Completes de P.J. Proudhon,* edited by G. Bougle and H. Moysset, Marcel Riviere Co., Paris, 1951, p. 101. Or see *Selected Writings of P. J. Proudhon,* edited by Stuart Edwards, Macmillan & Co., London, 1969, p. 159.

47. Bougle and Moysset, ibid., p. 125; Edwards, ibid., p. 163.

48. Max Stirner, *The Ego and His Own,* A. C. Fifield, London, 1912, p. 6.

49. In connection with this declaration, A. R. Louch's *Explanation and Human Action* and Michael Polanyi's *Personal Knowledge* and *The Tacit Dimension of Understanding* have been very instructive. A concrete and simple sample of this phenomenon of tautology is contained in Godfrey Leinhardt's example of the anthropologists (among whom was Darwin) who, while investigating the culture of the Tierra Del Fuego Indians, asked their informants so persistently and pointedly about the extent of cannibalism among them that the Fuegians with some humor and good manners began to elaborate full narratives of the phenomenon—all untrue! Darwin and the others "knew" them to be savages—an early stage of human evolution—thus they could not be far removed from cannibalism—a primitive form of sociality and subsistence. Of course most contemporary social scientists are much more subtle than their 19th-century counterparts but no less tautological, a fact somewhat signified by the recurrent theme of self-fulfilling prophecy in professional journals. Godfrey Lienhardt, *Social Anthropology,* Oxford University Press, 1967, p. 11.

50. Here is the one intellectual precedent if noit antecedent, for the theories of contemporary ethnologists such as Konrad Lorenz, Desmond Morris and Robert Ardrey who would hope to draw similar lessons for human society from the observation of "lower order" societies. Present efforts, however, are characterized more by persuasion and despair than the architectonicism of Proudhon and Kropotkin.

51. Stirner, *Ego and His Own,* p. 319.

52. Woodcock, *Anarchism,* p. 104.

53. Walter Kaufmann (ed.), *The Portable Nietzsche,* Viking Press, New York, 1968, p. 84.

54. See note 45 above.

55. Woodcock, *Anarchism,* p. 172.

56. As quoted in Woodcock, ibid., p. 110.

57. Ibid., p. 113.

58. Eric Hobsbawm, "Reflections on Anarchism" in *The Spokesman,* No. 7, London, November 1970, p. 13. Irving Horowitz in *The Anarchists,* his patronizingly hostile (Marxist?) introduction to a montaged presentation of anarchist theories and histories, suggests that the anarchists were heirs of Kant in the altruistic element in their thought. He pursues this analysis by systematically excluding Stirner, Nechayev and Nietzsche from the "classical anarchism" or Godwin, Kropotkin, Bakunin, etc., or submitting the former to analytical 'bloops'. Egoist anarchy is a deviant case, for Horowitz, to be associated more appropriately with "classical conservatism" than to the philosophies of the social revolutionists. Around the notions of property, violence, anti-intellectualism, rights over law, and anti-Marxism, Horowitz argues that the egoist and conservatives tended to converge and reinforce the others' position. (Hobsbawm in the article cited above also sees suggestions of an identity between anarchy and conservative economic theory.) "The aberration and absurdity it yielded (Horowitz is writing of the resistance to governmental interdiction pursued by American "individualistic" anarchists during the 1930s depression) is hence nothing but the logical outcome of the arguments it put forth." (p. 52). Horowitz thus fails to grasp this form of anarchism by its conceptual holds. Property outside of organized economic systems which are characterized by exploitation is a much more confined expression than its homonym posited on such systems; with fewer analytical codings it relates directly to another sense of property: an intrinsic element essential to the autonomy and survival of the described organism. Horowitz's claim for an antiviolence ethic shared by egoists and conservatives is either disingenuous or bad history. In identifying anti-intellectualism as a characteristic of egoist theory, Horowitz does not succeed in recognizing that these men were asserting an opposition to intellectualism as they understood it to mean sterile, immobilizing scholasticism and an instrument by which intellectual elites would deceitfully seduce and oppress their fellow individuals. However, the original intention of this note was to declare, contrary to Horowitz, that Kant vs. Hegel was no consistent character of anarchist theory, thought and action. There were approximations to Hegelian philosophy among the egoists in their pronouncement of the power of ideas over Reality.

59. Richard Johnson, *The French Communist Party Versus the Students,* Yale University Press, New Haven, 1972.

60. An interesting and significant ontological insight into the term "leader" emerges from a perusal of the anthropological materials on political organization and political authority. The term "leader" is succeeded by those of headman, chief, village elder, paramount chief, king, emperor, as one encounters, generally, social organizations of increasing size and more complex horizontal and vertical differentiations (though this relationship of size of population or that of density of population are not truly deterministic for the evolution of political authority—see Max Gluckman, *Politics, Law and Ritual in Tribal*

Society, Aldine Publishing Co., 1965, pp. 84-5). These typological distinctions are intended to suggest not only transformations into fuller authorities, other technologies of rule, critical elements of territoriality and sociology, but also refer to respective stylistic concomitants. The leader, usually associated with the relatively small, extra-familial (or familial extensions of) hunting bands characteristic of peoples like the Bergdama and Bushman of Central Africa, has typically a very definite style and "political range." His style is role-specific in that it relates almost exclusively to the male hunting group and the relatively superior hunting skills he brings to it. His selection as leader is ascriptive and his range particular. The small size of the group in "settlement," the relatively sparse density of population of the region, the kinship felt with other social groupings—part reinforcement, part resultant of exogamic marriage rules, the perception of the land as the most powerful of any hostile forces, all these factors integrate with each other to make warfare a quite remote element in the repertoire of the leader's living group. As such the process of institutionalization of fuller and more dominant leadership into rulership which to some degree is the concomitant of leaders of fighting or warring groups is absent. The leader is a domestic authority inasmuch as he has no function in the relationships between human groups. The enemy, again, is the earth, not other social organizations or groups and his skills are immediate to the interests of his group in its entirety since they relate to the extraction of survival out of the earth as hunting plain. Even the notion of leadership as a science or art with the implication of being and remaining leader is foreign to this example of leader from the anthropological literature. It would be an abuse of understanding and an analytical transgression to describe this experience as an "economic form of leadership" in any sense because the functions it prescribes are related to a precise role within the economic system and the suggestions of an evolutionary historicity lacks empirical data or validation. In current usage, even among social and political scientists, the term "leader" evokes much more powerful images with broader ranges certainly. For these analysts there seems to exist a metaphysics of leaders which is absent among those political anthropologists who are more deliberate in their choice of words and not the intellectual step-children of the former. Shortcuts in nominal and notational language are useful as long as they do not forfeit the sense of phenomenon complexity authentic to it, for such is one way to the loss of meaning so often painstakingly acquired. I am writing here of the anthropological precedent because it is an example which is more appropriate in spirit to the form and substance of "leader" least injurious to individual development. Terms like "political leadership" as they relate to political systems (parties, democracies, dictatorships, monarchies, oligarchies, etc.) seem quite horrendous and finally alien obstacles when this concern becomes central. When dealing with whatever variant of political leadership, it should be understood that this is a binary whose complementary term is followership *to some degree.*

61. Lewis H. Morgan, *Ancient Society,* Kerry & Co., Chicago, 1877.

62. Henry S. Maine, *Ancient Law,* Murray & Co., London, 1861.

63. Max Weber, *Theory of Social and Economic Organization,* translated by A. R. Henderson and T. Parsons, W. Hodge & Co., New York, 1947.

64. Robert Lowie, *The Origin of the State,* Harcourt, Brace, New York, 1927.

65. John Middleton and David Tait (eds.), *Tribes Without Rulers,* Routledge and Kegan Paul Ltd., London, 1958.

66. Ibid., pp. 1-1.

67. S. Nadel, *A Black Byzantium,* Oxford University Press, London, 1942.

68. A. R. Radcliffe-Brown, *Structure and Function in Primitive Society,* Cohen & West Ltd., London, 1952.

69. Max Gluckman, *Custom and Conflict in Africa,* Basil Blackwell, Oxford University Press, London, 1955.

70. A. Southall, *Alur Society,* W. Heffer & Sons Ltd., Cambridge, 1953.

71. Meyer Fortes, *The Web of Kinship Among the Tallensi,* Oxford University Press, London, 1949.

72. Edmund Leach, *Political Systems of Highland Burma,* Bell Co. Ltd., London, 1954

73. Middleton and Tait, *Tribes Without Rulers,* p. xi-xii.

74. Marvin Harris, *The Rise of Anthropological Theory,* Thomas Crowell, New York, 1968, pp. 514-538.

75. Middleton and Tait, *Tribes Without Rulers,* p. 3; see also Georges Balandier's reconstruction of J. Van Velsen's *The Politics of Kinship* in the former's *Political Anthropology,* Pantheon Books, New York, 1970, pp. 50-1, for an example of the persistence of ethnocentrism.

76. The term "Tonga" will be used generically to refer to the Ila-Tonga one of three principal groups of Tonga peoples (the Ila-Tonga, the Southern Tonga and the Valley Tonga). Since they possessed no political or territorial boundaries (". . .it is well nigh impossible. . .to fix the boundary between Tonga and Ila. . ." (Elizabeth Colson, *Among the Cattle-Owning Plateau Tonga,* Livingstone, Rhodes-Livingston Museum, 1949, p. 3), and are geographically dispersed, the several Tonga peoples are variously differentiated by their relation to other groups (e.g. the Ila, "Toka" or Shona, respectively) or by the geographic characteristics of their settlements (Plateau, West Nyasa, and Gwembe Valley, respectively). Toka and We are also terms found in the literature to refer to the second and third groups of Tonga.

77. Simon and Phoebe Ottenberg, *Cultures and Societies of Africa,* Random House, New York, 1960; and George P. Murdock, *Africa,* McGraw-Hill, New York, 1959.

78. Elizabeth Colson, *Marriage and Family Among the Plateau Tonga of Northern Rhodesia,* Manchester University Press, 1958.

79. Gluckman, *Politics,* pp. 81-122.

80. Ibid., p. 93.

264

81. Elizabeth Colson, *The Plateau Tonga of Northern Rhodesia,* Manchester University Press, 1962, pp. 1-65.

82. Ibid.

83. Gluckman, *Politics,* pp. 96-7.

84. Ibid., p. 97.

85. Ibid., pp. 94-5.

86. Ibid., p. 96.

87. Georges Balandier, *Political Anthropology,* Raymond Aron, *Progress and Disillusion: The Dialectics of Modern Society,* Pall Mall Press, London, 1968.

88. J.G.A. Pocock, *Politics, Language and Time,* Atheneum, New York, 1971, p. 278.

89. Erik Erikson, *Identity, Youth, and Crisis,* W. W. Norton & Company, New York, pp. 218-9.

90. I am referring here, of course, to Einstein's special theory of relativity and Heisenberg's principle of uncertainty. See conclusion of Chapter III.

91. Of interest here is Erikson's discussion of shame and guilt found in his works *Childhood and Society* and *Identity, Youth, and Crisis.*

92. Gluckman, see for list of secondary sources, pp. 121-2.

93. Ibid., pp. 98-9.

94. Ibid., pp. 100-1.

95. Ibid., pp. 110-1.

96. Thought flows quite directly here in at least four directions. First, I have in mind Popper's treatment of Plato's futile computations against the irrational numbers see *The Open Society and Its Enemies,* Vol. I, pp. 148-53, and Chapter IV. Secondly, Michael Polanyi's and A. R. Louch's treatises on explanation contained, respectively, in *Personal Knowledge* and *Explanations and Human Action.* Thirdly, the most contemporary of linguists, Noam Chomsky and his predecessors Ernst Cassirer and Ludwig Wittgenstein in their respective works, *Cartesian Linguistics, The Philosophy of Symbolic Forms,* and *Philosophical Investigations.* I have already mentioned the anthropologist-philosopher Claude Levi-Strauss and refer to his works, *The Elementary Structures of Kinship* and *The Savage Mind.* Each of these works deals with the arbitrarily drawn boundaries between the irrational and the rational in mathematics, Western scientific thought, language, symbol-use and mythology.

Chapter VI *Conclusion*

1. J. G. A. Pocock, *Politics, Language and Time,* Atheneum, New York, 1971, p. 286.

2. See Robert Nisbet, *Social Change in History,* Oxford University Press, London, 1969.

3. See among others, Reginald Green, *The Death of Adam,* Iowa State University Press, Ames, Iowa, 1959.

4. G. W. F. Hegel, *The Phenomenology of Mind,* Harper Torchbooks, New York, 1967, p. 78.

5. István Mészáros, *Marx's Theory of Alienation,* Harper Torchbooks, New York, 1970, p. 64.

6. Karl Polanyi, *The Great Transformation,* Beacon Press, Boston, 1944, p. 57.

7. Despite the fact that most of Levi-Strauss' work has been classically that of an anthropologist—focusing on "primitive" peoples like the Indians of the New World—the ontology for which he means to be significant is that which has been produced in the civil society: bourgeois culture.

8. Jürgen Habermas, *Knowledge and Human Interests,* Beacon Press, Boston, 1972, pp. 214-273.

9. Chapter V.

10. Woodcock has, interestingly, given a clue to this ironic relationship between liberal statist tradition and the libertarian *reaction* by noting that the use of anthropological data to legitimate the utility of the latter was generally specious: "The peasant communism of the Russian *mir,* the village organization of the Kabyles in the Atlas Mountains, the free cities of the European Middle Ages, the communities of the Essenes of the early Christians and the Doukhobors, the sharing of goods implied in the customs of certain primitive tribes: all these attract the anarchist theoretician as examples of what can be done without the apparatus of the state, and they draw him nostalgically to a contemplation of man as he may have been in these fragments of a libertarian past. The accuracy of the interpretations which Kropotkin in particular made of these early societies may well be questioned on the grounds that insufficient account was taken of the extent to which a tyranny of custom becomes a substitute for overt authority." George Woodcock, *Anarchism,* Meridian Books, New York, 1962, p. 25. Woodcock has, however, misrepresented Kropotkin who did indeed recognize as often "absurd" the basis for mutual aid, but who did fail to recognize its implications for *the nature of the ego* in such communities of "savages." (See *Mutual Aid,* Porter Sargent, Boston, 1902?, pp. 111-112.

11. Michel Foucault, *The Order of Things,* Tavistock Publications, London, 1970, pp. 377-378.

12. Marx's criticisms of Proudhon are especially instructive and revealing on this point. "In an advanced society the *petty bourgeois* is necessarily from his very position a socialist on the one side and an economist on the other; that is to say, he is dazed by the magnificence of the big bourgeoisie and has sympathy for the sufferings of the people. Deep down in his heart he flatters himself that he is impartial and has found the right equilibrium, which claims to be something different from mediocrity. A petty bourgeois of this type glorifies *contradiction* because contradiction is the basis of his existence. He is himself nothing but social contradiction in action. He must justify in theory

what he is in practice, and M. Proudhon has the merit of being the scientific interpreter of the French petty bourgeoisie—a genuine merit, because the petty bourgeoisie will form an integral part of all the impending social revolutions.'' *The Poverty of Philosophy,* International Publishers Co., Inc., New York, 1971, p. 193. See also Marx's ''Indifference to Politics'' in *Marx, Engels, Lenin—Anarchism and Anarcho-Syndicalism,* International Publishers Co., Inc., New York, 1972, pp. 94-99, especially, p. 99.

13. See Karl Marx, ''On the Jewish Question'' and ''Contribution to the Critique of Hegel's 'Philosophy of Right' '' in Robert Tucker's *Marx-Engels Reader,* W. W. Norton & Company, Inc., New York, 1972, pp. 25-51 and pp. 11-23, respectively.

14. Some brief recognition should be given to the mixture of dynamics which were realized in the Western anarchist tradition. That can be done most simply by subsuming those dynamics under two categories: 1) those anarchisms which had their roots in and were a reflection of the bourgeois society; and 2) those anarchisms that Kropotkin (and later writers such as George Orwell, Eric Hobsbawm and Franz Borkenau) would trace to older social order; e.g. medieval and post-feudal agrarian communalizations. The first, as was mentioned, found its most dominant expression in literature, theory and terror; the second, in traditional kin and cooperative social structures, e.g. village peasantry. To some degree these two dynamics would come together in the utopian and communitarian ventures of 19th-century England and North America. Yet too precise a periodization and location leads to error for it must be recalled that there were others at other times. The Boer movement in Southern Africa, strongly communitarian and anarchist, though ''of'' the 19th century had immediate roots in the 16th-century Huguenot rebellion.

15. Foucualt, *Order of Things,* pp. 261-62.

16. Of these three ways of knowing, Foucault has written: ''In relation to the 'human sciences', psychoanalysis and ethnology are rather 'counter-sciences'; which does not mean that they are less 'rational' or 'objective' than the others, but that they flow in the opposite direction, that they lead them back to their epistemological basis, and that they ceaselessly 'unmake' that very man who is creating and re-creating his positivity in the human sciences.'' Ibid., p. 379. The structure of this essay and Foucault's instruction are paradoxically fortuitous.

17. Alvin Gouldner, *The Coming Crisis of Western Sociology,* Avon Books, New York, 1970.

18. Pocock, *Politics, Language and Time,* p. 276.

Bibliography

Adorno, Theodor, and others. *The Authoritarian Personality.* Harper, New York, 1950.

Adkins, Arthur. *Merit and Responsibility.* Oxford University Press, London, 1960.

Allen, Gay Wilson. *William James.* Viking Press, 1967.

Almond, Gabriel. *Political Development.* Little, Brown & Co., Boston, 1970.

Almond, Gabriel, and Powell, G. Bingham. *Comparative Politics.* Little, Brown & Co., Boston, 1966.

Althusser, Louis. *Lenin and Philosophy.* Monthly Review Press, New York, 1972.

Anderson, William. *Man's Quest for Political Knowledge.* University of Minnesota, Minneapolis, 1964.

Antoni, Carlo. *From History to Sociology.* Wayne State University Press, Detroit, 1959.

Apter, David. *Ghana in Transition.* P. Smith, Gloucester, Mass., 1963.

——."Nkrumah, Charisma and the Coup" *Daedalus.* Summer, 1968.

——.(ed.). *Ideology and Discontent.* Free Press, New York, 1964.

Arendt, Hannah. *Between Past and Future.* Faber and Faber, London, 1961.

——.*Eichmann in Jerusalem.* Viking Press, New York, 1965.

——.*The Human Condition.* University of Chicago Press, Chicago, 1959.

——.*The Origins of Totalitarianism.* World Publishing, Cleveland, 1966.

Aron, Raymond. *Progress and Disillusionment: The Dialectics of Modern Society.* Pall Mall Press, London, 1968.

Aya, Roderick and Miller, Norman, (eds.). *National Liberation.* Free Press, New York, 1971.

Ayer, A. J. *Language, Truth and Logic.* Dover Publications, New York, 1952.

Bachrach, Peter. *The Theory of Democratic Elitism.* Little, Brown and Company, Boston, 1967.

Bakan, David. *Sigmund Freud and the Jewish Mystical Tradition.* Schocken Books, New York, 1969.

Balandier, Georges. *Daily Life in the Kingdom of the Kongo.* Meridian Books, World Publishing Company, New York, 1966.

——.*Political Anthropology*. Pantheon Books, New York, 1970.

——.*Sociology in Black Africa*. Praeger Publishers, New York, 1970.

Barbu, Zevedei. *Problems of Historical Psychology*. Grove Press, New York, 1960.

Barker, Ernest, (ed.). *The Politics of Aristotle*. Oxford University Press, New York, 1962.

Barrett, William. *Irrational Man*. Doubleday & Company, New York, 1962.

Bendix, Reinhard. *Max Weber, An Intellectual Portrait*. Anchor Doubleday, New York, 1962.

——."The Age of Ideology: Persistent and Changing" David Apter, (ed.). *Ideology and Discontent*. Free Press, New York, 1964.

——."Max Weber and Jacob Burckhardt" *The American Sociological Review*. April, 1965.

Berger, Peter L. "Charisma and Religious Innovation: The Social Location of Israelite Prophecy" *The American Sociological Review*. December, 1963.

Berger, Peter L. and Luckmann, Thomas. *The Social Construction of Reality*. Anchor Books, Garden City, 1966.

Berlin, Isaiah. "Machiavelli" *The New York Review of Books*. November 4, 1971.

Brown, Norman O. *Life Against Death*. Wesleyan Press, Middleton, Conn., 1959.

Bultmann, Rudolf. *History and Eschatology*. Harper Torchbooks, New York, 1957.

Braybrooke, David and Lindblom, Charles. *A Strategy of Decision*. Free Press, New York, 1963.

Campbell, Joseph. *The Hero with a Thousand Faces*. Meridian, New York, 1956.

Campbell, Norman. *What Is Science?* Dover Publications, New York, 1952.

Cassirer, Ernst. *The Myth of the State*. Yale University Press, New Haven, 1946.

——.*The Philosophy of Symbolic Forms*. Yale University Press, New Haven, 1953.

——.*Rousseau, Kant and Goethe*. Harper Torchbooks, New York, 1963.

Charlesworth, James, (ed.). *Contemporary Political Analysis*. Free Press, York, 1967.

Chomsky, Noam. *Cartesian Linguistics*. Harper and Row, New York, 1966.

Clegg, Ian. *Worker Self-Management in Algeria*. Monthly Review Press, New York, 1971.

Cohen, Jean. "Max Weber and the Dynamics of Domination" *Telos*. Winter, 1972.

Cohn, Norman. *The Pursuit of the Millennium*. Oxford University Press, New York, 1970.

Collingwood, R. G. *The Idea of History*. Oxford University Press, London, 1956.

Colson, Elizabeth. *Among the Cattle-Owning Plateau Tonga*. Livingstone, Rhodes-Livingstone Museum, 1949.

——.*Marriage and the Family Among the Plateau Tonga of Northern Rhodesia*. Manchester University Press, Manchester, 1958.

——.*The Plateau Tonga of Northern Rhodesia*. Manchester University Press, Manchester, 1962.

Comfort, Alex. *Authority and Delinquency*. Sphere, London, 1970.

Crocker, Lester. *Jean-Jacques Rousseau,* The Quest. *MacMillan Company, New York, 1968.*

——.*Rousseau's Social Contract*. Case Western Reserve University Press, Cleveland, 1968.

Dahl, Robert. *Pluralist Democracy in the United States*. McNally & Co., New York, 1967.

——.*Who Governs*. Yale University Press, New Haven, 1961.

Depelchin, Jacques. "Incipient Ideologies of the Lower Congo" unpublished paper, Stanford University, 1970.

Diamond, Stanley. "The Rule of Law Versus the Order of Custom" Wolff, Robert Paul, (ed.) *The Rule of Law*. Simon & Schuster, New York, 1971.

Dodds, E. R. *The Greeks and the Irrational*. University of California Press, Berkeley, 1971.

Drekmeier, Charles. "Knowledge as Virtue, Knowledge as Power" Sanford, Nevitt and Comstock, Craig, (eds.). *Sanctions for Evil*. Beacon Press, Boston, 1971.

Edelman, Murray. *The Symbolic Uses of Politics*. University of Illinois Press, Urbana, 1967.

Erikson, Erik. *Childhood and Society*. W. W. Norton and Company, New York, 1963.

——.*Ghandi's Truth*. W. W. Norton and Company, New York, 1969.

——.*Identity, Youth and Crisis*. W. W. Norton and Company, New York, 1968.

——.*Insight and Responsibility*. W. W. Norton and Company, New York, 1964.

——."The Concept of Identity in Race Relations" *Daedalus*. Winter, 1966.

Feyerabend, Paul. "Consolations for the Specialist" Lakatos, Imre and Musgrave, Allan, (eds.). *Criticism and the Growth of Knowledge*. Cambridge University Press, Cambridge, 1970.

Fiedler, Fred. *A Theory of Leadership Effectiveness*. McGraw-Hill, New York, 1967.

Findlay, J. N. *Hegel: A Re-Examination*. George Allen and Unwin Ltd., Lon don, 1964.

Fischer, George, (ed.) *The Revival of American Socialism*. Oxford University Press, New York, 1971.

Fortes, Meyer. *The Web of Kinship Among the Tallensi*. Oxford University Press, London, 1949.

Fortes, Meyer and Evans-Pritchard, E. E (eds.). *African Political Systems.* Oxford University Press, Oxford, 1940.

Foucault, Michel. *The Archaeology of Knowledge.* Pantheon Books, New York, 1972.

——.*The Order of Things.* Tavistock Publications, London, 1970.

——.*Madness and Civilization.* Mentor, New York, 1967.

Freud, Sigmund. *The Complete Works of Sigmund Freud.* Hogarth Press and Institute of Psychoanalysis, London, 1957

——.*Civilization and Its Discontents.* W. W. Norton and Company, New York, 1962.

——.*A History of Psychoanalysis,* Vol. I of *The Complete Works Of Sigmund Freud.* Hogarth Press and Institute of Psychoanalysis, London, 1957.

——.*Group Psychology and the Analysis of the Ego,* Vol. XVIII of *The Complete Works of Sigmund Freud.* Hogarth Press and Institute of Psychoanalysis, London, 1957.

Friedlander, Paul. *Plato.* Pantheon Books, Inc., Bollingen Series LIX, New York, 1958.

Fromm, Erich. *Escape From Freedom.* Avon Books, New York, 1966.

Geertz, Clifford. "Ideology as a Cultural System" Apter, David, (ed.). *Ideology and Discontent.* Free Press, New York, 1964.

Gellner, Ernest. *Thought and Change.* Weidenfield and Nicolson, London, 1964.

Georges, Robert, (ed.). *Studies on Mythology.* Homewood, Ill., Dorsey Press, 1968.

Gerth, H. H. and Mills, C. Wright, (eds.). *From Max Weber: Essays in Sociology.* Oxford University Press, New York, 1946.

Gluckman, Max. *Custom and Conflict in Africa.* Basil Blackwell, Oxford University Press, Oxford, 1955.

——.*Politics, Law and Ritual in Tribal Society.* Aldine Publishing Co., London, 1965.

Godelier, Maurice. "Myth and History" *New Left Review.* London, October-November 1971.

Godwin, William. *Enquiry Concerning Political Justice.* Edited by F. E. L. Priestley, Vol. II, University of Toronto, Toronto, 1946.

Gorz, Andre. *Strategy for Labor: A Radical Proposal.* Beacon Press, Boston, 1967.

Gouldner, Alvin. *The Coming Crisis of Western Sociology.* Avon Books, New York, 1970.

——.(ed.). *Studies in Leadership.* Harper, New York, 1950.

Gray, Alexander. *The Socialist Tradition.* Longman, Green & Co., London, 1946.

Green, Reginald. *The Death of Adam.* Iowa State University Press, Ames, Iowa, 1959.,

Green, T. H. *Principles of Political Obligation.* Ann Arbor Paperbacks, Ann Arbor, 1967.

Gregory, Richard. "Perception" Paterson, David, (ed.). *The Brain*. British Broadcasting Corporation, London, 1969.

Habermas, Jurgen. *Knowledge and Human Interests*. Beacon Press, Boston, 1968.

Harris, Marvin. *The Rise of Anthropological Theory*. Thomas Crowell, New York, 1968.

Hegel, G. W. F. *Early Theological Writings*. University of Chiago, Chicago, 1948.

———.*The Phenonmenology of Mind*. Harper and Row, New York, 1967.

———.*The Philosophy of History*. Dover Publications, New York, 1967.

Hirschman, Albert. "Underdevelopment Obstacles to the Perception of Change and Leadership" *Daedalus*. Summer, 1968.

Hobsbawm, Eric. *Primitive Rebels*. W. W. Norton and Company, New York, 1965.

———."Reflections on Anarchism" *The Spokesman*. London, November, 1970.

Huntington, Samuel. *Political Order in Changing Societies*. Yale University Press, New Haven, 1968.

James, C. L. R. "Colonialism and National Liberation in Africa" Aya, Roderick and Miller, Norman, (eds.). *National Liberation*. Free Press, New York, 1971.

James, William. *The Varieties of Religious Experience*. Modern Library, New York, 1929.

Jaspan, M. A. *The Ila-Tonga Peoples of North-Western Rhodesia*. International African Institute, London, 1953.

Johnson, Richard. *The French Communist Party Versus the Students*. Yale University Press, New Haven, 1972.

Joll, James. *The Anarchists*. Methuen and Company Ltd., London, 1964.

Jones, Stephen and Vroom, Victor. "Division of Labor and Performance Under Cooperative and Competitive Conditions" *Journal of Abnormal and Social Psychology*. March, 1964.

Kahn, Robert and Boulding, Elise, (eds.). *Power and Conflict in Organizations*. Tavistock, London, 1964.

Kaplan, Abraham. "Power in Perspective" Kahn, Robert and Boulding, Elise, (eds.). *Power and Conflict in Organizations*. Tavistock, London, 1964.

Kaufmann, Walter. *The Portable Nietzsche*. Viking Press, New York, 1968.

Kecskemeti, Paul, (ed.). "Introduction" Mannheim, Karl. *Essays on Sociology and Social Psychology*. Oxford University Press, New York, 1953.

Kermode, Frank. "Crisis Critic" *New York Review of Books*. May 17, 1973.

Kolakowski, Leszek. *The Alienation of Reason*. Doubleday and Company, New York, 1968.

Krieger, Leonard and Sterns, Fritz, (eds.). *The Responsibility of Power*. Anchor Books, Doubleday and Company, New York, 1969.

King, Preston and Parekh, B.C., (eds.). *Politics and Experience.* Cambridge University Press, Cambridge, 1968.

Kropotkin, Petr. *Memoirs of a Revolutionist.* Dover Publications, New York, 1971.

——.*Mutual Aid, A Factor of Evolution.* McClure, Philips and Company, New York, 1902.

Kuhn, Thomas. *The Structure of Scientific Revolutions.* Chicago University Press, Chicago, 1970.

——."Logic of Discovery or Psychology of Research" and "Reflections on My Critics" Lakatos, Imre and Musgrave, Allan, (eds.). *Criticism and the Growth of Knowledge.* Cambridge University Press, Cambridge, 1970.

——."Second Thoughts on Paradigms" Frederick Suppe, (ed.). *The Structure of Scientific Theory.* University of Illinois Press, Urbana, 1973.

Lakatos, Imre and Musgrave, Allan, (eds.). *Criticism and the Growth of Knowledge.* Cambridge University Press, Cambridge, 1970.

Lantenari, Vittorio. *Religions of the Oppressed.* Knopf, New York, 1963.

Laski, Harold. *The State in Theory and Practice.* Viking Press, New York, 1947.

Leach, Edmund. *Genesis as Myth and Other Essays.* Jonathan Cape Publishers, London, 1969.

——.*Political Systems of Highland Burma.* Bell Company, Ltd. London, 1954.

——."Anthropological Aspects of Language: Animal Categories and Verbal Abuse" Maranda, Pierre, (ed.). *Mythology.* Penguin Books, Middlesex, England, 1972.

Lenin, V. I. *The State and Revolution.* International Publications, New York, 1943.

Lerner, Daniel and Lasswell, H. D. *The Policy Sciences, Recent Developments in Scope and Method.* Stanford University Press, Stanford, 1951.

Levin, Harry. "Some Meanings of Myth" Murray, Henry, (ed.). *Myth and Myth-making.* Beacon Press, Boston, 1969.

Levison, Arnold. *Knowledge and Society.* Pegasus: Bobbs-Merrill Company, Inc., New York, 1974.

Levi-Strauss, Claude. *The Elementary Structures of Kinship.* Beacon Press, Boston, 1969.

——.*The Raw and the Cooked.* Harper Torchbooks, New York, 1969.

——.*From Honey to Ashes.* Harper Torchbooks, New York, 1973.

——."The Story of Asdiwal" Leach, Edmund, (ed.). *The Structural Study of Myth and Totemism.* Tavistock, London, 1969.

Leys, Wayne A. R. "Was Plato Non-Political?" and "An Afterthought" Vlastos, Gregory, (ed.). *Plato.* Vol. II, Anchor books, Doubleday and Company, Inc., New York, 1971.

Lichtman, Richard. "The Facade of Equality in Liberal Democratic Theory" *Socialist Revolution.* January, 1970.

Lindblom, Charles. *The Intelligence of Democracy.* Free Press, New York, 1 1965.

Louch, A. R. *Explanation in Human Action.* University of California Press, Berkeley and Los Angeles, 1969.

Lowie, Robert. *The Origin of the State.* Harcourt, Brace, New York, 1927.

Lukacs, Georg. *History and Class Consciousness.* The MIT Press, Cambridge, Mass., 1970.

MacGaffey, Wyatt. "The Religious Commission of the Bakongo" *Man.* 1970.

Maine, Henry S. *Ancient Law.* Murray & Company, London, 1861.

Malinowski, Bronislaw. "The Problem of Meaning in Primitive Languages" Ogden, C. K. and Richards, A. (eds.). *The Meaning of Meanings: A Study of the Influence of Language Upon Thought and of the Science of Symbolism. Harcourt, Brace Press, New York, 1945.*

Mandel, Ernest. Marxist Economic Theory, Vol. I. Monthly Review Press, New York, 1969.

Mannheim, Karl. *Essays on Sociology and Social Psychology.* Oxford University Press, New York, 1953.

Maranda, Pierre, (ed.). *Mythology.* Penguin Books, Middlesex, England, 1972.

Marx, Karl. Excerpts from *Das Kapital.* Tucker, Robert, (ed.). *The Marx-Engels Reader.* W. W. Norton and Company, Inc., New York, 1972.

——."On the Jewish Question" Tucker, Robert, (ed.). *The Marx-Engels Reader.* W. W. Norton and Company, Inc., New York, 1972.

——.*The Poverty of Philosophy.* International Publishers Co., Inc., New York, 1971.

——."Indifference to Politics" *Marx, Engels, Lenin on Anarchism and Anarcho-Syndicalism.* International Publishers Co., Inc., New York, 1972.

Masterman, Margaret. "The Nature of a Paradigm" Lakatos, Imre and Musgrave, Allan, (eds.). *Criticism and the Growth of Knowledge.* Cambridge University Press, Cambridge, 1970.

Melman, Seymour. "Industrial Efficiency Under Managerial vs. Cooperative Decision-Making: A Comparative Study of Manufacturing Enterprises in Israel" *The Review of Radical Political Economics.* Spring, 1970.

Meszaros, Istvan. *Marx's Theory of Alienation.* Harper Torchbooks, New York, 1970.

Michelet, Jules. *Satanism and Witchcraft.* Citadel Press, New York, 1971.

Middleton, John and Tait, David, (eds.). *Tribes Without Rulers.* Humanities Press, New York, 1958.

Mill, John Stuart. *Principles of Political Economy.* Longmans, Green & Co., 1909.

Miller, Norman and Aya, Roderick, (eds.). *National Liberation.* Free Press, New York, 1971.

Moore, Barrington, Jr. *Social Origins of Dictatorship and Democracy.* Beacon Press, Boston, 1966.

Morgan, Lewis H. *Ancient Society*. Kerr & Company, Chicago, 1877.

Mousnier, Roland. *Peasant Uprisings in 17th-Century France, Russia, and China*. Harper Torchbooks, New York, 1972.

Murray, Henry. *Myth and Mythmaking*. Beacon Press, Boston, 1969.

Murray, Margaret. *The God of the Witches*. Oxford University Press, London, 1970.

Myles, John. *The Political Ideas of the Greeks*. Greenwood Press, New York, 1968.

Nadel, S. *A Black Byzantium*. Oxford University Press, London, 1942.

Nisbet, Robert. *Social Change in History*. Oxford University Press, London, 1969.

Northrop, F. S. C. Introduction to W. Heisenberg's *Physics and Philosophy*. Harper & Row, New York, 1962.

Ogden, C. K. and Richards, I. A. (eds.). *The Meaning of Meaning: A Study of Language Upon Thought and of the Science of Symbolism*. Harcourt, Brace Press, New York, 1945.

Organski, A. F. K. Book Review. *The American Political Science Review*. September, 1969.

O'Shaughnessy, John. *Inquiry and Decision*. George Allen & Unwin, Ltd., London, 1972.

Ottenberg, Phoebe and Ottenberg, Simon. *Cultures and Societies of Africa*. Random House, New York, 1960.

Passmore, John. *The Perfectability of Man*. Duckworth & Company, Ltd., London, 1970.

Paterson, David. *The Brain*. British Broadcasting Company, 1969.

Pears, David. *Wittgenstein*. Fontana, London, 1971.

Pepper, Stephen. *World Hypotheses*. University of California Press, Berkeley, 1966.

Piepe, Anthony. *Knowledge and Social Theory*. Heineman, London, 1971.

Pirandello, Luigi. "Six Characters in Search of An Author" *three Plays by Luigic Pirandello*. E. P. Dutton & Company, New York, 1922.

Pitkin, Hannah Fenichel. *Representation*. Atherton Press, New York, 1969.

Plessner, Helmuth. "On the Relation of Time to Death" *Man and Time*. Pantheon Books, Inc., New York, 1957.

Pocock, J. G. A. *Politics, Language and Time*. Atheneum Press, New York, 1971.

Polanyi, Karl. *The Great Transformation*. Rinehart Inc., New York, 1957.

Polanyi, Michael. *Personal Knowledge*. University of Chicago Press, Chicago, 1958.

——.*The Tacit Dimension of Understanding*. Doubleday and Company, New York, 1966.

Popper, karl. *Conjectures and Refutation*. Basic Books, New York, 1962.

——.*The Logic of Scientific Discovery*. Basic Books, New York, 1959.

——."Normal Science and Its Dangers" Lakatos, Imre and Musgrave, Allan, (eds.). *Criticism and the Growth of Knowledge.* Cambridge University Press, Cambridge, 1970.

———.*The Open Society and Its Enemies,* Vol. I. Routledge, London, 1969.

Price, James L. *Organizational Effectiveness.* R. D. Irwin, Homewood, Ill., 1968.

Proudhon, P.J. *Oeuvres Completes De. P. J. Proudhon.* Bougle, D. and Moysett, H. (eds.). Marcel Riviere Co., Paris, 1951.

———.Selected Writings of D. J. Proudhon. Edwards, Stuart, (ed.). MacMillan & Company, London, 1969.

Radcliffe-Brown, A. R. *Structure and Function in Primitive Society.* West Ltd., London, 1952.

Reich, Wilhelm. *Mass Psychology of Fascism.* Farrar, Strauss & Giroux, New York, 1970.

———."What is Class Consciousness?" *Liberation.* October, 1971.

Robinson, Cedric J. "Malcolm Little as a Charismatic Leader" *Afro-American Studies.* September, 1972.

Rosinski, Herbert. *Power and Human Destiny.* Stebbins, Richard, (ed.). Pall Mall Press, London, 1965.

Rosenau, James. "Premises and Promises of Decision-Making Analysis" Charlesworth, James (ed.). *Contemporary Political Analysis.* Free Press, New York, 1967.

Rousseau, J. J. *The Social Contract and Discourses.* Cole, G. D. H. (ed.). E. P. Dutton and Co., Inc., London, 1950.

Rude, George. *The Crowd in History.* John Wiley & Sons, New York, 1964.

Rustow, Dankwart, (ed.). "Philosophers and Kings" *Daedalus.* Summer, 1968.

Sahlins, Marshal. *Stone Age Economics.* Aldiene-Atherton & Company, Inc., Chicago, 1972.

Sanford, Nevitt and Comstock, Craig, (eds.). *Sanctions for Evil.* Beacon Press, Boston, 1971.

Schaar, John. "Reflections on Authority" *New American Review #8.* New American Library, January, 1970.

Schapiro, Max. "A Note on Max Weber's Politics" *Politics.* February, 1945.

Schonfield, Hugh. *The Passover Plot.* Bernard Geis, New York, 1965.

Schroyer, Trent. "The Critical Theory of Late Capitalism" *The Revival of American Socialism.* Fischer, George, (ed.). Oxford University Press, New York, 1971.

Shelley, Mary. *Frankenstein.* Everyman's Library, London, 1818.

Shepperson, George and Price, Tom. *Independent African.* Edinburgh University Press, Edinburgh, 1958.

Simpson, G. G. *Principles of Animal Taxonomy.* Columbia University Press, New York, 1961.

Sinclair, T. A. *A History of Greek Political Thought.* Routledge and Kegan Paul Ltd., London, 1951.

Smith, M. A. *From Christ to Constantine.* Inter-Varsity Press, London, 1971.

Snell, Bruno. *The Discovery of the Mind.* Harper Torchbooks, New York, 1960.

Snyder, Richard, Bruck H. W. and Sapin, Burton, *Decision-Making An An Approach to the Study of International Politics.* Princeton.

Sohm, Rudolf. *Outlines of Church History.* McMillan & Company, Ltd., London, 1904.

Southall, A. *Alur Society.* W. heffer & Sons, Ltd., Cambridge, 1953.

Sparshott, F. E. "Plato as Anti-Political Thinker" *Plato.* Vlastos, Gregory, (ed.). Anchor Books, Doubleday and Company, Inc., New York, 1971.

Stirner, Max. *The Ego and His Own.* A. C. Fifield, London, 1912.

Strout, Cushing. "William James and the Twice-born Sick Soul" *Daedalus.* Summer, 1968.

Sullivan, Walter. *New York Times.* March 28, 29 and 30, 1972.

Terray, Emmanuel. *Marxism and "Primitive Societies".* Monthly Review Press, New York, 1972.

The Times Literary Supplement. "Adorno: Love and Cognition." Number 3705, March, 1973.

Tucker, Robert. *The Marx-Engels Reader.* W. W. Norton & Company, Inc., New York, 1972.

——.*Philosophy and Myth in Karl Mrx.* Cambridge University Press, Cambridge, 1971.

van der Leeuw, G. "Primordial Time and Final Time" *Man and Time.* Campbell, Joseph, (ed.), Pantheon Books, Inc., Bollinger Series XXX, New York, 1957.

Van Der Sprenkel, Otto B. "Max Weber on China" *Studies in the Philosophy of History.* Nadel, George, (ed.), Harper Torchbooks, New York, 1965.

Vansina, Jan. *Kingdoms of the Savanna.* University of Wisconsin Press, Madison, 1966.

Vernant, J. P. *Les Origines de le Pensee Grecque.* Paris, 1962.

Vlastos, Gregory. *Plato,* Volume II. Anchor Books, Doubleday & Co., Inc. 1971.

Walker, Jack. "A Critique of the Elitist Theory of Democracy" *The American Political Science Review.* June, 1966.

Wallace, Anthony. "Revitalization Movements" American Anthropologist. Vol. 58, 1956.

Walter, E. V. *Terror and Resistance.* Oxford University Press, New York, 1969.

Weber, Max. *Ancient Judaism.* Free Press, New York, 1967.

——.*Economy and Society.* Bedminster Press, Inc., New York, 1968.

——.*Theory of Social and Economic Organization.* MacMillan Co., 1947.

Wells, Harry K. *The Failure of Psychoanalysis.* International Publishers, New York, 1963.

White Hayden. "Foucault Decoded: Notes From Underground" *History and*

Theory. Vol. XII, No. 1, 1973.

White, Leslie. "The Social Organization of Ethnological Theory" *Rice University Studies.* Vol. 52, No. 4, 1966.

Whyte, William Foote. "Informal Leadership and Group Structure" *Studies in Leadership.* Gouldner, Alvin, (ed.), Harper, New York, 1950.

Wittgenstein, Ludwig. *Philosophical Investigations.* B. Blackwell, Oxford, 1963.

——.*Tractatus logico-philosphicus.* Routledge and Paul Kegan, London, 1922.

Wolf, Eric. *Peasant Wars of the Twentieth Century.* Harper & Row, New York, 1969.

Wolff, Robert Paul. *The Rule of Law.* Simon & Schuster, New York, 1971.

Wolin, Sheldon. "Paradigms and Political theories" *Politics and Experience.* King, Preston and Parekh, B.C. (eds.), Cambridge University Press, Cambridge, 1968.

——.*Politics and Vision.* Little, Brown & Co., 1960.

Wolpert, Jeremiah F. "Toward a Sociology of Authority" *Studies in Leadership.* Gouldner, Alvin, (ed.). Harper, New York, 1950.

Worsley, Peter. *The Trumpet Shall Sound.* Schocken Books, New York 1968.

Woodcock, George. *Anarchism.* Meridian Books: The World Publishing Company, Cleveland and New York, 1962.

——.*William Godwin.* Porcupine Press, London, 1946.

Index

ology, 150
charismatic leadership, 110, 247 n.3
concept of, 111-12
messianic myth and charismatic figure, 149, 156-57, 255 n.90
the political and charisma, 155-56
politicization and charisma, 153-55
submission of charismatic figure, 151-53
Weber on Charismatic figure, 149-50
Christianity
and the irrational, 86
Godwin and Christian rationalism, 176, 259-60 n.39
Collingwood, R.G., 78, 119
Cohen, Jean, 155-56
Cohn, Norman, 83, 101-04, 240-41 n.9, 245 n.73
Colson, Elizabeth, 196
Comfort, Alex, 63, 68-70
Crocker, Lester, 165, 258 n.16

Dahl, Robert, 13-15
Darwin, Charles, 261 n.49
Decision Making, 64-70
incremental decisions, 66
indeterminate decisions, 68
pure decisions, 65
Democratic Notion, 15-18
Aristotle on, 224-45 n.23
Athenian democracy, 173, 259 n.31
and Christianity, 16-17
Godwin on, 172-75, 258 n.18
as ideology, 47
modern democracy, 21
representative democracy, 19-21, 225 n.24
representative democracy and bourgeoisie, 19
Dialectical Reason, 133
the dialectic and history, 139
Diamond, Stanley, 4, 24, 29
Dodds, E.R.
on Archaic Age of Greek culture, 144
on chronology of Greek thought, 253 n. 68
on Classical Age of Greek culture, 144-45
on physis and nomos in Greek thought, 142-44
on social crisis of the Archaic Age, 254 n. 81
on Socrates, 142
Dostoevsky, F., 82

Drekmeier, Charles, 232 n.59
Edelman, Murray, 41-44
Edinger, Lewis, 236 n.42
Einstein, Albert, 108-09
Elites and Leadership, 62-63
Epistemology
epistemological transitions, 138-39, 251-52 n.58
nature of Western epistemology, 207-09
of scientific discourse, 136
Erikson, Erik, 69
on ego-ideal, 152
on myth, 129
on reification in psychoanalytic tradition, 201
Evans-Pritchard, E. E., 190-92
Experimental Psychology, 36, 231-32 n.58

Fascism, 96
Feyerabend, Paul, 22, 227 n.33, 239 n.5
Fiedler, Fred, 50
Fortes, M., 190
Foucault, Michel, 141, 213, 267 n.16
and conditions of possibility of knowledge, 137
countersciences, 6
epistemological transitions, 138-39, 251-52 n.58
and the epistemology of scientific discourse, 136
on Greek thought, 147
on history, 131-32, 139
on Marxism, 216
on thought, 136-40, 251 n. 53, n.58
Freud, Sigmund, 92-98, 111, 243 n.38, 244 n.40, n.50, n.52
Fromm, Erich, 99-101

Gandhi, Mahatma, 203
Geertz, Clifford, 129-30, 250 n.37
German Romanticism, 181
Gluckman, Max, 195-97, 203-04
Godelier, Maurice, 140-41
Godwin, William, 168-77
on Athens, 173, 259 n. 31
background and training, 170-72
and Calvinism, 170
and Christian rationalism, 176, 259-60 n. 39
on democracy, 172-75, 258 n. 18, n. 27
and Kropotkin, 174
on political authority, 172, 175, 260 n. 40